SILENT WOUNDS
The Hidden Cost
of War

Published by: Virtual Life Solutions, LLC.

Visit
www.SilentWounds.com
to purchase additional copies of this book and for more information about our products and services.

JAMES W. DANIELS, JR.,
EMILY KUHLBARS HOWDEN,
&
RICHARD ARDEN KUHLBARS

SILENT WOUNDS
The Hidden Cost
of War

Cover Design

RICHARD ARDEN KUHLBARS, II

2007

A Personal Message
From a Veteran of Iraqi Freedom

It is an honor to write you this personal note, and to highly recommend "Silent Wounds" to you. This is an important book. After over fifty years of combined uniformed care and concern for Soldiers and family members, retired chaplains Colonel Richard Kuhlbars and Colonel James Daniels are making perhaps their greatest contribution to the health and well-being of those service and family members who served and continue to serve in our Nation's military.

"Silent Wounds" is written for those who have suffered directly or indirectly the horrors of modern warfare and have been wounded by the experience. The key is the recognition of the soul as a critical component of our human composition, a reality long ignored and disregarded by the physiological and pharmaceutical approach to mental health. The soul, that unique "personal essence and inner identity," is the place of wounding. This wounding is dramatically portrayed in the story of Luke and Jennifer. Masterfully woven throughout "Silent Wounds," the narratives provide the "flesh and blood" to the concepts and principles presented. And these concepts, using available tools and leveraging technology, empower the wounded Warfighter, Veteran, and family member to take control of their lives and begin the work of recovery.

"Silent Wounds" is written for the professional caregiver as well. The concepts have been thoroughly researched and documented, with an extensive bibliography. The narratives provide the caregiver insight into the wounded soul before them, and the discussions give resources readily available for their use in assisting in healing and recovery. "Silent Wounds" provides practical counsel leading to recovery, healing, and hope for the wounded soul. This is an important book, and will make a difference in the lives of countless Warfighters, Veterans, and family members who avail themselves of its counsel!

Rev. Robert F. Land

What Warfighters, Veterans, and Family Members are saying about "Silent Wounds."

"This book is a must read if you fall into any of the following categories: Veterans, spouses of Veterans, children of Veterans, chaplains, ministers, helping professionals such as counselors, social workers, psychologists, psychiatrists or medical professionals such as nurses, doctors, or medical technicians, those working with law enforcement, firemen, prison wardens, guards, and so on and so on. This book is about war, but it is really about trauma. It captures how a "Gung ho" kid ends up with PTSD and what his family does to help bring him back."

Robert M. Hardee, Jr.
LISW, Vietnam Veteran

"Silent Wounds reminds us that all veterans are living Souls and that they all have a sacred story to tell. This book does an excellent job of presenting the deep suffering that is a legacy of war. The writers are commended for reminding us of both the shape and nature of some of this suffering and challenging us to open to our returning veterans the possibilities of healing that only sensitive hearts and ears can bring."

Rev. David Canada
Chaplain (LTC), U.S. Army, Retired

"Another thing... The numbers and statistics concerning suicide that you use in the introduction absolutely blew my mind. More soldiers died by suicide after Vietnam than died in the combat of the Vietnam War. These stats create an urgency in the reader and make your book extremely important."

Family Member

"I read "Silent Wounds" while on deployment in Iraq. The author's premise startled me: "... every Veteran and Soldier is silently wounded." Me? Am I being silently wounded too? I had never considered the possibility. Like all who answered our nations call to war, I only thought of my physical self. I wanted to come home alive ... with my body intact. But we are more than just a material being ... this I knew to be true. I have not experienced the direct horrors of war, as did Luke; but I have heard the rockets fly overhead, seen the flash of the mortar's detonation, heard the startling explosions, and felt the percussion shake my surrounding. Stray rounds have passed within yards ... I live in a City of Death. Fear is a daily companion, for death is indiscriminant and random and one never knows if they may be next ... I grieve and rage at the senseless killing of my fellow service members and innocent Iraqis by misguided Islamic zealots. My anger borders on hatred. I have grown suspicious of all dark haired swarthy-skinned people I see ... I have been silently wounded. I owe a debt to Kuhlbars, Howden, and Daniels, for "Silent Wounds" has awakened me to this reality and helped prepare me for its possible manifestation when I get back to 'the world.'"

Iraq War Veteran

"We sleep safe in our beds because rough men stand ready in the night to visit violence on those who would do us harm." (George Orwell). We who sleep safely in our beds are indebted to our Warfighters, Veterans, and their Family Members. Our Nation, as a Community, has a special obligation to care for those who are wounded in service to the Nation. While physical wounds from the weapons of war are amazingly well addressed by the medical community, there are other wounds, less well addressed, but just as life threatening. Rough men have souls, and their souls are more vulnerable than their bodies. Warfighters, Veterans, and their Family Members have sacrificed themselves to wounding from the delicate internalization of conflict between duty and morality, the trauma of loss, and from the numbing uncertainties of separation. The needs of the soul must also be addressed as part of our obligation to our wounded. "Silent Wounds, The Hidden Cost of War" is a significant installment on the debt we owe our Warfighters, Veterans, and their Family Members. It provides an azimuth for the journey leading to discovery of the spiritual self, healing and a productive life."

Joseph R. Taylor
LTC, U.S. Army, Retired
Vietnam Era/Cold War Era Veteran

"We cannot afford, emotionally or economically, another generation of veterans who have lost touch with their souls because of the trauma of war. The men and women of our armed forces who have endured the stress and distress of war and who have been wounded in ways both visible and not, deserve our best efforts to recognize and lend healing to those injuries. The work of Ms. Howden and Chaplains Daniels and Kuhlbars presents a profound and potent protocol to restore the balance of personal and spiritual health for veterans, their families, and their communities. Silent Wounds holds great potential for caregivers in the military, for counselors in civilian communities, and for pastors and churches as they seek to support the soldiers, sailors, and airmen who have survived the unutterable horrors of war and are now dealing with the memories and emotions of an unforgettable past. This book is an essential element in the toolkit of remedies for injured souls."

Rev. Dr. Terry Bradfield
Chaplain (COL), U.S. Army, Retired

"When I began reading "Silent Wounds," I was desperately searching for clues to help me understand my dad, a WWII veteran. Even as a little girl, I sensed my daddy was battling silent demons. He always took such excellent care of his family – my mom, my brother, and later my little sister. He played with us, told us funny stories, and always, always had hugs anytime we needed them. Yet, there were times he seemed so very, very sad and so far away. I guess I did not have the vocabulary or understanding to really question him, but I do remember asking, "What's wrong, Daddy?" His response was always the same. "Nothing, Baby. Everything will be just fine. We have to believe that everything will be just fine." I knew in my heart that wasn't true and I hurt for him.

Thirty years later, the wounds that he had so efficiently hidden all my life began to manifest themselves. He developed an undiagnosed trembling in his torso and arms. He began to experience bouts of depression, and being in crowds, especially noisy ones, really bothered him. Finally, he began participating with some other WWII Vets from our little town in a therapy group. I couldn't believe this. Daddy had always "stuffed" any emotions he might be feeling about anything unpleasant. He wouldn't talk about what was discussed in the groups, but he did say, "I thought I had seen some terrible things, but some of those boys saw worse things than I did." He had talked about some of his war experiences, but these were always funny ones. Now he mentioned a few that weren't at all humorous. Even then, I'm sure he gave us the "cleaned-up" versions and kept even more unpleasant events from us. All along I had believed that his tremors were from an unexplained source that the doctors could not discover – until a few years ago when I drove Mom and Dad to Daddy's appointment at the VA. I knew that he never missed an appointment with a certain doctor. He called her "my doctor" and always said she made him feel so much better. I am so dense. She was a psychiatrist and I listened with a sore heart as my daddy talked to her about bad dreams and other things he remembered – in very vague terms, of course, to continue sheltering us. He said, "I don't think I'm a bad person; why do I keep having these dreams?" For the first time I really realized how much my daddy had been hurting all of his life and how he had kept us safe from his hurts and any others that he could. I felt so inadequate and hollow. I don't know how he survived let alone made it possible for his family to thrive.

"Silent Wounds" helped me to begin an understanding of all that he had done for us, our family, and our country. I have always known – and now I am sure of it – that Daddy is a hero. There are so many parts to this puzzle that are still missing and that I'll probably never find, but I do know this: No matter what happens, I can always look to Daddy as a model and inspirations to having lived life as well as it can be lived.

Nevertheless, there is no happy ending to this story. He is still hurting and I can't fix it. I just wish with all of my heart that his wounds could be soothed. Maybe if this book and the insight it brings had been in place for my dad, he wouldn't still be aching. I pray that for some other "Daddy" this book will provide healing and take away the hurt."

Julie Taylor
Family Member

"This book had to be written. The souls of our War Veterans were crying out for it. It gives a penetrating view into the trauma suffered by our combat veterans and their families through the eyes of a soldier who experienced the horrors of close combat in Iraq and his wife. It helps us to understand that all combat veterans experience silent wounds that change them. Often those wounds are so profound they cause the disintegration of the soul itself disrupting or even preventing return to "normal" life. The result is a crisis of identity and meaning. The combat veteran has been transformed, but to whom and what meaning does life hold now. Contemporary pharmaceutical and psychological treatments are often ineffective precisely because they fail to understand or accept the reality that the soul, our inner being that defines who we are, is damaged or as some combat veterans express it "lost."

Beyond bringing clarity to the suffering of the combat veteran and the veteran's family, "Silent Wounds" presents a new paradigm for healing, a healing that focuses on the re-integration of the soul, and discovering the meaning of one's life in the new reality of post combat existence. It does not present a shallow, self-help formula, or quick fix. Such profound wounding belies shallow approaches and cannot be healed quickly.

The authors present a pathway offering hope and renewal of the soul that if followed will bring effective healing to the soul of the warrior and the warrior's family over time. Having counseled with combat veterans, including several suffering from PTSD, and visiting many of our wounded and their families, especially at Walter Reed, I can tell you that "Silent Wounds" is right on target. I can also tell you that having counseled those who suffered traumatic loss from Hurricane Katrina and other tragedies, this book has application beyond the military even though that is its primary focus. "Silent Wounds" is a wonderful gift to our courageous soldiers, airmen, sailors and marines and their families who truly give their all for us."

Rev. Dr. Sherrill F. Munn

This book is dedicated
To the memory of

Chaplain, LTC, (retired) James W. Daniels, (April 7, 1928 - May 9, 1996), Veteran of World War II , Korea (Navy) and Vietnam (Army Chaplain) who passed away from complications of Agent Orange exposure in Vietnam.

T/SGT (retired) Emil Arthur Kuhlbars, (November 10, 1922 – 21 February 1997), Veteran of World War II (Army) and Vietnam (Air Force).

SM/SGT (retired) Jackie Elmer Murdaugh, (January 7, 1935 – August 24, 1994), Veteran of Vietnam (Air Force).

ACKNOWLEDGEMENTS

We would like to thank the many Souls who mentored us throughout our careers. Their leadership, experiences, and stories enriched our own lives and enabled us to offer this testimony of the sacrifices of our Warfighters. We acknowledge the influence of several key authors who are quoted herein who themselves shared their stories of their silent wounding. We also acknowledge the great sacrifice of Soldiers, Marines, Sailors, Airmen, and civilians who gave their life's work, their welfare, their lives, and ultimately their Souls in Service to their Country. To our friends and families who acted as our best critics and kept us on the right path we give our deepest love and thanks. We honor the loving support of our spouses who lived with us over the years: Elsie Daniels, Truman Howden, and Frances Kuhlbars.

In our research, we found that a great number of individuals and institutions were doing great work for our silently wounded Warfighters. We want to be sure that everyone understands the great effort and exceptional work being done by military Chaplains and Chaplain Assistants who labor selflessly in support of the spiritual needs of our Warfighters on the battlefield and to their family members who wait at home. We acknowledge the dedicated and tireless daily effort of medical and mental health professionals, social workers, peer counselors, clergy, and other key caregivers who also give of their life's work in support of the healing of our wounded Warfighters and Veterans. We especially wish to thank all those unsung heroes, the volunteers who care and work to provide the love, support, care, and often materiel needs of Warfighters, Veterans, and family members in so many small but significant ways. Our Institutions are serving us well. We all, as a whole community, need to acknowledge and believe in our own collective power to support our Warfighters, Veterans, and family members.

During our years of research, we read many great articles, studies, and books, some that can be found in our Notes and Selected

Bibliography. We want to highlight and acknowledge three authors for their inspirational works and their support and concern for the deep silent wounding of our Warfighters, Veterans, and their family members. Their books are exceptional and we recommend them to everyone who is interested in understanding and supporting Warfighters, Veterans, and family members who are silently wounded. Thanks to Lee Alley for his sacrifice and service and writing the book "<u>Back From War- Finding Hope & Understanding In Life After Combat</u>." (Exceptional Publishing. 2007); to Elio Frattaroli, M.D. for his insights in healing the silent wounds in his in-depth work, "<u>Healing the Soul in the Age of the Brain</u>." (Penguin Books, N.Y. N.Y., 2001) and we highly recommend his website www.healingthesoul.net; and a final word of thanks to Edward Tick, Ph.D., for his ground-breaking and enlightening work, "<u>War and The Soul</u>." (Quest Books. 2005).

There are several organizations and individuals who have supported our effort and believed in our ministry. We offer grateful thanks to the United Methodist Endorsing Agency and Pat Barrett, Tom Carter, Laura Flippen, and Dave McLean. For his mentorship and support, we thank Herm Keiser the chairperson of the National Council on Ministry to the Armed Forces (NCMAF), and Jack Williamson the Executive Director.

Specifically we want to acknowledge the following dear friends that helped us along the way with their feedback, experiences, and their own stories: Nonia Gay Jones, Mary Slaback, Dr. Louise Burpee, DVM., Dr. Paul Flowers, PhD., Dr. Robert Raguso, PhD., Dr. Gregory Forter, PhD., Rev. Dr. Dave Canada, DMin., Rev. Dr. Terry Bradfield, DMin., Bob Land, Rev., Dr. Sherrill Munn, PhD., Bud and Susie Whitehouse, Bob Hardee, Joe and Julie Taylor, Dr. Martha Rutledge, Lindell Anderson, Richard Rios, Monsignor Jerry Haberek (who championed the original idea for "Healing the Soul"), and Robert Fulcher.

ABOUT THE AUTHORS

<u>About James W. Daniels, Jr.</u>: Chaplain (Colonel-Retired) Daniels served local churches in Maine gaining significant experience in the pastoral ministry before entering active duty as an Army Chaplain. He brings over 34 years of experience providing professional military religious support to Soldiers, leaders, and their families. His early experience as a Chaplain was with the mechanized Infantry, where he walked with Soldiers on the ground. The Army recognized his ability to provide strategic leadership by assigning him to key Army staff positions in the Chaplaincy. With a Masters in Business Administration, Chaplain Daniels served as a Chaplain military comptroller, providing the resources, supplies, equipment, and funding necessary for the religious support of troops in harm's way. Later, he was the program manager for ecclesiastical supplies and equipment at the Defense Logistics Agency that supported the surge into Iraq and Afghanistan with religious supplies for the Soldiers on the ground. He attended the Army Senior Service College earning a Masters in Strategic Studies. His last assignment was Director of Plans, Policy Development, and Training for the Army Chief of Chaplains located at Headquarters, Department of the Army, Pentagon. He was instrumental in leading the formulation of military religious policy, religious planning, mobilization support, and ensuring that every unit deployed with a Chaplain to Iraq and Afghanistan. Chaplain Daniels is a subject matter expert in the delivery of military religious support to include pastoral care and counseling to Soldiers in the land maneuver warfare environment. His expertise extends to the formulation and delivery of military religious support and services, family life ministry, strategic professional support to the Command as principle religious advisor, crisis management, training, and military religious support planning and operations, and policy formulation. He holds a Master of Divinity (Bangor Theological Seminary), Master of Business Administration (W. VA Wesleyan), and Master of Strategic Studies (U.S. Army War College) degrees. He is an ordained Elder in the United Methodist Church, Retired.

<u>About Emily Howden:</u> Emily is no stranger to the effects war has on family members. She is the product of an Army family, describing her "hometown" as a variety of Army posts both stateside and abroad. Both of Emily's grandfathers were war veterans and her father is Chaplain (Retired) Kuhlbars, co-author of this book. She married her high school sweetheart, fellow Army brat, and current U.S. Soldier. Emily experienced the trauma of war first hand, as a military dependent living in Heidelberg, Germany, during the first war with Iraq; she is currently experiencing the strain of being a military spouse during Operation Iraqi Freedom. Emily is a graduate of Heidelberg High School, Heidelberg, Germany. She will graduate from the University of North Carolina at Pembroke in May 2008, with a Bachelor of Science (Biology) and a Bachelor of Arts (English.) She finished applying to veterinary school this fall and will receive their decision in 2008.

<u>About Richard Arden Kuhlbars:</u> Visionary Colonel (Retired) Richard Arden Kuhlbars is the founder of Virtual Life Solutions, LLC. Before starting Virtual Life Solutions, LLC, Ric served in the United States Army Chaplaincy holding various positions requiring unique and specialized skills. It was during his military service that he developed his understanding of and the need for a methodology to sustain 'life skills' with the capacity to immediately translate the educational, training, or counseling insights into behavior. He has come to understand the emerging role of the Internet and technology in how today's society increasingly trusts the virtual venue to meet a significant proportion of the full range of human needs. Ric understands that multi-media technology represents a "self-help" economy with unlimited potential. While leading the re-design of the chaplaincy into the twenty-first century, he became aware of the critical need to equip military chaplains with the proper skills to address the most urgent need of Soldiers, the healing of their souls. His foremost concern throughout his distinguished military career was caring for Soldiers and their families. His passion empowered him to write about his vision and develop tools extending from that vision. His purpose is to offer practical, usable, and accessible

skills, enabling people to overcome the painfulness of the worst of human conditions and consequently live successful, fully healed lives. Ric was the visionary for the U.S. Army Chaplain Corps in this arena. He has extensive experience and training in leadership development, spiritual readiness/training, crisis intervention, force management, acquisition, virtual training, and computer products along with a critical array of professional and academic credentials. He holds both a Master of Theology degree from Southern Methodist University, and a Master of Strategic Studies from the US Army War College in Carlisle Pennsylvania. He is an ordained United Methodist clergyperson with an educational background in social psychology.

ABOUT THE GRAPHIC DESIGNER

About Richard A. Kuhlbars, II: About Richard A. Kuhlbars, II: Richard has the rare and unique combination of technical and artistic talents that make his innovative work connect. He brings concepts to life in the virtual and interactive realms. He has a background in education and business. He taught computer graphics in the prestigious Fairfax County, Virginia school system. Many of the students he taught and mentored have gone on to media production and filming careers. He was the creative force behind an innovative self-assessment software system, which is currently being used to assist Veterans heal from the trauma of war. He recruited and led a team of actors, videographers, graphic designers, writers, crewmembers, computer technicians, audiovisual experts, and many others to create this marvelous product. The phenomenal technical engineering, graphics, and product design of this product is not simply the result of his talent and expertise but also of his shared passion for caring for people. Richard is a graduate of Virginia Commonwealth University with an emphasis on 3-D graphic design. He has expertise in 2d animation, video, motion graphics and web design. Richard brings an untiring commitment to the mission of VLS and a fervent desire to help in whatever way possible to improve the quality of people's lives through virtual and digital technologies. He is active in Habitat for Humanity and serves on the board of the Goochland County Chapter.

Contents

FORWARD

Ric, Emily, and Jim do all combat veterans a much-needed service by describing the deep wounds to the Soul that these special folks carry. Indeed, many of us not involved in the military forget about the fact that all of our veterans are living and breathing Souls.

This book does more than paint a realistic picture of the struggles our Veterans face, however. Without using the technical jargon of any particular discipline they place the struggles of the suffering Veteran within the context of issues brought before the church for healing and redemption. Many years ago, Charles Gerkin drew upon the work of Anton Boisen, the father of Clinical Pastoral Education, to write his monumental work on pastoral care, The Living Human Document. Gerkin did an excellent job of fleshing out the ideas that had been the foundation of Boisen's life work. His basic premise was that every human being – every Soul in the language of Ric, Emily, and Jim – was a living human document whose story was as sacred as any document that our faith had canonized. Every living human document was worthy of respect, study, reflection, and interpretation. It thus became the role of the pastoral care giver to listen faithfully to the sacred stories being told by those who present themselves. I have the feeling that the writers of this wonderful book are in a sense serving as an extension of the ideas set forth by Gerkin and Boisen.

Through stressing the importance of the community for direction and healing, they will remind all pastors and church people that the church is not only the community of the faithful, but is also the Body of Christ. It is a sacred community called together for life and healing. It is also often through the sharing of the Word that life and healing become possible. Remembering Gerkin and Boisen's challenge to view every person as a living sacred document we may begin to grasp the powerful opportunity for healing that the church holds as a vital part of its mission.

I became an Army Chaplain in the late 70s. The War in Vietnam had just ended. Back in those days, there were many people in the military suffering with what was soon labeled as Delayed Stress Syndrome. Over a period of years, I was blessed to know a number of these men and women. Eventually these special people, some of the work then being done by the Veterans Administration, and much prayer and reflection helped me to see that their relationship to their chaplain was often helpful when it became a penitent/priest relationship. They often knowingly or unknowingly sought the forgiveness that would restore their sense of value in themselves, their lives, their community, their nation, and their faith. It seemed to me then, and it seems to me now, that it is not only they who need forgiveness, but also all who live in a society engaged in making war.

The metaphor of a stained glass window has helped me to understand the lives of combat veterans and their spiritual journey of healing. In the story of the Garden of Eden, we learn about what the church calls original sin. I have come to understand this as a loss of innocence that all of us go through as we mature. For some of us this loss of innocence is forever tied to experiences of trauma that we witness or participate in. Consider that our lives are a beautiful stained glass window. Through it, the warmth of God's love can radiate. It illuminates images of sacred people and events. In time, the window shatters. For those who experience the violence and evil of war the shattering is always traumatic. We then spend the rest of our lives trying to put the window back together. A Veteran telling his/her story is like a person trying to put a jigsaw puzzle together. Broken pieces are picked up and held against the window to see where they fit. At first the shards of glass may cut. In time, the Veteran learns how to handle them without danger or pain. If the Veteran can step back from the window, he/she may find that others around them are trying to put together the pieces of their windows, and that all of the windows are actually a part of a much larger window. In so doing, the isolation that is so destructive to the Soul is overcome.

Churches, pastors, family members, and other interested persons will not find easy answers here. Indeed, by definition the damage to the Soul and the processes that lead to healing are very complex. However, as stated above, the reader will surely finish the book with a deeper understanding of the wounds veterans wrestle with, and with the need for healing. The reader will also come away with much to ponder about what the church and other instruments of healing have to offer and how they may best offer it.

For those of us who were born in the first half of the Twentieth Century, the authors' references to the cyber community will present a special challenge and opportunity. The authors certainly understand the world of cyberspace and cyber-relationships far better than I do. They move me toward a deeper understanding of this part of the world that our suffering Veterans know and feel so much a part of.

This book is much needed. I appreciate the hard work my friends Jim, Emily, and Ric do here. It fills a real need in my life and work, and I am confident that it will fill the same need in the church, the nation, and the world.

David M. Canada[1]

Chaplain (Lieutenant Colonel, Retired)

Doctor of Ministry

Author, Editorial Advisory Board the Circuit Rider Magazine,

Honorary Member the Army's Society of Medical Merit,

Advanced & Supervisory Clinical Pastoral Education (CPE)

Residencies,

Licensed Nursing Home Administrator

"The diagnosis of ailments that degrade a person's ability to perform, either in combat or upon return from combat are real ailments. However, I think we need to really look at how we treat those ailments. I don't know that the treatments have really changed or improved to support our current conditions. There is a lot of horror on the current battlefields, IEDs, eviscerations, limbs, and heads being mangled and severed; and the truth is these things do adversely affect Soldiers. We have to figure out how to treat the Soldiers (get them grounded in their faith, the bad guys don't have a problem with their faith). The other part of this deal is the leaders need to be grounded. Well, anyway, we got to figure this out, and get our Soldiers healthy."

Robert J. Fulcher, Jr.
Colonel, Retired
Battalion Commander, Gulf War

PREFACE

"I left the military forty years ago, and I have worked hard to demilitarize my self. I'm older now, and war is no longer exciting or glorious to me. I know that even if you return alive, battle scars are inevitable, not just on the body, but on the soul."[2]

Shepherd Bliss

We served the Army Chaplaincy as the Director for Combat Developments and the Director of Plans, Policy Development, and Training as our country entered the War on Terrorism. These jobs entail developing policy at the Army level and the structuring of the chaplaincy to meet the requirements and needs of the Army. We were in the midst of designing the chaplaincy for the 21st century when this war began. We saw Warfighters and family members touched by the trauma of war and began to ask ourselves, "What the role of the chaplain is in the healing process?"

We were aware of the effects war has on the whole person and the whole family. Early in our observations, we understood the impact of silent wounding. We experienced it when our fathers returned home from War World II and Vietnam, and we experienced it with today's Warfighters. We knew "Post Traumatic Stress Disorder" (PTSD)[3] treats the wounding as a stress disorder, but it does not consider the whole person. We also knew that war touches everyone. We became concerned about a deeper, more pervasive, wounding…what we saw as a silent wounding of the Soul. This affects everyone who experiences the trauma of combat. We started calling this form of "PTSD:" "Post Traumatic Soul Disorder" (PTSoulD).

By conducting intense research and asking ourselves challenging questions, we became aware that the trauma of war wounds people to the core of who they are. It silently wounds their Souls. We had a new generation of Warfighters and their family members with silent wounds. It was out of this realization that our concept of healing the Soul began. Our walk with struggling Warfighters and their families helped us learn that the traumatic impact of war inflicts silent wounds upon the Soul and that we need to address them with an extraordinary effort. Therefore, we turned our efforts to the research of the deeper trauma of war, the irrevocable life changing experiences of combat and what is now being described as a silent wounding of the Soul. This is a broader, more universal experience than "PTSD" as a stress disorder. We saw this as a disorder of the Soul.

We discovered two basic issues. One was that our Veterans seek forgiveness from their families, friends, communities, and their Nation for the things they see and do in combat. This forgiveness has both a secular and a spiritual implication. The second issue was the increasing instances of behavioral dysfunctions to include alcohol and drug addictions, dysfunctional anger and hostility, paranoia, anxiety disorders, irrational fears, social and relational problems, and a pervasive all encompassing silent desperation that left untreated often leads to premature death by suicide as a symptom of combat trauma and a delayed casualty of war. Studies found that over 60,000 Warfighters died from suicide following the Vietnam War.[4] That is more than were actually killed in action during the war. By 1998, that number had risen to over 100,000 Veterans who died by suicide.[5] Another study found that the children of Vietnam Vets had twice the suicide rate of their peers. When we saw that, the Iraq and Afghanistan Vets are following a similar post-combat pattern:

> "Hundreds of troops have come home from war, left the military and committed suicide. That is the finding of preliminary Veterans Affairs Department research obtained by The Associated Press that provides the first quantitative look at the suicide toll on today's combat veterans. The ongoing research reveals that at least 283 combat veterans who left the military between the start of the war in Afghanistan on Oct. 7, 2001, and the end of 2005 took their own lives. The numbers, while not dramatically different

from society as a whole, are reminiscent of the increased suicide risk among returning soldiers in the Vietnam era."[6]

Kimberly Hefling

We understood immediately that we needed to do something about the escalating suicide rates of our Veterans and their family members.

Our Warfighters and Veterans need our collective forgiveness for what they see and what they do in the name of patriotism and world peace. They need our help and support to find healing, meaning, and purposeful living. As a community, we must not abandon them to their pain, grief, loss, and desperation. Left untreated and without intervention, their pain, grief, loss and desperation escalate throughout their lives, and they become uncounted casualties.

There are many words used to describe military service members. They are Soldiers, Airmen, Sailors, Marines, and Coasties. In today's war, we must consider the fact that Department of Defense civilians and contractors continue to play a significant role in the war on Terrorism and are silently wounded by the trauma of war. We have decided to use the term, "Warfighter," as a universal literary reference for all Armed Services personnel. Warfighters become Veterans through their experiences in wars, both hot and cold. As Warfighters re-integrate back into their daily lives as Veterans, they discover that they have been changed, deeply and silently wounded in mind and Soul, and they cannot return to life, as they knew it.

You will also see us using the acronym "WVFM." "WVFM" means Warfighter, Veteran, and family member. "WVFM" is used for the ease of reading. Its use is not intended to reduce the significance of the silent wounding that Warfighters, Veterans, and family members experience from the trauma of war.

The story of Luke and Jennifer is a fictional portrayal of thoughts, events, feelings, and experiences of a typical Military couple. Any similarity to actual events, people, or experiences is truly coincidental. The story itself may be fictional, but the story depicts real events, real feelings, and real experiences.

> "...war is indeed universally traumatizing. Because of this inevitable trauma, . . .Unlike our veterans today, warriors were reintegrated into civilian life with elaborate rituals that involved the whole community and imparted transformative spiritual wisdom."[7]
>
> Edward Tick

INTRODUCTION

"It was a condition I first experienced after serving as a marine in Vietnam. I was never the same person after placing the first body in a body bag in Nam. And every day after that, there was just more death and destruction. I was changed; I was different from the man I used to be and there was nobody I could tell. I was afraid to talk because I was afraid to cry. If I started to cry, I might never stop."[8]

Melvin Mason

Our concern is about healing our Veterans and Warfighters as they return from combat. Veterans and Warfighters experience pain, grief, loss, and desperation as a result of their combat experience. Combat trauma irrevocably changes a person. We refer to these elements of trauma, pain, grief, loss, and life-changing experiences as the silent wounding of the Soul. This silent wounding of the Soul leads to ongoing behavioral dysfunctions to include alcohol and drug addictions, dysfunctional anger and hostility, paranoia, anxiety disorders, irrational fears, social and relational problems, and a pervasive all encompassing silent desperation that left untreated or without intervention often leads to premature death by suicide as a symptom of the combat trauma and a delayed casualty of war. "PTSD" and "mild traumatic brain injury" (mTBI)[9] are a part of the story. But today we find that treatment of "PTSD" and "mTBI" is isolated to the more obvious, some say extreme, examples, and manifestations of these injuries and disorders of combat trauma. Post Traumatic Stress Disorder, commonly and historically known as Nostalgia, Soldier's Heart, Shell Shock, War Neurosis, Combat Neurosis, Combat Fatigue, Combat Exhaustion, Battle Fatigue, Combat Stress, and "PTSD," is often used to label every trauma disorder displayed by our Veterans and Warfighters. Historically, that may have been the case.

Today, diagnosis and treatment of "Post Traumatic Stress Disorder" (PTSD) has become narrow and more focused on the immediate and obvious symptoms of "PTSD" and "mTBI" that require hospitalization, medication, psychotherapy, or all three. "PTSD" is one set of symptoms of combat trauma. Our concern is about another set of symptoms that we call the silent wounding of the Soul. We suggest that this is a deeper and more universal symptom of the experience of combat. While the typical military and VA medical institutions focus on the more obvious symptoms of "PTSD," we discovered that the personal silent wounding that takes place as a result of experiencing combat trauma is largely neglected. This silent wounding affects everyone exposed to combat trauma including Warfighters, Veterans, their family members, their friends, their communities, and our Nation that sends our Warfighters into combat. We suggest that this silent wounding of the Soul affects every personal characteristic of the whole person. Typical care and treatment of "PTSD" does not consider the whole person or the process of finding meaning and purposeful living.

We are concerned about the silent wounding of the Soul that we have come to label a Soul disorder rather than a stress disorder. A disorder of the Soul is a life-changing experience that engenders ongoing grief, pain, feelings of loss, and a quiet pervasive sense of desperation. The Soul disorder will remain long after the more acute and obvious symptoms of the stress disorder are dealt with through medications, hospitalization, and therapy. When Warfighters and Veterans are released from the hospitals, have phased out their therapy sessions, and have reduced or eliminated their medications, they then must take up the healing of the Soul. We have come to call this ongoing silent wounding the "Post Traumatic Soul Disorder" (PTSoulD).

We suggest that the history and treatment of "PTSD" and now the other signature injury of Iraq and Afghanistan, "mTBI," address only one facet of the concept of the silent wounding of the Soul. In 1980, the American Psychiatric Association's Diagnostic and Statistical Manual, Edition III, defined a new behavior illness category: post-traumatic stress disorder, now commonly known as "PTSD."[10] For many years, "PTSD" became the label of most post-combat illnesses and symptoms of combat trauma. It became a label for such a broad spectrum of symptoms that we were generally confused about what it is and how it should be treated. "PTSD" was treated as anything from a stress disorder to a severe behavioral mental health illness. This confusion is understandable in light of the evolution of "PTSD" and subsequent methods of treatment.

Dr. Jim Goodwin, Psy.D, in his work "The Etiology of Combat-Related Post-Traumatic Stress-Disorders" describes the evolution of PTSD.[11] Through World War II and well into the Korean War, what is now labeled "PTSD" was thought to be a psychological breakdown due to the actions of combat. As the intensity of combat increased, the psychiatric injuries increased. As combat intensity decreased, psychiatric injuries also decreased, and then appeared to go away after combat stopped. As a result, it was treated as an injury with the end state of either returning to duty or being discharged as unfit. For example, during World War I it was called "shell shock" and associated with the physiological damage resulting from exploding artillery shells. After the Warfighters went home, no follow-up was done to track the symptoms. They were thought to have stopped when the war stopped.[12]

The Vietnam War changed the perceptions of "PTSD." Symptoms, common among all Veterans and Warfighters, with a wide variety of combat experiences, were being observed long after the actual combat experiences ended. The common symptoms included anxiety, flashbacks, dreams of combat experiences, depression, uncontrolled anger, and loss of relationships, isolation, and other related symptoms. Surprisingly, the post-Vietnam era research discovered that a variety of non-combat related events created similar symptoms. Victims of such events as natural disasters, plane crashes, and other traumatic events presented similar "PTSD" symptoms as combat Veterans.[13]

One of the key findings common to most "PTSD" studies

is that shared experiences, relationships, connections to fellow Warfighters and Veterans and the sense of community created a buffer for "PTSD" symptoms. During WWII Warfighters were connected through the classic "Band of Brothers."[14] They experienced war together, survived together, and in the years following the War, they re-connected and told their stories. The WWII Warfighters found support in their connections with each other that are still maintained to this day through reunions and Veterans' organizations.

These Veterans went on to hold significant jobs and became public servants, lawyers, doctors, clergy, etc. 1LT Lee Alley has a great quote in his book, "Back from War" about looking in the wrong place for Vietnam Vets. He suggests that many of us have bought into the propaganda and stereotypes about Vietnam veterans, but the reality is many of them went on to be public servants and hold critical jobs.

> "I began to realize I was looking for you in the wrong places. I was looking where Hollywood tried to influence us all to look for Vietnam veterans. 'Look for the down and outs. That's where you'll find them'. Not so! Just absolutely plain not so. I have found you and continue to find you as the good husbands and fathers, the doctors, clergy, lawyers, teachers, farmers and all the other fine, reputable and honorable people you have always been and continue to be . . .The Vietnam vets have quietly become the backbone of America."[15]
>
> Lee Alley

During Vietnam, Warfighters were given an end-date for their assignment in combat and were rotated as individuals, not as parts of a unit. Survival in combat became an individual effort. Once home, the Veterans believed they would forget about their war experiences and return to life as they knew it before they deployed. The Vietnam Warfighters experienced a profound sense of personal isolation. Those that survived until their end-date found upon returning home that their trauma had only just begun. They had few on-going unit connections and returned to their lives disconnected and in isolation with their trauma. This became fertile ground for festering "PTSD" symptoms. A recent phenomenon for the Vietnam Veteran is the advent of the virtual community that is reconnecting them. They are rediscovering a community of fellow Veterans and Warfighters and finding outlets for their stories.[16]

> "The Gulf War (90-91) was lauded as an operation causing little loss to U.S. forces. As of May 2002, more than a decade later, the VA had recognized a total of 262,586 veterans disabled due to Gulf War duties and 10,617 dead of combat related injuries and illnesses since."[17]
>
> Edward Tick

Today's Warfighters and Veterans of the Global War on Terrorism (GWOT) and the Iraq and Afghanistan Wars continue to suffer the trauma of "PTSD." However, recent research is changing how the military and VA diagnose and treat "PTSD." This change has created a welcome focus on the more severe symptoms and has led to treatments that are more effective. It has also created a gap in recognizing the deeper affects of combat trauma on the Warfighter and Veterans. We believe that there is now another story that must be told. Once the military and VA started to focus on the more obvious and extreme symptoms of "PTSD" and "mTBI," what was neglected is the more subtle, deeper, and more hidden silent wounding that takes place. We call this the silent wounding of the Soul. A silent desperation takes over and becomes all-encompassing.

The symptoms of the silent wounding of the Soul often mimic the more obvious "PTSD" and "mTBI injuries." Veterans and Warfighters return home with vague behavioral issues, painful memories, stress, and other disorders that the medical world classifies as mild stress and does not immediately treat. Veterans and Warfighters often mask their symptoms in order to get home more quickly. They do not yet realize the extent of their wounding. This Soul disorder is life changing. While Warfighters are engaged in combat they learn to adapt to the stress, chronic fear, lack of sleep, and the lifestyle of combat and field conditions. Upon their return to home life they begin to realize the extent of the changes that have taken place in their lives and in their Souls. Their "Post Traumatic Soul Disorder" (PTSoulD) becomes apparent as they attempt to return to life, as they knew it and discover that nothing is the same. Warfighters, Veterans, and family members seek out the connections within the community of other Warfighters, Veterans, and family members who share the pain, grief, loss, and silent desperation.

In the Global War on Terror, personnel assignment policies continue to treat Warfighters as individual assets, but the evolving virtual community is keeping them connected unlike any time in the past. The increased reliance upon National Guard and Reserve Warfighters creates the contemporary dilemma of the impact of relatively short combat experiences sandwiched between routine home lives. The Guard and Reserve Warfighter can be home one month and in combat the next, and home again a year later. It is easy then for the individual Warfighter to believe that the home life did not change in their absence. The common belief is that they would be deployed for 12 months or so and then return to their lives, as they remembered them. After all, they were the police, the firefighters, the bankers, the businesspersons, the husbands, and the wives of their communities. They had to believe that they would return to life, as they knew it.

Today, the emotional and mental symptoms of war are still tinged by perceptions of poor training, disciplinary problems, personality issues, weakness of character, and even cowardice. "PTSD" is relegated to an extreme behavioral mental health illness or a medical injury. Everything else is seen as mild stress reactions from which Warfighters should recover relatively quickly. "PTSD" victims still cannot escape many of the stereotypes and stigmas of mental health - that somehow, the person is faking it, and the condition isn't real. If it is real, it is not something we talk about. And if we do talk, it is always something the other guy has - the one who can't cut it in combat.[18]

Many experts in combat psychiatry have come to believe that modern warfare is simply too traumatic and stressful for Warfighters to withstand for too long.[19] The best-trained Warfighter will succumb to the trauma of war sooner than later. Sometimes this will be displayed as extreme symptoms of "PTSD." However, less obvious, our premise is that every Warfighter and every leader will experience the silent wounding of the Soul and the companion physical, mental, emotional, social, and spiritual breakdowns.

Combat trauma as a silent wounding of the Soul has only recently emerged from the research and study into the symptoms of "PTSD" and "mTBI." Certainly, these two injuries have physical as well as mental symptoms. Both are facets of a silent wounding of the Soul. However, when treating "PTSD" and "mTBI," the silent wounding of the Self, of the whole person, remains largely ignored.

Even people of great faith experience the trauma of war and are changed by it.[20] The media has written numerous stories of military chaplains who are so wounded by the trauma of war that they lose their faith or adopt the destructive behaviors of escapes such as alcohol abuse to try to cover up the pain they feel from their emotional wounds. We know military chaplains who were so silently wounded by the trauma of war that they chose behavior that destroyed their careers and marriages. These stories confirm for us that no one is exempt from being touched by the horror of war.

We believe that what requires treating is not just "PTSD" in its traditional or historical sense. We will leave that to the medical and psychotherapy professions. What we believe needs attention is the silent wounding of the whole person. What requires treatment is "PTSoulD" in its life changing silent wounding sense. We believe that a silently wounded Soul is a subsequent and lingering symptom of combat trauma. The focus of this book, therefore, is on discussing the nature of this Soul disorder and discovering healing of the silent wounds of the Soul. Healing must occur in the context of self-awareness and community. The silent wounding is life changing and as a result is a lifelong healing process. It involves a sense of the Self and one's Soul. By default the silent wounding of one's Soul also becomes a spiritual issue. This is true whether one believes deeply in a religious faith or has none at all. The core premise is that we all have a sense of our Soul. The concept of the Soul, the silent wounding of the Soul as a symptom of combat trauma, and the healing of the Soul, is not a popular concept for treating Veterans and Warfighters throughout the military, government, and medical institutions. At best, the silently wounded are treated with medications and left on their own. At worst, they are ignored.

We have a combined 12 years of experience at the policy and strategic levels of the Department of the Army. We have seen both the military chaplaincy and the medical and mental health professions struggle with how to address the trauma of war. Recent research indicates that these two domains are now starting to come together. Prominent combat psychiatrists are saying that the trauma of combat results in a silent wounding of the Soul. The military chaplaincy is coming to a deeper understanding of their role in healing the silent desperation that engulfs the lives of our Warfighters, Veterans, and family members. The purpose of this book is to show how these worlds can work together to heal the inner pain, grief, loss, and desperation experienced by our Warfighters and Veterans. The Healing of the Soul is a life saving event. Our research indicates that far too many Warfighters and Veterans take their lives post-combat because they can no longer live with the memories, the pain, the grief, the loss, and the desperation. We all have a role to play and we must work together to do something about that.

"In this I disagree radically with the vast majority of

psychiatrists today, who are so entranced with the powers of modern medication that they concern themselves with symptoms rather than souls, treating the chemically imbalanced brain but ignoring the experiencing self."[21]

Elio Frattaroli

Spirituality and the Soul are not the common domains of the medical and mental health models for treating the symptoms of combat trauma. Too often, spirituality and the Soul are relegated to the world of religion and then equated to a variety of attitudes from open and joyful acceptance, deeply personal feelings and beliefs not subject to discussion, or to perceptions of power, control, and manipulation. Certainly combat trauma has traditionally not been treated as a spiritual or moral dilemma. "Psychotherapists are trained not to talk much about spirituality or morality in the first place. But these are precisely the characteristics we must address in order to evolve strategies that facilitate identity reconstruction and soul restoration."[22]

When we change the perceptions of combat trauma symptoms to a silent wounding, we discover that one facet of the wounding is a sense of grief and loss. This grief and loss is not only the witness to the loss of life that occurs in combat, but also the loss of innocence and the loss of Self. The sense of grief and loss harbors deep within our Souls. The Warfighters, Veterans, and family members' reactions to the trauma of combat are a profound sense of loss, grief, and guilt. This, along with the vivid memories of combat, is the silent wounding and the disorder of the Soul. We need to find the path to our healing, to grieve, to acknowledge our loss, to confront our guilt, and to decide to live once again. Left untreated or without intervention, this silent wounding leads to behavioral dysfunctions to include alcohol and drug addictions, dysfunctional anger and hostility, paranoia, anxiety disorders, irrational fears, social and relational problems, a pervasive all encompassing silent desperation, and premature deaths as additional, post-combat casualties through suicide.

We believe that there is a new generation of Warfighters, Veterans, and family members (WVFM) with silently wounded Souls who are at risk of life-long behavioral dysfunctions and often pre-mature death through suicide. This is a significantly profound and perhaps arrogant thing to say. But with the current attitudes about spirituality, the Soul, and healing, those silently wounded by the trauma of war are not finding healing in the traditional methods. They are suffering from all of the symptoms of "PTSoulD" in their own right as much as anyone suffering from the more traditional symptoms of "PTSD." However, when we engage the "WVFMs" to tell their stories about their silent wounds and their quiet desperation, they have a story to tell and are eager to do so. It becomes a cathartic event. Telling their stories is a critical step to finding healing, finding meaning in their lives, and moving on to purposeful living.

Warfighters, Veterans, and family members who are survivors of combat trauma speak universally about being silently wounded in their Selves and their Soul - living lives of quiet desperation. We are dealing with a moral trauma that silently wounds the Soul. Healing is finding balance in our lives and returning our sense of Self to health.

Thus, this is a story of the silent wounds from the trauma of war and of healing. This is also a story of preventing additional post-combat casualties through suicide and diverting lives from ongoing behavioral dysfunctions and pervasive all encompassing silent desperation. Warfighters, Veterans, and family members are silently wounded and their lives are changed as a result of combat trauma. Their whole persons are affected, different from "before," and changed. This is a story of learning how to heal and to live with the changes. This is a story of remembering, understanding the Self, finding meaning in the wounding, telling the stories, and finding healing through connection within a community of relationships. The trauma of combat changes Warfighters and Veterans, and they cannot get the old Self back, or return to life as it was before combat. They will never forget. They will endure the changes for the rest of their lives. They will have pain, grief, and loss the rest of their lives. Warfighters and Veterans lose their innocence in combat, and that innocence is forever lost.

The trauma of war is a story of the whole community. It is only within the connections of the whole community that healing is truly possible. The individual Warfighters and Veterans first and foremost seek acceptance, understanding, and forgiveness by the community that sent them to war. They crave acceptance and understanding for the horrors they witnessed and forgiveness for the horrors they committed. The Warfighters and Veterans seek to tell their stories within a community that nurtures and supports them. They seek to find meaning in the pain, grief, loss, and desperation they experience. Warfighters and Veterans, and family members seek connection within community. The community then bears witness to their stories, their trauma, and their pain, grief, loss, and desperation. We all, then, accept responsibility for the silently wounded Warfighters and Veterans, and their family members.

WHAT IS THE SOUL?

"The fashion nowadays is to use the word mind instead of soul (to avoid any spiritual connotations) and to believe that either mind or soul is really just another word for brain. This belief-that anything we might call mental or spiritual is really only a by-product of brain activity- is the hallmark of our current "Age of the Brain." It helps us answer academic or scientific questions about the mind and mental illness. But it doesn't provide much of an answer for the questions we really care about: Who am I? and What is the meaning of my unique experience as a human being."[23]

Elio Frattaroli

At the core of every human being is a Soul. The Soul is the set of beliefs, values, morals, traditions, and ideas that form the living personal characteristics that define who we are as persons. Healing the Soul involves coming to terms with one's personhood. Each Warfighter's or Veteran's sense of Self or personhood is unique. They each see, hear, interpret, and act in different ways in their own understanding of their core personal characteristics and how they are manifested in their Souls.

The Soul is the personal essence that is unique to each of us. It is what we call the Self. The Soul is what makes the person unique. The Soul is that unique combination of personal characteristics coming together to incorporate the inner sense of awareness of a person. The Soul is our sense of inner identity and what makes me, me, and you, you. The Soul is the unification and focus of all that a person is in life. When the Soul is wounded so then is the person.

HEALING POST TRAUMATIC SOUL DISORDER CONCEPT

"In practice, this means that you always have within you the resources necessary to solve the problems that confront you. Healing the soul means becoming able to access those inner resources easily and at will."[24]

Elio Frattaroli

First and foremost, the focus is on healing. What we are calling a disorder of the Soul requires a life-long commitment to healing that will have significant effects. Healing will have significant effects. One such effect is that Warfighters, Veterans, and family members find meaning in their pain, grief, loss, and desperation. Another effect is relief from the ongoing pervasive desperation that clouds their lives. When we find meaning, we can learn to cope with our pain. Another effect is turning from inner despair to living for the greater good. Healing the Soul is about connecting again to life, family, and community through purposeful living. The core accumulative affect of healing the Soul is to prevent post-combat deaths through suicide.

We believe that every Warfighter and Veteran is silently wounded and can live a life of quiet desperation. Combat trauma silently wounds the Soul in many ways that are unique to each individual person. The degree and depth of the grief, loss, pain, and desperation might vary from Veteran to Veteran and Warfighter to Warfighter, but the pain is real and alive for each individual. For some, the wounding remains silently within and creates great emotional pain and desperation. It is a deeply silent disorder of the Soul. Too often, Warfighters and Veterans never deal with the grief, loss, pain, and desperation in an honest and essential way. The memories, pain, and loss can lead to life-long behavioral dysfunctions and pre-mature death through suicide. When hurting occurs within us, there must be careful and deliberate work, on Warfighter's and Veteran's, and family member's parts, to touch the

Soul and let healing begin. Confronting the silent wounds and the disorder of the Soul is a matter of life.

The Soul becomes wounded when the sights, sounds, and smells of combat create a deep pain and leaves Warfighters feeling profound loss and grief. This describes the disorder of the Soul. As a result, they manipulate their behavior to mask the feelings of loss and the grief. They engage in many behavioral dysfunctions to include alcohol and drug addictions, dysfunctional anger and hostility, paranoia, anxiety disorders, irrational fears, social and relational problems, and a pervasive all encompassing silent desperation. When this behavior becomes destructive and continues without intervention, the Veteran is in danger of ultimately taking his or her life to stop the pain. The effort of Veterans to mask their pain does not take it away. Just as getting drunk does not take away the pain, it only masks it so they can survive another day. For Warfighters and Veterans to remove the pain in their spirits and the wounds of their Souls, they need to reach deep within themselves and examine what is taking place in their lives. That takes a great deal of personal courage. It takes as much courage to heal as it does to face the fears of combat in the first place.

When Warfighters, Veterans, and family members feel the profound sense of loss and pervasive grief, they develop subsequent attitudes and behaviors that reflect their silent wounds rather than who they really are. They display these attitudes and behaviors in each of the personal characteristics of their whole person. Healing the Soul is about the deliberate choice to deal with the grief, loss, pain, and desperation with honesty and thoughtful exploration, self-examination, and personal reflection.

Healing the Soul involves Warfighters and Veterans intentionally challenging their attitudes and behaviors and asking themselves why they think, believe, and act as they do. The process of healing will challenge them to determine if they are living in such a way that reflects a hurt Self, a pained spirit, and a silently wounded Soul. The silent wounding results in poor decisions, bad behavior, an unhealthy sense of Self or personhood, dysfunctional emotions, and a deepening of the silent wounds in their Souls. Thus, healing the Soul is about bringing the personal characteristics of Self into balance, finding meaning in suffering, and making life choices in honest and deliberate ways to achieve purposeful living.

FINDING MEANING IN THE SILENT WOUNDING

"I have to accept my new reality and go on with my life."[25]

Anonymous, Iraq War Veteran Amputee,
Interview of Army Staff Sergeant

Healing begins when Warfighters and Veterans choose to assign healthy meaning and purpose to their grief, loss, pain, and desperation. This is the beginning of healing. They find meaning in order to move on to purposeful living. Finding meaning and purpose in life's traumas and most difficult experiences affirms that Warfighters and Veterans ultimately have the choice of how to behave because of the experience. It is a personal decision. They can choose to be a victim of the pain or wrongfulness and allow the Soul to go without healing. Yes, they can choose to remain a silently wounded Soul. On the other hand, they can determine to find a purpose in the pain, loss, grief, and suffering and in doing so, claim the power to begin their own healing, reconnect with their communities, and ultimately save their own lives. Healing the Soul begins when Warfighters and Veterans find purpose in their grief and suffering and the suffering or pain does not diminish their lives. It does not mean the memories go away nor does it mean that they will be free of grief, loss, pain, and desperation. Healing the Soul is a lifetime process. They will, however, learn how to live with these changes in their lives and find ways to serve the greater good.

An Army Chaplain recalled the story about an Army Staff Sergeant he recently visited in the Walter Reed Medical Center. This Soldier's story is a poignant example of a man making a choice to heal his Soul. He lost a leg above the knee in Iraq to an improvised explosive device (IED). His other leg was shattered. He had gone through many surgeries in an attempt to save the leg. The Chaplain asked how he was handling all he was going through. He answered, "It's been tough. At times, I really get down and depressed, but I've decided not to let it beat me. I have to accept my new reality and go on with my life." [26] He made the decision to take the path of healing of both body and Soul.

This book will help Warfighters, Veterans, and family members understand that it is possible to make such a decision in their lives. In fact, it will help anyone who has experienced deep personal wounding. The silent wounding of the Soul transcends the trauma of combat. It is a condition common to the human experience. Healing is the process of finding meaning and seeking purposeful living. Healing is about saving lives.

Part One.
Remembering
The Silent Wounds of War

"To be wronged is nothing unless you continue to remember it." [27]

Confucius

INTRODUCTION

"Although the world is very full of suffering, it is also full of the overcoming of it."[28]

Helen Keller

Many Warfighters and Veterans can tell us the day, the hour, or the act when they remember losing their Souls. Others may not be able to point to a specific time or event, but remember the series of experiences like a movie being played out in their minds. Veterans of World War II and Vietnam remember, as do Veterans of today's Iraq and Afghanistan Wars and the Global War on Terrorism. They are connected by their memories of war trauma. The act of remembering is a consistent issue concerning the trauma of war and a result of "Post Traumatic Soul Disorder" (PTSoulD).

Rather than being simply a stress reaction or a behavioral mental health issue, the silent wounding that occurs can be described as a "person" changing experience that fundamentally and irrevocably changes who Warfighters and Veterans are as persons. This is what some care-giving professionals are beginning to call a silent wounding of the Soul. The act of remembering and telling their stories provides a connection between Warfighters, Veterans, and family members; it is both a reflection of the trauma and a part of the healing process. In order to heal "WVFMs" need to tell their stories to themselves and to others. They will not be who they were ever again. But they can begin to heal the person they have become. When they cannot or do not tell the stories of their memories, those memories overwhelm them, and they engage in life-long behavioral dysfunctions and may eventually experience pre-mature death, most often by suicide. They become uncounted war casualties. And so, to walk the path of healing, begin by remembering.

REMEMBER THE DAY

"Perhaps someday it will be pleasant to remember even this."[29]

Virgil

LUKE

I remember that day like it was this morning. The day I lost my Soul. I was on patrol. Shotgun in the hummer. I remember it was hot. The wind was blowing and sand was in my teeth and I was bitchin' to myself about it. Can't even chew a piece of gum without crunchin' on grit. Then it happened. I remember it like this morning, and it was over a year ago. But first, let me tell you about being young once.

I remember the day I graduated from high school. Felt free. It was a new feeling. I could do whatever I wanted. After all, I had the whole summer ahead of me. My girl, Jennifer, and me. We graduated together. Yeah, we had thought about college but we decided to stay around home. So I got a job helping my old man in the store. Had a car. Jennifer started talking about getting married. But I didn't think we would make it on what I was makin' at the store. I was out with some of my buddies that August and for fun, we decided to join the Guard. We heard it was easy going. Besides, most everyone in town was in the unit. All my friends were in it and most of my family.

At first the Guard was just fun. A chance to get together with friends as we worked out the training. We didn't take things too serious in the beginning. Things changed when we went to Basic. Maybe we changed. We ended up at Jackson and I remember most the feeling of becoming a warrior. Not at first. But we changed during those weeks together in Basic. I remember getting our berets. That was cool stuff. We stood tall together. We thought we were really warriors. Cocky as hell. One of the really cool things we did is learn about all of the technology in the equipment we had. Not much different from the video games we sat around playing or the texting we did on the web. Same stuff we did all the time.

It wasn't long after we returned home that the unit got orders to deploy. To be honest we knew about what was going on in Iraq but we really didn't pay a lot of attention. It was still far away and didn't affect us. We thought that our unit wouldn't be affected by it all. It hadn't been called up since the 60's. And then they never made it out of the training base before being sent home again. So it was a shock when the captain said we had deployment orders. And then we were excited. The next days and weeks were a blur. Before long, we were through our deployment train-up and on our way to Iraq. We were young then. We took on the world.

§§§§

A young Warfighter deployed today could be home in Baltimore or Boston by the weekend as a Veteran, with the thanks of a grateful Nation. How does a man or woman who was on patrol in the streets of Iraq just weeks ago adjust to being on hometown streets, at the family dinner table, in the arms of their loved ones, so soon after the experiences of combat?

The silent wounds of war that affect the daily transitions needed from the front lines to the front stoop are often hidden and not easily solved. Our Warfighters, Veterans, and family members often have limited, if any, day-to-day support. Certainly, our Guard and Reserve Veterans who are located far from standard medical and VA facilities are left with extremely limited options. Traditional training, transition programs, and suicide prevention programs are expensive in either standard facilities or as exported programs, depend heavily on resources, and are focused on utilization of caregivers. "WVFMs" need help and support with the healing process in their own homes, taking advantage of their own inner strengths, and at times, of their own choosing. They find connection within their hometowns, not within the medical and VA centers.

In the past, the emotional and spiritual wounds of war

may not emerge for months or years after Warfighters return home. Today they are evident almost immediately as a result of the real-time connections through the Internet. We find that the advent of technology and the virtual community keeps Warfighters, Veterans, and family members connected to each other, but also connected to the traumatic events they experienced. Thus, the trauma of war and the symptoms of their silent wounds become evident immediately upon their reintegration back into the home front. Especially for National Guard and Reserve Warfighters, the expectation is that they will return to life, as they knew it prior to their deployment. They expect to return home and step back into their jobs and resume their family relationships as if nothing happened. When they return, they discover nothing is like it was before. Everything has changed because they have changed. The common experience remains that as Veterans, they often do not recognize their emotional and spiritual scars in them, and when they do, they are reluctant to ask for help, often for fear of being labeled as weak or broken. When left untreated, "PTSoulD" can lead to premature death.

The DoD Mental Health Task Force released its final report June 15, 2007.[30] The 14-member task force spent a year compiling and evaluating research data and testimony from experts and advocates and conducted site visits to 38 military installations worldwide. They found that mental health problems still carry a stigma that remains pervasive in the military and additionally, it deters those who need care from seeking it. Long-term silent wound problems were not even on the map. The group highlighted the urgent need for action to address the "signature injuries" from the current conflicts and the trauma of war. It is more evident today than in the past that combat trauma affects Warfighters, Veterans, and family members within their Souls. It is also evident that there are not enough traditional methods of care to meet this new understanding of their emerging needs.[31]

Going from home to an operational theater and into combat

involves a loss of innocence. When Warfighters subsequently redeploy from places like Iraq and Afghanistan, they often have a difficult time adjusting to life back at home. Warfighters, as Veterans, attempt to return to their lives as they were. Living for months in a high-stress, high-adrenaline, fear-laden environment can have a cumulative effect on the physical, emotional, mental, social, and spiritual state of an individual. Dealing with the loss of comrades, one or two at a time, and fighting against elusive insurgents, that sometimes include women and children, is difficult at best and can be quite traumatic, during both the deployment and long afterward.

We find that non-traditional approaches to healing help Veterans and Warfighters at redeployment and during their reintegration into home-life. There is a marked increase of use and dependence on technology to reach literally every facet of life. The web not only continues to flourish, but also, more importantly, is becoming a part of mainstream culture. Veterans, Warfighters, and family members today are a part of the evolution of virtual communities where they find connection and support. They are finding connection in the virtual world and as a result are telling their stories in that world.[32]

WE TOOK ON THE WORLD

"Let us not look back in anger or forward in fear, but around in awareness."[33]

James Thurber

LUKE

When the unit got the notice to deploy, we didn't have much time to think about things. The days prior to our move to the mob site were full of getting ready. We got equipment and did a lot of training. We were introduced to a lot of the Army's on-line training. We got extra computers set up in the Armory and most of us spent a lot of time there. In basic, we got hooked big time on the Army game "America's Army." We got into "Shadow Warriors" also. We played them both a lot, killing time in the Armory. What we didn't know at the time was our captain thought it was good training. We thought we were getting away with something.

Most of us were family and friends in our small town. We ran the businesses, and we were the police and fire departments. My squad leader was the local bank manager. My brother was our platoon leader. So the town went into crisis mode almost immediately. Jennifer and I started making plans to get married. We wanted to do that before I left. Just seemed like the right thing to do. We had about two months from the notification to when we were to report to our deployment mob station for training. No one would say anything at the time but we were all scared. But then I remember we were scared we would not measure up. That somehow we would fail. No one thought about being killed although that was in the back of our minds. We just didn't talk much about it. We started looking more at what we were to expect in Iraq. All the stories. We got on the net and blogged others to get the scoop. We had some web geeks that put together a website for all of us to stay in touch with our families and friends at home. I started a blog to tell my story. Looking back, my entries were cocky and smart. Didn't see it then but I do now. We were going to do it different. Most of my friends did up a blog also. And then we started sharing it all on the website. We really had a great network going then. And when

35

we hit the ground in Iraq, we were in full blog with everything we did put up on the net. We had pictures, movies, and everything. We were able to email back home all the time. Having just got married, I was able to keep in touch with Jennifer every night. It was still like we were dating in high school when we used to text each other in class. I don't think the fact that we got married had sunk in yet. It was one big blur and one big party. But then we didn't have enough time to get used to the idea. Jennifer was into going to church a lot. I tagged along because that was where Jennifer was. I didn't think much about what all that meant to me…all the talk about the spirit and prayer and stuff. Now I do. Do I ever. But we were cool then. We didn't need a prayer.

JENNIFER

I thought I knew what was coming— months upon months of letters, fear, and deep unutterable longing. Tears streamed down my face, and I tried not to fall apart as he kissed me. I whispered "Goodbye," but I could barely bring myself to let go of his fingertips as he joined the line of Soldiers. I sighed. I swallowed.

My eyes wandered the curves of his body, the green bag slung over his shoulder, his shaved head. My eyes rested on his shoulders and then moved to the scar on his chin. I tried desperately. I tried desperately to memorize every last inch of him, one more time. I'd been memorizing him for weeks—studying his face, finding every mole, every freckle, every worry line, and every scar. He didn't understand my insistence on taking pictures of him cooking, sleeping, talking to a friend, or sleeping with the dogs. But I was making sure that I wouldn't forget—that in the middle of the night, or mid-afternoon, I'd be able to feel his face touching mine, his lips calming me, his arms holding me close.

He turned his head towards me. His soft eyes searched me; fear crossed them, sadness, longing—love. A half smile, a wave, and those blue eyes were gone. The Soldiers began to board the plane, and I saw him turn back to wave, but it was too far for me to see his face.

I knew Luke was deploying to Iraq when we got married. And at first, I thought I could handle it. I envisioned myself as a newly wed Army Guard wife, strong and supportive of the Warfighter I married. I was always the independent type, and that's what made Luke so crazy about me. In high school, we were friends that started dating kind of on accident. He left flowers in my locker, slipped love notes between the pages of my textbooks, and text messaged me during class. We spent so much time talking. He talked, and I listened. I talked, and he listened. We left nothing out. On our first date, we spent the evening revealing the worst things about ourselves to each other in what we called "The Question Game." Any question was permitted and the only rule was straight-up honesty. I'm sure it sounds like the first date from hell, but it was so natural to us and, that's how we started.

The closer we got to graduation the more Luke talked about getting married. He was so sure about "us," always telling me to trust in "us." He wanted kids with me, a family to support and take care of. Even though he'd never say it, he hated working in his dad's store; he needed something that was just his, something to be proud of, and something that would pay the bills. When he joined the guard, I didn't really think about the possibility of him deploying. We were still kids. The infamous 9/11 attack happened our senior year in high school; it hardly occurred to me that it could affect our lives so directly. We got married a few weeks before he left. I'll never tell him this, but part of me just couldn't handle the idea of never being his wife. In case he didn't come back, I wanted every possible moment I could have with him as a married couple, even if it only was a few weeks. We just couldn't wait until he came back. I wasn't sure that he would.

> "Luke, I'm just so sad. I don't know what I'm gonna do when you are gone and I can't talk to you every day." "Jennifer, it's my job. You knew this was going to happen when we got married. I don't know what you want me to do." "Stop trying to fix this. You can't fix it Luke. I don't want you to do anything or say anything. I just need you to know what is going on inside my head."

It's amazing how much tension there was between Luke and me those last few weeks before he left. We wanted to savor the moment, but we couldn't focus on anything but him leaving. I was a veterinary assistant at a local animal hospital and on my drive to work each day I listened to the radio. Most days I listened to reports like "three Soldiers killed in Iraq today." Names, ranks, and ages were listed. "This past month was the deadliest for American troops since the start of the war on terror." There's so much talk about what the Soldiers are sacrificing and what they must feel like over in Iraq. I felt like my world was falling apart, and no one was noticing. People never hesitated to remind me that we have a volunteer army and that if I pray hard enough everything will just work out.

When it came to dealing with Luke's deployment, I had good days and bad days. On bad days, I would cry all the way to work, and even the word "deployment" could initiate more tears. I felt exhausted and completely disinterested in anything outside of spending time with Luke. Everything that used to seem important paled in comparison to the fact that he was leaving for twelve months. I felt like I was not only losing my best friend, but also that I was preparing to lose a part of myself. On good days, I spent little time contemplating deployment. Good days consisted of grocery shopping with my husband, walking the dogs, making dinner together, telling jokes, and laughing at each other. Good days were almost like comic relief, a sub-reality distracting us from the impending deployment and all that it entails.

It was the Saturday after payday, and we made our usual trip to the grocery store. Our conversation was light, and we were in good moods from sleeping late. I was thinking about how okay I felt and wondering why I had been such a mess during the week when Luke bumped into a guy from his unit in the parking lot, and they started talking about Iraq. John had been to Iraq three times and was negotiating a divorce with his wife. "They don't even have a dining facility where we're going. A unit deployed there two or three months ago, and no one has heard from them yet. They don't even have internet access. Did you hear about the three Soldiers that are missing? Yeah, that's where they were kidnapped." The sick feeling I'd had early in the week descended almost immediately. Good day gone bad.

We got in the car in silence, and I did everything I could to hold back tears. Neither of us said anything, and we didn't need to. I had assumed from the start that internet was a given and never contemplated the concept of waiting for weeks at a time to know if Luke was alive or not. It was as if every time I got a handle on the idea of Luke leaving, I was presented with another insurmountable challenge. It was hard for me to comprehend twelve months without instant messaging, cell phones, and email. Ironically, once Luke arrived at his base in Iraq the internet was readily available.

At first, we thought Luke's unit was deploying to Afghanistan. When we got married, we thought his unit was leaving in January, after the holiday season. We would be together for his birthday, Thanksgiving, Christmas, and New Year's. The holidays seemed far away and thus, so did his deployment. One day at work, I noticed a new text message on my cell phone. "We need to talk," was all Luke wrote. My stomach sank. When he walked in the front door that night, I said, "How soon are you leaving?" "October and I'm going to Iraq." I felt as though the oxygen in my lungs was draining out. No Thanksgiving. No Christmas, birthday, or New Year's. I would spend every one of our first married holidays alone. That day at work, Luke's unit was given a different deployment date and a different deployment destination. "I'm leaving for the field next week. We'll be gone two weeks."

It was all I could do to deal with him leaving for twelve months. The deployment was practically upon us, and a lot of Luke's time would be spent away from home in training. I felt as though all our time together was gone, and I didn't know how I would get through the days and nights when he went to the field, let alone to Iraq.

I had nightmares about a chaplain coming to my door to tell me that Luke was dead. I decided I wouldn't answer the door if a chaplain ever came knocking. I would never let a stranger say those words to me. My dad was about the only person in the world I thought I could hear that from. Maybe because he was the man in my life up until the day Luke and I got married. Maybe because I felt that if he told me, I could just fall apart and it would be ok to fall apart if he was there. Or those words coming from his mouth would be somehow less terrible than from a stranger in ACU's. I never told Luke that I thought about things like that. He wouldn't ever let me talk about him dying over there. He always said there was more chance he'd get in a wreck on the way home from work than that he'd die in Iraq. Regardless, I couldn't shake it off. My fear was real to me, and yet, he didn't want to, or maybe he just couldn't bear to, address it.

§§§§

The shift back to life at home is never going to result in returning to life before deployment. Family members are affected when the Warfighter "abandons" them during the deployment. The return of the Warfighter may result in spousal abuse or the abuse of other family members. As a way of coping in such situations, Veterans, Warfighters, and family members turn to destructive behaviors. This can be as dangerous and life-threatening as substance abuse and alcoholism, or as benign, but just as destructive as financial abuse or developing behaviors such as an obsessive-compulsive disorder. In some cases, Warfighters and Veterans have committed atrocious acts upon their return to home station. All these problems have plagued Veterans as long as there has been war, and it represents an often hidden part of the cost paid by Veterans and Warfighters serving their nation in combat around the world.

There is a need to address issues centered on common re-integration problems of Veterans who return from deployment and the silent wounding they experience. Warfighters are often described as America's most deployed combat system. Yet, beneath all of the sophisticated technologies, weapons systems, tactics, and techniques, there are human beings with hearts and Souls. Warfighters, as any system under such extensive and intensive deployments, require maintenance and even repairs. They need healing after their loss of innocence from being exposed to the challenges and sights, sounds, and smells – the absolute horrors - of war.

We found that Warfighters and Veterans need help examining the changes in their lives. Combat trauma damages a person's ability to feel, think, and behave as they did before. As changed, silently wounded persons, their pain, grief, loss, and desperation affect and influence their relationships with family members and others. Their "PTSoulD" reflects their inability to handle anger, guilt, and other emotions after returning. Warfighters, Veterans, and family members need help examining their life changing experiences as part of the healing process.

A WAR AND A GAME

"Fear not that thy life shall come to an end, but rather fear it shall never have a beginning."[34]

Cardinal Newman

LUKE

I remember that for the first few weeks things were really routine. Not much different from the weeks of training back home. We got to know the mission we had. The territory we covered. At first, what we saw and did was interesting. New things to see and do. It wasn't long before the heat and dust started getting on our nerves. And the smells. Everything smelled old, dead, and like burnt rubber. When the routines stretched out, we started spending more time on the net when we were off. That is where I learned that Jennifer wasn't doing so good at home. We spent nearly every night emailing each other. Even got into playing games. She always beat me at cards and that got old but I didn't say anything. Something like 200 games to my one or two. Maybe I wasn't really thinking about the games. As I look back, I think we were all too distracted. Every odd sound, every bang, every out of place shout and we would all look up. I tried not to let on but I think that Jennifer knew. And she kept sticking it to me in cards. One thing for sure…Jennifer and I probably talked more over the net than we did face to face. In the emails, we could tell each other only what we wanted, or thought we wanted, each other to hear. It was the camera connections that were the hardest. Jennifer would look into my eyes and seem to know the truth. And the website with all the pictures. Of course, they were pictures of the worst things to see. Couldn't explain those away.

I found out Jennifer was pregnant one night soon after we got settled in country when we were emailing each other.

JENNIFER

Luke barely talked about being in Iraq or what it would be like when he was gone. He always talked about how much cash we could save

43

with the extra money from the hazardous duty pay, and what type of house we would be able to afford when he got back. Luke focused on "when I get back," when I could barely think that far. My anxiety was about him leaving and being gone for twelve months, and God forbid—what if he never made it back? If the possibility of his own death ever occurred to him, he never mentioned it to me.

Time was ticking away in my mind, and I grieved the loss of each day. If I was ever annoyed with Luke or him with me, I felt racked with guilt for wasting the only time we had left in a random argument. Luke had a hard time understanding where I was coming from and why I all of a sudden feared and hated spending even short amounts of time without him. I couldn't understand why he was so okay with the whole situation. I don't know why he couldn't just tell me the truth—that he was scared too, just in a different way. I think he was worried about me more than anything—worried that I wouldn't check the oil in my car, that I would lose too much weight once he left, or hold back my life, and spend too much time alone. I think another part of him had more faith in my strength than I did, and he knew I could handle what was to come, even if I didn't.

He told me one night that he was scared; he just doesn't know I remember it, and we never talked about it again. Late on a Saturday night, we were on our way home from a friend's birthday party. A few martinis had loosened me up, and personal anguish was flowing from my mouth. I was sharing with him the unsolicited advice I received from family members on both sides of our family. Prayer will get you through. Trust in the Lord and everything will be okay. I was in an utter panic. Trust what? Pray for what? A prayer that Luke would come home wouldn't necessarily bring him home. I knew that much, and so did everyone else. They just weren't willing to put it out there. Everyone wanted to make me feel better, but they didn't want to address the real issues I was dealing with. I was terrified and no one would acknowledge the reality of my fear. As the words poured out of me, he turned to me and said, "I'm scared too, but I think we've just got to trust in us." In the three words, "trust in us," he provided the type of comfort that only he could give me.

When Luke's unit started spending a lot of time in the field, I had a hard time driving home after work and getting to sleep at night. I dreaded darkness and going to bed without him. I put the dogs in bed with me, locked all the doors, closed all the blinds, and locked myself in our bedroom, with my cell phone under my pillow. If I couldn't get Luke on my cell phone, then I would talk to my mom until she went to bed. When the phone calls were over, and there was no one left to call, I was forced to turn out the light and lay in bed. If a neighbor drove up on our street I'd jump out of bed and peer through the blinds. If another dog barked and mine got excited, I panicked. At some point each night however, sleep won the battle. Every morning that I awoke without Luke, I turned to the dogs and whispered, "We made it." No one broke in. No one hurt us. We're alive, and the darkness is gone. I was relieved to see the daylight.

Right after we got married, Luke and I rented a house with a fenced yard for our dogs. It was a good size for us, and it was located in what seemed to be a relatively safe neighborhood. The closer and closer it got to Luke's deployment date, the stronger my urge for military connection. I wanted to know other wives and families who had been through what I was about to experience. I wanted someone to go the grocery store with, to have dinner with, and to depend on when I was scared or lonely. Moreover, I wanted to experience the deployment with someone who was experiencing it at the same time. I didn't want to do it alone.

I developed a relationship with Calley, a wife of one of the guys in Luke's unit. We spent hours talking about our fears and thoughts. We decided to alternate dinner at each other's houses once the guys left, to get through the deployment together. I agonized over having a good place to live—a place with friendly, supportive neighbors—a place that felt safe and secure. I dreaded living in a house by myself. I dreaded going to bed in an empty house and cooking dinner for one. I thought about moving home with Mom and Dad, but I didn't want to leave "our home." We had a home of our own, with our dogs and our stuff, and I wanted to be in that space, even if I didn't want to be alone.

Even before Luke left, I could picture every room in our house without him. I pictured myself going through the motions—waking up, feeding the dogs, letting the dogs out, starting the coffee, showering, getting dressed, playing with the dogs, drinking the coffee, driving to work, and coming home to the dogs each day. If I didn't have my dogs, "Sandy" and "Maggie," I would have felt worse. They were irreplaceable comfort in every aspect of the deployment, even before Luke left. They licked tears; they snuggled under my chin. They curled up on the couch and under the covers. They were the only thing that made being alone feel remotely bearable.

I questioned my sanity more often than I'd like to admit. I felt enraged, depressed, terrified, and I could encounter a range of emotions in a matter of hours on any given day. I found it more and more difficult to fake a smile and generate a friendly "how are you." No matter how many people I talked to, or friends I had, the type of hole that was being cut out of me could only be filled by Luke. There was something about his spirit that awakened mine. There was something about that sweet space we called "us," a place of peace, warmth, and stillness, and I didn't want to lose it.

We heard stories about Soldiers returning from Iraq all the time. Luke was at another Soldier's apartment one night and they heard the sound of very nearby gunshots. A Soldier was firing a gun off in his apartment; he seemed to believe he was still in Iraq. His wife made it out safely, but we never heard what happened to them after that. Callie told me about a husband waking up at night and putting his wife in a chokehold before realizing he was in his home and his wife was the person beside him. Would Luke be changed when he came back? Would I be changed by his deployment? Would we be robbed of our innocence in such a way that we would never be the same? What would he experience and how would it change who he was? What would happen in my life while he was away, and would I be the same young wife he knew when he left in the first place? Would we even know each other when we were re-united?

Luke and I wanted a family, but we didn't want one until his time in service was up and he was safe at home. When I saw the positive blue stripe on the test I bought at the local drugstore, I thought it was a fluke. I thought I was late because of the stress of him leaving. I wasn't sleeping or eating right, so it seemed natural that my hormones might be a little off. After ten tests and ten more blue stripes, I collapsed on the bathroom floor. I could have waited until he called again, but I knew he'd want to know, and I didn't want to wait. I sat down at my computer, "babe, I don't know how, but we're pregnant. I guess God had different plans for us than we did." I left out the fact that I thought getting pregnant was God's way of telling me that Luke wasn't going to make it back after all. I had thought it through, and if Luke never came back, I would pray to be pregnant with his child somehow, because then maybe I wouldn't be losing him completely. I wanted a boy.

§§§§

We exercise our healing within community. We cannot heal the silent wounds in isolation. The virtual world is becoming a trusted agent of community and information, as well as a source of support and assistance. The rise of virtual communities, on-line education, instant messaging, and blogging offer great promise for Warfighter, Veteran, and family member care and support. Today the virtual community is real, alive, and fulfilling legitimate needs for maintaining connections among "WVFMs." Making a connection with others is a key step toward healing. Often, it is even a critical life-saving step.

The extraordinary discoveries and advancements in virtual technologies and information exchange continue to mainstream into day-to-day activities. The virtual community is alive and well. Web-based activities and interaction are mainstream in today's society.

In 2005, Nintendo presented Amy Jo Kim's findings[35] concerning emerging trends relevant to understanding the critical placement and integration of technology. Today's youth trust, engage, and have immediate and sustained access to technology;

they exhibit an increasing level of global participation through the use of technology as well. Connected communities are changing. Community is no longer a sense of place, but rather a connection between people, including website social networks and buddy lists on mobiles. Emerging connection in communities is now rapidly moving from PCs and laptops to cell phones and Ipods. The home desktop computer system is the first communications device to research, seek, and establish the virtual community. Now, the cell phone is the emerging primary technology that builds and connects communities. Today's virtual world allows the individual to connect to others, formulate theories, test their theories, and discover their own personal and community cultures.[36]

Warfighters deployed to Iraq have the opportunity to play Internet games in "real time" with family members living in the States. We know of couples that use game playing to maintain contact during the deployment. The Internet allows them to spend quality time together while they are thousands of miles apart. Families of sport enthusiasts can play "fantasy" football and other games from any location in the world. Today the Internet is enabling Warfighters and family members to stay connected in ways not possible during the lengthy deployments and separations of the past.

The following remarks are from Douglas Lowenstein, President, Interactive Digital Software Association, spoken at the 2003 Serious Games Conference, Woodrow Wilson Center, Washington, DC:

> "The Department of Defense has been using game design principles for a decade to better prepare America's armed forces for war. Contrary to some of the exaggerated rhetoric one hears about military sims, the Pentagon does not use video games to train Soldiers to fire weapons or desensitize them to killing enemy Soldiers. Instead, they use video game simulations to teach tactics, build teamwork, and enhance decision-making. Games put the

Soldiers in realistic environments and real life situations, adding highly evolved artificial intelligence that is capable of mimicking the behavior and response of the enemy. The result is that the games enhance the prospects that Soldiers and officers, when confronted with comparable real life threats, will be better able to make the decisions that protect one another and accomplish critical missions because, in effect, they've already been there and done that." [37]

The dark side of this is that Warfighters and Veterans remain connected to the traumatic experiences that caused their wounding. Family members are actually getting too much information, causing them to live in a constant state of fear of losing their loved one. They find themselves glued to the news hoping to catch a glimpse of their loved one. When they don't, they fear the worst. They also see and hear the trauma of combat through the virtual world. We live in a visual, multi-media world, and we do not propose changing that. What we do propose is gaining an understanding of how this world affects us, keeps us linked to silent wounds, and how we need to live with these influences on our lives. The bright side is that the virtual world enables Warfighters, Veterans, and family members to connect with others, tell their stories, find meaning, and begin the healing process. We must deal with both sides of this modern day tool for connection.

THE HOME FRONT

"The human being who lives only for himself reaps nothing
but unhappiness. Selfishness corrodes. Unselfishness
enables, satisfies. Don't put off the joy derivable from
doing helpful, kindly things for others." [38]

B.C. Forbes

LUKE

Looking back sometimes, I marveled about the families and spouses at
home. After several months in country, my buddies said their spouses
were doing everything. They cooked, took care of kids, mowed the
lawns, fixed the cars, even acted as electricians. I wondered what will
be left for me when I got home. One thing I knew…money was tight.
At least that was what Jennifer told me all the time. Like I could get
a second job or something. And it wasn't like we were paying out a
mortgage. We argued about where all the money was going. I think
Jennifer did some research in what kind of help we could get for food
and basic household items. I felt ashamed about this. So I took it out
on Jennifer. Everything was tight — money, bills, groceries. It' wasn't
nearly enough, Jennifer explained. I knew that if the car broke down,
we couldn't just call someone, take it to the garage, and have them fix it.

We went to a lot of classes and briefings before I deployed. So many it
is now all a blur. Briefings and paperwork. That's all I can remember.
We even went to a retreat with the chaplain and had a bunch of briefings
about how to talk to each other. Jennifer and I were just married so
this didn't sink in at the time. Jennifer kept poking me to make points
about what the chaplain said but I didn't pay much attention. I didn't
think we needed all of that. We were doing OK. It was a cool free
weekend away and I wanted to skip out and play.

Jennifer kept telling me about the networks the spouses set up back
home. They did it all on the web. They blogged about everything
they were doing and what was going on in country. I think they knew
more about stuff happening than we did. It was a running joke that if
we wanted to find out what was happening, we just needed to tune into

51

CNN or work the net. I guess I shouldn't have complained. We did the same thing in country. In fact, we made it a point to post what we learned for our buddies. Warnings, what we saw, what we heard, what to avoid. We learned a lot from each other. Maybe Jennifer learned from the other spouses.

I know one thing; none of us wanted anyone to know that we were having any trouble. Especially at home. But every day I seemed to get angrier about what was happening and what we did and saw. The one bright spot was the birth of my daughter. Jennifer and I had been video web messaging for some time and we were sharing what was happening with her pregnancy. I was out on a patrol when the word came through that she had gone into labor and we had a daughter. I was flying high. Got a lot of ribbing from my buddies. Had to buy cigars from the PX for the whole world. At least for a few days, the anger retreated and my thoughts turned to a new family. But I was soon frustrated that I couldn't be there to help. And I started wondering if I would ever see my daughter for real.

JENNIFER

Before Luke left, I was introduced to the "FRG," Family Readiness Group, in his unit. At first, I felt strange. I appeared to be the youngest one there, and one of the only ones without several kids running around. I felt sick when they told us we had to have Luke's will written before he left. In the Army community, they don't sugarcoat the possibility of death like family members and other civilians. In the Army, death is always a possibility. I hated that way of thinking at first, but the more I got to know the other wives, I began to realize that I wasn't the only one who was scared or who felt alone.

The FRG set up a website when the guys left, and we were able to access pretty up-to-date information about where the guys were and what was going on. We also had a phone tree, just in case of an emergency. Most of the time our FRG meetings were focused around the children. We would meet at Chucky Cheese's or a big playground. We accessed the website for informational purposes, and we got together for companionship. I didn't feel very connected to these women until I found out I was pregnant. When I found out I was pregnant, all of a sudden I became part of this sisterhood of Army Guard wives and their babies. They made being pregnant very real to me. They had all been through it, some of them more than once. And they all knew what it was like to get through a pregnancy alone. The first time I got "morning sickness," Marty a mother of three, came over to the house to check on me and help me get the dogs fed and let out. We weren't a glorified support group— as some people described us—we were family.

We were women who mowed lawns, checked the oil, changed light bulbs, lighted grills, paid the bills, managed the money, and killed spiders. I became one of these women, and I was, as Luke would say, "damn proud." In some way, these women helped me find meaning in the daily sacrifices that come with being an Army Guard wife. We were in it together, and we would do whatever it takes to get to the day when our husbands came home.

§§§§

A recent study reported in the July 2004 of the New England Journal of Medicine (Vol. 351: 13-22, No. 1, July 1, 2004) entitled, "Combat Duty in Iraq and Afghanistan, Mental Health Problems, and Barriers to Care,"[39] made several alarming discoveries. The research has shown that exposure to combat results in considerable risks of mental health problems and impairment in social functioning and in the ability to work. And yet, the report also discloses that many gaps exist in the understanding of the full psychological effect of combat.

The study indicated that most of the psychological screenings for war trauma, major stress, and generalized anxiety disorders rely upon self-reports by the Warfighter. As a result, impairment in work, at home, or in interpersonal functioning was categorized as "very difficult" to be measured by questionnaires. Subjects in the study continually and consistently identified strong reservations and perceptions of stigma barriers in using traditional programs and care giving for help.[40]

The use of the virtual community can significantly enhance the capabilities to address these critical needs and simultaneously be integrated into the preparation before redeployment. Veterans learn things differently and at different speeds. Traditional classes and briefings often turn off Warfighters, Veterans, and family members because they are bored with them and resent being lectured to.

Most military and Veteran programs do not deal with the trauma and disorder of the Soul that results from the horror of combat. Veterans, Warfighters, and family members will not always find help through traditional programs to assist them with life solutions after deployments.

One of the core principles of healing the Silent Wounds is the individual must desire to find help, to find meaning, and to live a purposeful life. Individuals must want, seek, and engage help for help to be beneficial. The most effective help occurs when the individual is very comfortable with the process and believes that the help has value in their lives. The virtual world provides that level of comfort. The virtual community and the help found on the web is available to the Warfighter, Veteran, and family member in their own private space and time.

In his article, "Looking Into Online Therapy," Mark Griffiths[41] suggests that there are pros and cons of online therapeutic approaches that we can apply to the help "WVFMs" receive from the virtual community. These pros and cons illustrate the culture, expectations, and attitudes of today's generations who are comfortable with the virtual community. He lists several pros for on-line counseling such as convenience and cost effectiveness. Online help reduces barriers that may prevent people from seeking more traditional support such as social stigma.[42]

Warfighters, Veterans, and family members benefit from the help and support they find in the virtual world. The information and interaction on the web reaches the physically disabled, geographically isolated, and/or those who do not have access to a nearby caregiver. In addition, the virtual world reaches "WVFMs" who are embarrassed, anxious, and/or too nervous to talk about their problems face-to-face with someone.[43]/[44]

At the opposite end of consideration are the following cons observed by Griffiths[45] As Internet help and support services grow, so also do the legal and ethical issues for this type of caregiving.

The virtual community gives rise to legal and regulatory concerns and may compromise any expectation of privacy and confidentiality. In addition, the virtual community may not recognize if the individual needs referral to more direct care such as therapy, medications, or hospitalization.[46]

Our research in combat trauma suggests that the more effective on-line support includes the virtual communities that connect Warfighters, Veterans, and family members with each other. In these on-line communities, the "WVFM" can share their stories with others and receive the understanding and support that buffers the symptoms of their "PTSoulD."[47]

SIGHTS, SOUNDS, AND SMELLS

"My wounds have taken much from me, but they have also become gifts that transformed me."[48]

Shepherd Bliss

LUKE

There are things that I will remember forever. I know I will and forever hasn't gotten here yet. Almost but not. When the unit first arrived in Iraq, we saw more of the war on TV than the area we ended up. Our time would come, though. As the weeks passed, I grew frustrated. Our mission was important, yet I felt like I was being left on the sidelines.

Before moving out each day, I locked a magazine of ammo into my weapon and placed Jennifer's photo on the windshield of my hummer so it would feel like she was with me. Within minutes of leaving the FOB, we encountered our first Iraqi village.

The drive became tense quickly. Iraqi civilians were standing in the middle of the road to try to force us to stop so they could sell us trinkets. We were tempted to slow down but stopping would make us a target for attack. We fought our instinct to slow down, and we sped through the Iraqi civilians, who always scattered in time.

Sometimes the scenery we encountered on our patrols was a thing you would expect to find in Iraq -- herds of camels and sheep, destroyed military equipment and rubble where houses used to be. As we were on the move, we heard about insurgent attacks that continued to cause a steady flow of casualties among other units. As I look back, those early days were heaven compared to what would come.

Many days, aside from dodging Iraqi civilians, the only danger we faced was from the blinding dust, which increased our chances of getting lost or having an accident. To this day, my watch is still encrusted with sand. I often walked up to groups of kids and gave them some candy.

We came across an Iraqi town we had bombed the heck out of. Kids

57

would run out of the broken down houses and wave at us as we passed. They were known to pull out handguns so we had them in our sights at all times. Unfortunately, one of the vehicles right behind us ran one of them over and killed him. Iraqi's would drive past us, which was very nerve racking. We were aware that they were probably soldiers that were looking for an easy target they could ambush.

I don't remember what day it was, but I was in the FOB, working outside on the hummer cleaning things up and we heard the nerve-wracking wine of incoming and an explosion went off right across the street. It was about fifty yards from me. Nobody got hurt but that was a wake up call...

The roads around our FOB where we patrolled were littered with debris, burned out cars, hidden bombs that were called IEDs. One day we lost the first sergeant, and after that, the casualties never stopped. While on the streets we slept in abandoned houses, and we often went weeks without a shower, and days without sleep. We went on raids at night, kicking in doors and searching houses to the sound of gunfire and screams.

I remember that I had never felt such excitement in my life. Although we didn't see it then, the pressure, fear, and exhaustion began to smother us all. The squad survived several IED blasts. We started sucking on aerosol cans of Dust-Off to get high, and a new guy who came in accidentally died. I remember quitting the Dust-off. Lack of sleep mixed with the random IEDs and incoming shots scrambled our brains. We all wore it on our faces, in how we walked, and how we talked. It wasn't long before everything was in slow motion. Except the dread. The fear kept us on an edge that exhausted us. No one really ever slept anymore. And no one admitted that they were afraid.

I can still remember every detail; I can smell the burning vehicles and burning flesh in the air. I can hear the thunderous explosions from the artillery and air strikes and my heart beating uncontrollably. I remember the fear of the unknown and fear of the sky dense with thick smoke. I remember the feeling when I laid my eyes on a dead Iraqi for the first time. Chills ran down my spine as I gazed into the eyes of the mangled man. We were patrolling through a small village looking for insurgent activity.

The locals did not want to fight us head on but that day they changed their minds. Thoughts like that ran through our minds and poisoned our brains. We were always alert, but it seemed we were never alert enough. A fellow Soldier stepped on a land mine, shortly after my Platoon Sergeant was shot and killed a couple feet from where I stood. I moved behind a wall because I still heard bullets ping off our assault vehicle. I don't think I will ever get used to that whip-snap-crack sound of bullets flying past me. My Platoon Sergeant had been shot. I knew him. He was a deputy sheriff back home. I think most everyone in the platoon got a speeding ticket from him at one time or another. I got to my knees and began to remove his gear. He had stopped breathing. As I noticed his wound, the medic arrived to assist me. He had been shot in the chest on the edge of his body armor. I applied pressure to the oozing wound as the corpsman prepared some gauze. He never woke up.

I was always wondering who would be the next to get shot or shot and killed. I knew that none of us were immune to death but we tried hard not to think about it. At any given moment, a pull of the trigger could change the life of anyone of us. We all lived in suspense. Like we held our breath for 12 months.

I will never forget the day that death seemed inevitable. A few weeks after my platoon sergeant was killed, we got into a vicious firefight with some insurgents in a building in another village. As I moved down the street shooting everything, it was kill or be killed. An insurgent jumped from around the corner, and before I could get off a round, he fired off a burst. I remember my panic when he jumped out; I froze for a split second. My heart rushed as I fired back and then he fell to the ground. I feared that he would get up and try to kill me again so I put several more rounds in his body. When he finally stopped moving, a feeling I can't describe took up residence in my gut, and it still lies within me today.

Bullets and rockets flew from every direction. Bodies were lying on the street sides. Blood was everywhere. Some of my close friends were shot and another one was killed before my eyes. Another scene that will haunt my dreams forever. I kept thinking to myself; when will this end? Will I get to see Jennifer again?

The twelve-month deployment claimed the lives of 50 soldiers in our brigade. Two committed suicide in country. Three more within months of returning home but they weren't counted as combat casualties. I lasted eleven months in country before I was changed forever. That was the afternoon I watched my platoon leader, my brother, get blown apart by an IED hidden in a roadside trash pile. I remember my knees buckled and I vomited in the reeds before I was ordered to help collect body parts. My nightmare was seeing arms and legs go flying. I saw the body armor stay in place. No arms, no legs, no head. Just the body armor. It should have saved him. We should have been invincible. My nightmare grew to see my friends without arms and legs. I woke up in a shaking, cold sweat, checking my own arms and legs. A few days after the attack I was sent to the combat-stress trailers, where I was given antidepressants and time to rest. After a week, I was still twitching and sleepless. The Army decided that my war was over.

JENNIFER

I had the strangest dream while Luke was in Iraq. Luke and I were in the back of a truck or some type of military vehicle. Sand was blowing all around us, and we were squinting to keep it out of our eyes. Luke and I were at the very back of the truck. He was facing me and I was facing ten or twenty other Soldiers that were sitting with us. All of a sudden, we were under attack by Iraqi insurgents. It was as if we were in the center of an explosion. All around us, I saw images of fire, and I heard the firing of enemy weapons. I wrapped my entire body around Luke, protecting him. He didn't resist me. It was so clear to me that covering him would keep him safe from harm, that somehow I was protecting him from something. I looked back and saw the faces of the other Soldiers. They seemed to understand why I was there and why I was protecting Luke. In my dream, I understood too.

It's the everyday things that made me miss Luke the most. Every time I did laundry, I missed his undershirts, his sweaty uniform, and the way he always left his socks rolled in dirty little balls. Every time I put away clothes, I'd see his part of the dresser—two drawers that no longer opened and closed. I even resented how clean the house was—how in order things were. It was such a façade, the way my life appeared to be in impeccable order. I learned to get through each day, and I eventually learned how to sleep through the nights, only waking to my alarm clock. I learned how to light the grill and how to re-program the cable, replace light bulbs, and kill bugs that I never would have dreamed of attacking when Luke was home. These were bittersweet victories. On the one hand, I was proud of these newly acquired abilities, and on the other, they were details in my life that indicated the absence of Luke.

I focused all of my energy into my pregnancy. I checked out every book on pregnancy nutrition from the library. I prepared all my meals and all my snacks accordingly. I wanted to give my baby the best of everything, and I believed that giving the baby a healthy womb was the best way to start. For the first time in a long time, I was caffeine-free. Giving up caffeine was one of the hardest parts of the pregnancy for me. At first, I would have taken morning sickness over missing my cup of coffee any day. But as time went by, I conquered caffeine-addictions in the same way I conquered my persistent longings for Luke—day by day.

The day my water broke, I missed Luke with an entirely new fervor. I didn't panic or cry; I just deeply wanted him to be with me in person. I felt his presence in a remarkable way that day. We were sharing the birth of our first child, even if we were worlds apart. I could hear his voice in my mind, soft and whispering, encouraging me through each contraction. It was a day we had dreamed about. It was a day we never dreamed he'd miss. "Sadie" introduced herself to me after eight hours of labor. Immediately I saw her strength in the blue eyes she inherited from her Daddy. She had a tuft of strikingly dark, curly hair. We named her "Sadie," after my grandmother, the strongest, most steadfast human being either of us had ever known. From that day on, it was just the two of us-- Sadie and me—counting down the days to Luke's return.

§§§§

The technological advances in protecting Warfighters in combat have done a phenomenal job keeping our Warfighters alive. While this protection shields the torso, it does not shield the extremities of arms and legs. Even the best protection technology does not shield the brain. One of the causes of "mTBI" is pressure waves from bomb blasts that course through the brain creating injury. These injuries slowly manifest in impaired judgment, thinking, and reaction. Subsequently, we have an emerging generation of Veterans who are paraplegics, quadriplegics, and patients with brain injuries. These very young men and women in many cases have their self-sufficiency stolen from them. Even though we have made great strides with prosthetic limbs, the lives of these Warfighters are irrevocably changed both physically and also mentally, emotionally, and spiritually. Beneath the physical injuries are silently wounded human Souls. Behind these Warfighters and Veterans are equally wounded families. Their expectations of a reasonable sense of self-sufficiency are now changed. The everyday activities that they used to enjoy, are no longer possible. The families of these unquestionably brave men and women suffer deeply and silently. They are thrown into a situation they did not ask for and do not welcome. Their Souls, silently wounded beyond expression, yearn for understanding and a path forward.

Our findings suggest that Warfighters deployed into combat consistently express their sense of minute-by-minute fear. Deployed Warfighters perceive that there is no safe place or safe zone. When troop gyms, mess halls, and sleeping areas are attacked and bombed and life is lost, there is a perpetual fear for safety that does not subside. It takes a dramatic and lasting toll on the human Soul. They carry a snapshot of the tremendous fear that many live with daily as the only life they know.

What has traditionally been inspiring to Warfighters, in such traumatizing conditions, is the idea of going home. Home is after all where we are safe and untouched by the world of pain and harm that we have experienced. Once we are home, we feel at ease. Imagine the fear that lingers in the homes of Warfighters today who are now faced with the uncertainty of potential multiple, back-to-back deployments. Where there was once a sense of security and well-being, there now resides a lingering, cold fear of notice of the next deployment. The memories remain vivid. When left untreated, Veterans' and Warfighters' memories, their fear, their pain, grief, and loss will overwhelm them; they remain silently wounded, and they succumb to "PTSoulD" by commiting suicide.

"I was too scared to be in a room by myself, much less to walk to school alone, or sleep without my bedroom door open all the way. The Soldiers that lined my school playground, wearing combat helmets, with machine guns under their arms, ignited my childish imagination. I was convinced my family and I were in grave danger.

At dinner, in our tiny kitchen, as we huddled around the table, I contemplated what would happen to us when the "bad guys" came and made us their slaves. Even in my worst imaginings my mom, my dad, and my brother, as well as our little puppy, Cuddles, were right next to me. My first grade mind was incapable of fathoming life without the four of them. We would be slaves together when the bad guys got us.

At least my daddy was still home—he hadn't gone off to "Saudi" like some of my friends' daddies. All I knew was that something bad was happening in that "desert storm" and that daddies had to go away in tan versions of their regular uniforms. When Retreat went off every day at 5 P.M. and my playground friends and I stood still and put our hands over our hearts, I knew that we were part of something very brave and very special—even if it was scary."[49]

Emily

Children of today's Veterans are no longer assured in the same way as they once were when the deploying family member left and returned after a single event and that was the end. This cloud of uncertainty silently creates a deep pain in children's Souls that they do not know how to express. Today's military families no longer take comfort in that lifestyle. This abiding uncertainty and tenuous lifestyle gives rise to a very deep pain and silent wounding few truly understand. Such an ongoing sense redefines the home. This redefining has a tremendous and abiding effect, especially upon children. Those who live in such conditions cannot survive for long. On the other hand, if they do, they adopt to dysfunctional patterns and diminished joyfulness.

CONCLUSION

"I also need to say something about wounds: there are the physical wounds for which the Purple Heart is awarded. But, there are also the mental and emotional wounds that can't be seen . . . all these things will haunt a combat soldier for the rest of his life. The learning to live with all these things is very hard to do, but it is also very important to do."[50]

Lee Alley

Remembering is a critical symptom of "PTSoulD." Remembering is also an essential part of healing. Today's Warfighters can be returned home in a day. From Iraq to the front porch in the time it takes to catch a plane and fly, the Warfighters return home essentially alone. They bring their stories with them. Their memories are fresh, raw, and full of the emotions and trauma of combat. They attempt to resume their lives with little understanding of the trauma they endured and the emerging symptoms of their wounded Souls. All they have are the memories. Once home they are struck by a harsh reality. Both the families that remained at home and now the Veterans themselves continue to be bombarded daily by the horrors of the war by the news, the web, and the connections they maintain with their friends. They will remember forever what they experienced in combat. The Veteran makes it home, but the harsh reality remains that they have irretrievably been changed, and their lives will never be the same.

There are a number of perceptions about combat trauma and its affects on Warfighters, Veterans, and family members. One is that most combat trauma is really a mild stress and burn out that will resolve with rest, or it is a link to a pre-existing personality disorder. Another is that military and government agencies offer adequate transition guidance. The military and VA do offer many programs and both are working on resolving the more obvious and extreme issues and symptoms, as well as healing of physical and mental injuries. However, our traditional institutional care does not reach disorders of the Soul.

Most military and government programs do not recognize the slow emergence of the so-called "soft" injury -- that is, injury that is not immediately obvious as physical or mental health. Most programs target the immediate and obvious needs. The silent wounds of the Soul emerge more slowly; so slowly sometimes that many do not distinguish between wounded behavior and normal behavior. They simply think things changed. For example, Vietnam Veterans are currently struggling to recognize and provide treatment for a range of combat trauma injuries that are just now emerging, 30 years later following their return home.

Most traditional programs do not provide the deep, long-term care required to begin the healing of "PTSoulD." The military's primary concern is to return Warfighters to combat or if found unfit for duty, to discharge them. In the case of National Guard and Reserve Warfighters, they are returned home when their deployment clock runs down. The military knows how to treat the Warfighter who lost limbs, and they can treat the Warfighter who exhibits obvious "PTSD" and "mTBI" symptoms, but they have a much more difficult challenge when it comes to treating the Warfighter whose life is turned upside-down as a result of his or her "PTSoulD." When "PTSoulD" is left untreated and the Veterans become a post-combat casualty by suicide, they are not even acknowledged as a casualty of war. They do not receive the honors of the Warfighter killed in action. They are the silent wounded and the unacknowledged casualty.

Part Two.
Wounded Self --
Wounded Soul

"Veterans often remain drenched in the imagery and emotion of war for decades and sometimes for their whole lives. For these survivors, every human characteristic that we attribute to the soul may be fundamentally reshaped. These traits include how we perceive; how our minds are organized and function; how we love and relate; what we believe, expect, and value; what we feel and refuse to feel; and what we judge as good or evil, right or wrong. Though the affliction that today we call post-traumatic stress disorder has had many names over the centuries, it is always the result of the way war invades, wounds and transforms our spirit."[51]

Edward Tick

INTRODUCTION

"To change and change for the better are two different things."[52]

German Proverb

Combat trauma changes us. The greater the trauma is, the deeper the change. Recent combat trauma studies reveal that the single most common symptom is the change to the personality, the change to who Veterans are as persons. The common thread is that the trauma of combat irrevocably changes the whole person. Traditional treatment methods ignore the whole person. They only treat the specific symptoms. When Warfighters are redeployed, they carry back with them the traumatic experiences in their memories. They are changed persons.

As the Warfighters and Veterans begin to re-assimilate and return to home routines, their silent wounds emerge in their behaviors. The sights, sounds, and smells of their environment continue to trigger traumatic memories. The instant information culture of the virtual world continues to keep the combat experiences fresh in their thoughts. The web blog and video messaging connections remain with their comrades both in and out of the combat zone. The silent wounding of the Soul is kept raw and begins to fester. The Warfighters and Veterans must now learn to live with the changes that occurred in their lives and their personhood. They are different persons now than they were when they first deployed. The first step is to understand that things change.

THINGS CHANGE

"Everything changes, nothing remains without change."[53]
Buddha

LUKE

Physically the war in Iraq was over for me, but emotionally I doubted the war would ever end. There were sights or smells or sounds that brought me back to that day on the road outside of an Iraqi village. There were pictures or words that brought me back to all the conversations with my brother and my friends. I felt angry. Deep. The anger isolated me from everything and I felt numb. The anger knotted up my stomach. I didn't have time to check in with Jennifer before I was lifted out. Somehow, I didn't much care at that point. I couldn't face one more decision, question, or platitude. While I was in the stress trailer, the chaplain visited. I saw him a lot but did not really talk with him. He stopped by my stretcher and just started talking. Then he prayed and left. I think my anger blocked him out. I was even angry with God. How could God allow this to happen? I think the chaplain knew that my brother was blown apart. But I was too angry to acknowledge he was even there.

On the C-17 that headed out to Landstuhl, I think I was pretty much numbed up by the stuff the Docs gave me before I left. Even with the numbness, my dreams still came and my thoughts kept swirling around. And, I felt naked without my weapon and my gear. I felt close to panic. I didn't have anything physically wrong with me. No IV drips or bandages or blood. I felt like I failed. I felt like everyone was thinking that I was weak and abandoning my friends in need. I felt ashamed. But I couldn't sleep or when I did, even with the drugs, I could still see and smell my brother coming apart…in slow motion. Then I got angry all over again and started pounding my fists on the stretcher. That got the medics stirred up. Another shot.

I finally slept. And when I woke up, I was being carried across the tarmac to waiting ambulances and transporters. Fell asleep again and woke up in a locked down psych ward in Landstuhl. A nurse handed me some hospital stuff and said to change. I didn't want to get out of my uniform. My uniform was the last thing I had that kept me connected to my brother and my friends. It took me hours to change. The nurse harassed me all the time and I just kept lashing out in anger. As I look back I think she needed her own combat pay after the likes of me. They took my belt and shoelaces. That hit me hard. What were they thinking I was going to do?

I was mixed in with some real cases. I can remember that much. I thought I was OK. I didn't understand that to everyone around me I as sensitive as a landmine. The smallest thing set me off into a rage. A rage filled with fear at the same time. I didn't want to talk, I didn't want to eat, I didn't want to cooperate. That first night in Landstuhl, my dreams were filled with arms and legs. I could taste blood in my mouth. I could smell burnt flesh. I was scared of everything and felt like I was crawling out of my skin. I couldn't stop the movie in my head about my brother stepping on that bomb. Endless loop. My gut churned. I felt sick all the time.

My stay at Landstuhl lasted two weeks and I was lifted back to Walter Reed. Back in lock-down my long deep nightmare continued. That is what I felt like…trapped in a long nightmare. After a week in Walter Reed, they stabilized me. At least I wasn't lashing out at everything and everyone. Jennifer was in touch but I don't remember a thing about what we said. My brain was fried. A black ball of mush surrounded by barbed wire and sandbags. I couldn't remember what things were like before I left for Iraq. My brain felt like a blackboard that was erased and all this crap was written back on. Each night the movie continued in my head. Each hour I woke up in desperation, making sure my legs and arms were still there. One time I actually grabbed my head to make sure it was still attached. Now I can laugh a little about that one. At the time I wasn't so sure it was still there.

Sometime in the middle of the second week, they let me out of lock-down and I was turned over to outpatient psych for on-going treatment. I was still the casualty without a scratch. In outpatient, I began the longest winter of my life. The weeks passed in Walter Reed filled with psych sessions, group sessions, and boredom. They gave me back my belt and shoelaces.

Physically I turned into the same mush as my brain. I must have gained ten pounds laying around and eating junk food. The meds didn't help much. All the tranquilizers just encouraged me to lie around and eat junk food. I was in a fog half the time. I was put up in Mologne House.

All that time Jennifer was working to keep in touch with me. The first few weeks it was hard to pay attention. Somewhere deep inside I knew she was there and I clung to that thought like an anchor in the middle of a rip tide. I just don't remember being all that open with her. Or responsive. That came later. I am glad she stayed with me through those nightmare days. She managed to get a room in the Fisher House for a part of the time I was in Walter Reed. Then she was in a local hotel.

JENNIFER

When I got the email from the chaplain, I didn't know what to think. All it said was that he would be contacting me by phone or in person regarding Luke. It said that Luke was safe and stateside, and more details would come when the chaplain and I met in person. I had never heard of getting an email from the chaplain or him coming to your home, unless your husband was dead.

Chaplain Blaine knocked on my door the next afternoon. My dogs met him at the door, and Sadie gurgled at him from the living room. I was nervous and a little edgy because I didn't know what to expect. I was glad he had emailed first. If he had just shown up, I would have thought Luke was dead, and I probably wouldn't have let him in. I made him coffee and he explained to me that Luke's platoon had been attacked while out on patrol, and Johnny, Luke's older brother, was killed in the attack. Luke was staying at Walter Reed and being monitored. He was suffering from Post Traumatic Stress Disorder— nightmares, flashbacks, paranoia, rage, and even fear. "When can I see him?" was all I said. I was given an address, and within the hour, I had packed Sadie in her car seat and phoned my neighbor to look out for the dogs.

The drive was strange. I knew Luke was hurting, and the loss of Johnny would have been more painful for me if I wasn't so grateful that my husband had survived. I knew the loss of his brother would torment him. I didn't need an explanation on Luke's reaction to Johnny's death. Luke was the protective type when it came to Johnny. I knew that whatever had happened, Luke was blaming himself for not bringing Johnny home with him. The chaplain spared me the details of the attack, and it was quite some time before Luke was ever able to speak of them to me. Luke was alive and Sadie was giggling in her lilac overalls. In a matter of hours I would be in the same area code as Luke, and maybe even beside him. I didn't care what shape he was in. He was my Luke, he was Sadie's daddy, and it was about time the three of us were together in the same room.

Tears streamed down Luke's face when Sadie and I entered his room at Walter Reed. He picked her up first, smiled at me, grabbed my arm, and pulled us both into his arms. He was still my Luke. His eyes met mine and I saw something I had never seen before in his eyes—regret, anguish, and maybe—a little hope. "I've got my girls now," he said quietly. We sat on his bed side by side, and he held Sadie in his arms.

He was quiet each day when we visited, but his eyes told me that someday I would understand what had happened to him, what terrible moment in Iraq had shaken his spirit to this extreme. It probably would have been even quieter if we didn't have Sadie to talk about. He wanted to know everything about her. He wanted to be holding her for the entirety of the visits. He was madly in love with his little girl in overalls. Luke was different and I know his nightmares were torturing him, but Sadie and I weren't leaving without him. This time Luke was fighting a battle that the three of us could fight together.

§§§§

Our findings suggest that Veterans of recent wars, such as those in Iraq and Afghanistan, may have more difficulty readjusting to home life than Veterans of past wars, to include Vietnam. Helping professionals suggest that this may be the result of the globalization of technology where the details of war are available instantly, worldwide, by the Internet with the simplest of equipment. A cellphone camera can capture and transmit the most horrific of events nearly instantaneously across the globe. We suggest that when Warfighters and Veterans try to assimilate back into life, as they knew it before deployment, they discover that they are different persons. It does not matter what the wounding is that takes place; all Warfighters and Veterans return wounded in their Souls. They are silently wounded if they return otherwise unscathed, or without physical wounds, missing limbs, mental illnesses or brain injuries. The life changing silent wounding is universal to the very experience of the sights, smells, and sounds of combat. "PTSoulD" affects every characteristic of the whole person.

Fear is one debilitating, wounding factor in the combat environment. Fear about the unknown, the what if, the next explosion, or the next bullet can physically and mentally exhaust a Warfighter. Uncontrolled fear, combined with deep fatigue, can create a combat statistic just as surely as receiving a physical wound. And both create Post Traumatic Soul Disorder (PTSoulD). Fear remains for years after a Veteran redeploys back to their home life and debilitates the family as well.

Because Warfighters witness extreme acts of violence during war, whether it is the maiming and murdering of fellow Warfighters or of civilians, they develop extreme responses to normal events when attempting to re-assimilate back into home life. The terror factor in the Global War on Terrorism uses horrific acts of violence to foster a climate of fear and create trauma casualties. The family experiences the fear of losing the Warfighter spouse.

As Veterans deteriorate, they become more and more obsessed with the trauma of their combat experiences. Their dreams and their flashbacks become more real and more vivid. This creates a descending spiral of despair that can end in chronic dysfunctional lifestyles or suicide unless helping intervention occurs. Our research suggests that strong personal intervention is most successful. The Veterans project their fear and trauma on others around them including their families. This becomes a trap for everyone.

This pain, grief, loss, and quiet desperation affect not only the Veterans but also the many different people that they are in contact with, from their most intimate spouses and friends to those casual relationships that recoil from their random anger and acts of despair and frustration. This is why "PTSoulD" affects all aspects of our lives. Combat trauma symptoms consistently disrupt every characteristic of the whole person. Without intervention, what starts out as mild symptoms of "PTSoulD" that are expressed in our day-to-day behaviors becomes an almost unchangeable characteristic of our basic personality. The Warfighters, Veterans, and family members are changed and different people. However, intervention and healing can prevent them from descending into the chaos and unbearable pain that often leads to dysfunctional behaviors and lifestyles and when left untreated, premature death by suicide.

As family members and friends reunite with Warfighters and Veterans, they need to understand that it is normal for relationships to experience difficulty, and they need the time to readjust to being together again. Just being apart from their families and friends creates change. Warfighters and Veterans come back not only as changed people, but changed as silent wounded Souls.

> "She jumps, giggles, and squeezes her cheeks with her tiny little fingers. Her four-year-old body expands with joy. Her Daddy is coming home today. She thinks she remembers him. It was a year ago when he left. She knows she remembers him. He's big—tall, taller than her. Blond hair, blue eyes, and a smile. Sometimes he has that little hairy thing under his nose that sits on his lip. It's scratchy when he kisses her. She doesn't think she likes

76

it very much. But she thinks she likes him. She thinks she remembers.

Her big brother helps her make the banner for outside. "I thought you were good at coloring," he says when she carefully fills in the letters he draws for her. She thinks she is good at coloring, but now she's worried. Daddy will see the bad coloring and not like it, not like her.

Mommy ties plastic ribbons around the tree in the yard and on the patio light. She looks at them. Daddy's coming home. She jumps and smacks her hands together. A little grin trickles across her face. Daddy's coming home. Mommy says they don't have to count Sundays anymore, or cross off the days on the calendar. Mommy always does that with her. But not anymore, she says because Daddy is coming home.

Her ringlet-curls bounce in the van as she smiles and sings to Old MacDonald. Today is a special day Mommy says. She bounces with joy. She walks on her toes into the airport, hand in hand, with Mommy and big brother.

She doesn't smile when she sees him. She doesn't bounce. She doesn't speak. Her body stops all movement. She stands behind Mommy. She lets big brother say hi. She looks at the ground. Daddy's home she's told, but she doesn't understand.

Daddy hugs her. Daddy picks her up in the air and kisses his little princess. She feels the caterpillar on his lip fuzzy on her cheek. She remembers the fuzzy. Daddy's home."[54]

Emily

When the Warfighter and Veteran return home from a combat deployment they face the moment of reunion with their families. This is a time of euphoria and relief that masks the pain, grief, loss, and life changes that took place in both the Warfighter and the family members. It will take time for these changes to emerge. When they do emerge they will need support and care to begin to recognize the disorder of the Soul. With help "WVFMs" will all live with their silent wounding. The purpose is to find meaning in the changes, renewed purpose in our lives, and lasting healing in our Souls.

PERSONAL CHARACTERISTICS OF THE WHOLE PERSON

"I believe that humans possess a spiritual as well as a physical dimension, and that there are very real differences between brain, mind, and soul."[55]

Frattaroli

One way to understand the changes that take place in Warfighters, Veterans, and family members is to understand who they are in terms of core personal characteristics. When we see what happens to the parts, we can understand what happens to the whole. We all can picture who we are through the images and behaviors of five core personal characteristics of our Self. Each of these core characteristics we build into who we are as a person. They encompass our thoughts, behaviors, ideas, and physical appearance, our experiences, desires, and dreams. The infinite combinations of these characteristics are what make each of us so wonderfully unique. These characteristics of our personhood are physical, emotional, mental, social, and spiritual. Each of these characteristics should be in balance with each other, maintained, and healthy. That sense of balance is also unique to each of us, although we do point to some common core needs such as health, well-being, and happiness. Who a person is and what makes him or her whole is unique to that person.

The trauma of combat and disorder of the Soul that result causes the personal characteristics of the Warfighters, Veterans, and family members to be out of balance. The depth and degree of the unbalanced characteristics reflects the depth and degree of "PTSoulD." When one or more of these personal characteristics are not healthy, not present, or not maintained, then a person becomes unhealthy. For example, physically we need to take care of our bodies to the best of our ability. We must provide food, clothing, and shelter for ourselves. We know this. We don't always do it well. But we can understand what makes us physically

79

healthy or unhealthy. It is harder to understand this with the other characteristics. Spiritually a person decides to believe in a higher power or God. Therefore, we decide to love God, understand that God loves us, and we learn to then love ourselves. Emotionally we are in charge of our own emotion; no one can make us "feel." Mentally or intellectually, we have the ability to think and make our needs known to others. Socially, giving to others and receiving from others is a necessity for our personal well-being.

When our core characteristics are wounded, neglected, unhealthy, or unbalanced, we are unhealthy and wounded as persons. Combat trauma wounds and damages the core characteristics of Warfighters and Veterans. That is the damage to the Soul. Many things, controllable or uncontrollable, create an unhealthy self just as many decisions we make lead to a healthy self. Diseases, poor habits, stress, drugs, alcohol, abuse, and, yes, pain, grief, loss, and trauma are all things that can lead to an unhealthy person.

Imagine our sense of self as a finely balanced art mobile hanging from the ceiling. The core characteristics are the objects hanging on our "Self-mobile." All the pieces are in balance along the various arms of the mobile. The core characteristics of who we are naturally sway and jump with the breezes and currents that life sends our way. But we settle back into a sense of health and balance. Hang a bottle on the arm with the physical characteristic, representing alcoholism, and we can readily visualize just how seriously our "Self-mobile" would fall out of balance and become seriously "unhealthy." Hang a "brain injury" on the mental characteristic and we can readily envision how our healthy and balanced sense of Self becomes unbalanced and unhealthy because of the injury. Take away a limb from the physical and again we can envision what happens to our Self-mobile.

In response to our lack of balance, we then have to adjust the balance of the other pieces of our Self-mobile, if that is possible, or get rid of the bottle to be healthy and in balance again. With some injuries, extreme adjustments are necessary to become balanced and healthy again. In some cases, we can never readjust our balance; we can only learn how to live with the unbalance. Sometimes we need help to determine that the injury or the bottle is causing us a great deal of pain; our personhood is not in balance, and we are unhealthy in life. Sometimes we need help from someone else to hold up the arm of our Self-mobile that is burdened with the bottle, or with pain, or grief, or loss. Sometimes we can never recover and eventually we fall into catastrophic disarray.

To some degree, we all live with things that cause us to be out of balance. A completely balanced and healthy Self is an ideal few reach. We each live our lives constantly adjusting to things about which we can do little or nothing. We learn to live with being "unhealthy." Our struggle is to identify those things that we can do something about, and then begin a healing process.

What we do in life, our behaviors, reflect the health and balance of our core characteristics. When we experience life-changing pain, hurt, and trauma, the wounds affect the very sense of who we are – our Self – our Soul. How we respond to the pain, hurt, and trauma is actually our choice to make, as difficult as that may seem. The examination of our core characteristics allows us to review our choices and begin a path to healing the silent wounds to Self and Soul. This self-examination helps us understand our lives and how the pain of traumatic events affects us. It is not an easy thing to do.

The disorder of the Soul is reflected in our behaviors and our attitudes. "PTSoulD" impacts what we do, how we act, the decisions we make, how we take care of ourselves, and how we relate to others. Healing begins when we take the risk to examine our behaviors and decide that we need to make changes in our lives.

PERSONAL CHARACTERISTIC OF THE SELF: PHYSICAL

"There is beauty in everybody. You are born with it. It's just a matter of what you do with it, and if you lose it, it's like losing your soul."[56]

Francesco Scavullo

LUKE

As the days and weeks passed, I became a physical wreck. I was so tired all the time. I mean deep tired. I slept ten hours a night and felt like I could sleep ten hours a day. Slept but didn't sleep. My sleep was full of nightmares. I was gaining weight and losing my fitness. I was once proud that I could max the PT test every time. But while I was at Walter Reed, I couldn't do a pushup to save my life. I felt really strange walking down the hill to the ward. The guys in wheel chairs spun past me in a flash. At least they seemed confident and actually looked like they were having fun…if you didn't think too much about not seeing legs sticking out from the seat. They would gather around the little bus stop shelter at the bottom of the hill and smoke cigs before they went into the wards. There I was…the patient without a visible wound…with all my arms and legs intact. I was just missing my head.

I had to wear those robes and gowns a lot. I felt really stupid. Vulnerable. I wanted my uniform back. The psych Doc said we could wear them if someone got one for us. I thought Jennifer might bring me an old one from home or maybe buy one for me at the PX. At least I could look better than I felt.

I used to run a lot, but I couldn't walk up a set of stairs without feeling dead. That really scared me deep down inside. It was like I was losing an important part of who I was. It was like I was giving up. Worse yet, I felt like I was betraying my brothers still in country. Like I couldn't hold up my end anymore.

There were a lot of us in the psych clinic. I guess company makes

83

misery less miserable. But they were all weird. Half the time we all slept, waiting for our turn with the counselor. We were about as interested in each other as we were in ourselves. Numb. Physically numb. Emotionally numb. Except for the anger.

I guess that I really didn't care. I turned into mush in no time. Gained weight like crazy. Ate more junk food than I can ever remember. I remember that I was always into healthy food thanks to my Mom... and Jennifer. Jennifer was always on my case about eating at the hamburger joint. And I was angry. Angry all the time. Angry and tired. And the movie kept playing in my head. Blinding flash and numbing concussion. Body parts. And the smell. I smelled that stink every time I walked into the cafeteria. And I ended up not eating. Instead, I hit the quick-mart for chips and cookies and canned stuff. Then I spent all my time either sleeping or trying to sleep or staring off into a deep dark hole.

After a few months, the Army had me on a dozen different meds. By then I had gained 30 pounds and was too tired all the time to do PT. I ate gummi bears by the handful. To heck with PT anyway. What good did it do my brother? He was torn apart anyway. One night I rummaged around in my ruck that somehow made it back with me. There was a pile of sand in the bottom. And the outside was stained. And I threw-up in my trashcan.

JENNIFER

Sometimes I could see my best friend in Luke's eyes. Other times it was as if Luke was absent from his own body. I didn't agree with the anti-depressants they were feeding him, but my opinion didn't seem to matter. The doctors insisted that Luke needed the rest that the anti-depressants provided. But I knew what was wrong with Luke. It wasn't his body or his brain that was giving him trouble; it was his soul. Somehow, Luke lost touch with his own spirit over in Iraq, and he needed help finding it. How could drugs that sedated his spirit help him find it? Why did they want to subdue the very thing he was searching for? I felt like they wanted to cover up or hide the pain that the war in Iraq created in Luke. Was it a dirty secret that war troubled the Soldiers that fight it?

Every time he got upset or rowdy, they came in and drugged him up. I vomited in the hallway the first time I saw them hold him down and inject him with one of their magic potions. That was my husband they were holding back. That was my husband they were trying to quiet. He needed to let that anger out. He needed to yell or scream or do whatever it took, and they pushed him down. And I could do nothing to stop them. Tears streamed down my cheeks and the acidic vomit burned my throat. Luke's nurse noticed me after she finished holding my husband down for the injection. "Are you okay Mrs. Smith?" Was I okay? Was she so completely diluted that she thought I was okay with watching my husband get treated like a complete mental case? "I'm fine," was the only response I could manage.

After they gave him the anti-depressant, it was like his Luke-ness disappeared. It was as though they took him right out of his body, away from me. I didn't care if he needed to yell or scream or throw things at the walls. Obviously, he was dealing with something. Something that happened in the war that he was sent to fight. Was it a terrible thing to be torn up over the loss of your brother and countless members of your community? Was it so wrong to freak out a little bit? This wasn't his fault. He didn't choose to go to Iraq or to watch his brother and his friends die.

I sat with Luke after I washed my face, after the drug-bearing physician and his assisting nurse had left the room. I tried to hold his hand, but he let it fall, without grasping mine. I wanted him to know that I was there, that I was safe, that I would never try to shut him up. His eyes told me that it didn't matter who was sitting beside him; he didn't know the difference. He couldn't form a word or recognize me as Jennifer, his girl, his wife. First, the war took him away, now drugs created the separation between him and me. Every time I caught a glimmer of Luke in the midst of his own agony, in the midst of his own rage, they quieted him. He didn't even know I was there.

I spoke to the nurse and scheduled my visits around when his daily drugs had more or less worn off. I couldn't bear to see him when he hadn't the faintest idea that I even existed. When he was over in Iraq, he at least called me to talk or messaged me online. I knew I mattered to him and that he wanted to feel my presence in any way possible. Now that he was "home," it was like I barely existed at all. I refused to bring Sadie to visit the Luke-less body that persisted for hours after taking the anti-depressants. I never wanted her to feel the desperation of her own father not knowing who she was. I didn't want her to ever feel un-noticed, un-important, or unwanted.

As quickly as Luke was gaining weight, I was dropping pounds almost daily. The stress of visiting Luke and keeping Sadie content was depleting my appetite. I lacked any control of what was going on and I felt as though the details of my life were spinning out of my reach. At some point, everything would drop to the ground and shatter, and I would be the only one left to gather the pieces. On the drive to Walter Reed, I was full of anticipation. I thought my Luke was home. I thought he was safe. I thought he was still Luke. But Luke hadn't come back, and he was hardly safe; he was hardly himself. Even when I did force myself to eat, I often ended up vomiting after many visits with Luke. If he was still in Iraq, I would be counting down the days until his return. Now he was back, but he wasn't back at all, and I was unsure if or when I'd ever talk to my husband again.

§§§§

 The trauma of war creates very obvious physical wounds. This is the most known and talked about part of combat wounding. The picture of the Veteran with two missing legs running with the President is more dramatic and interesting on the News than the picture of the Warfighter with his head in his hands because he can't think straight anymore due to traumatic brain injury. Lost limbs, disfigurement, scars, and burns are all the horrible wounds of war. Lives are traumatized by these wounds. We spend the most money, time, and effort on the obvious physical wounds of Warfighters and Veterans. We can all see these wounds. These are also the wounds that change the way Warfighters and Veterans think, act, and behave. These are also the wounds that traumatize family members and so deeply change their lives. What is now normal? How do Warfighters, Veterans, and family members now live their lives?

The physical Self includes what may happen to the Warfighter in war. Debilitating wounds, missing limbs, disfigurement, burns, each transforms the physical body. Warfighters, Veterans, and family members recover. They come to understand a new normal. They learn to live with who they have become. They learn to survive, find meaning, and live. They can heal in their physical Self as well as in their Soul. This is not an easy path to endure. The consequences of NOT learning to cope with the changes in their physical Self are life threatening.

During our visits to Walter Reed and other military and VA medical centers, we witnessed firsthand the trauma of war. Today's wars in Iraq and Afghanistan are producing many unique wounds due to the technology of Warfighter protection. Now Warfighters are losing limbs and facing disfigurement where in the past they would have lost their lives. Saving lives is a great thing and a tremendous accolade to the advancement of technology. We believe that this new pattern of wounding has taken everyone, including the medical systems of the military and the VA, by surprise. It took the system several years to react. Now we have a generation of new Veterans with the wounds of lost limbs, disfigurement, and other physical displays of the trauma of war. The physical characteristic of the Self is now affected by combat. In turn, this has affected each of the other characteristics of the Self. What happens to the physical self also silently wounds the Soul.

While we are doing exceptional work and making tremendous strides in treating the physical wounds of modern combat, we still must remember the "PTSoulD" that occurs in tandem. It does not do much good to provide the latest in technical wizardry for arms and legs if the Warfighter's Soul remains so silently wounded that they fall into debilitating despair.

The family members of these physically wounded Veterans and Warfighters are also silently wounded in their Souls. They carry the burdens of caring for the Veterans and Warfighters as they rediscover how to live again with new realities of their physical Selves. It is the family member who carries the greater emotional and spiritual burden. This is not just a process of caring for the recovering and rehabilitation process. This is rather a process of discovering their new lives together. It is coping with the irrevocable changes that have taken place as a result of the trauma of combat. In this case, they are discovering a new normal together due to their physical changes. The same process takes place with the other personal characteristics of the Self. Combat trauma changes the person. The Soul is silently wounded. Veterans, Warfighters, and family members alike need to rediscover, life, healing, meaning, and purposeful living.

The sights, sounds, and smells of combat affect the physical sense of Self. Silently wounded Warfighters, Veterans, and family members struggle to understand that they are responsible for their physical recovery and physical health. Often they think of this as just another uncontrollable symptom of combat trauma. "PTSoulD" creates such deep life-changing pain, grief, loss, and desperation that they seek to mask their suffering by what they do physically. They turn to both illegal and legal drugs, alcohol, bizarre behaviors, dangerous acts, and physical expressions of denial. They take their physical Selves for granted and neglect themselves until it is too late. When they are silently wounded, "WVFMs" just do not care about themselves anymore. Their outward physical characteristics reflect their inner suffering.

There are many things Warfighters, Veterans, and family members cannot control, such as the internal and external accidents of injury, trauma, disease, and aging. They can not control the physical wounds of war. They can only do their best to buffer the affects of these wounds and accidents of life. In some cases the events of combat that create physical changes such as lost limbs or bodies ravaged by the effects of disease, battle, or physical wounding present some of the most extreme challenges "WVFMs" will face short of death.

For the Warfighters, Veterans, and family members, understanding the relationship between their sense of who they are as a whole person and their physical personal characteristic is a fundamental starting point for healing their Souls. The way they cope with their physical wounds and take care of their physical Selves is a direct reflection of their silently wounded Souls. How the "WVFMs" perceive their physical Self and take care of their physical being affects how they think of themselves and how they behave.

When combat trauma causes "PTSoulD," Warfighters, Veterans, and family members do not have a healthy sense of their physical Self. They reflect the pain, grief, loss and desperation by doing those things that hurt their Selves physically; they are somehow convinced they do not deserve goodness in their lives. "WVFMs" are deceived by their silent pain, grief, loss and desperation.

The destructive physical dysfunctions are learned characteristics of the disorder of the Soul. Silently wounded Warfighters, Veterans, and family members learn to do things through their physical characteristic that they believe masks their pain, grief, loss, and desperation. These changes in their physical characteristic soon become so much a part of them that they soon define who they are. This is the almost stereotypical picture of the Veteran who is an alcoholic or drug addict. These destructive behaviors are reinforced through the physical characteristics of touch, taste, smell, sight, and sound. Combat trauma is all about touch, tastes, smells, sights, and sounds. When deeply caught up in "PTSoulD," the Warfighter or Veteran will find any means to turn off the touch, the taste, the smell, the sight, and the sound of combat trauma.

Warfighters, Veterans, and family members are reminded constantly of the trauma of war as the things that they touch, taste, smell, see and hear trigger the memories of the war trauma that silently wounded their Souls. Everyday acts become memories of the horrors of combat. The friend who was killed drinking a cup of coffee. The fellow Warfighter who was physically wounded while standing next to you engaging in friendly banter. The Warfighter who was telling a joke one minute and attempting to stem the loss of blood from a missing arm the next. Silently wounded Veterans can never again engage in these everyday acts, drinking coffee, engaging in friendly banter, the telling of a joke, without remembering.[57] Physically wounded Warfighters and Veterans are always reminded of their combat trauma when they struggle with their artificial limbs and relearn how to do the everyday chores of life. Silently wounded Warfighters and Veterans are always reminded of their combat trauma when they struggle with the everyday touch, tastes, smells, sights, and sounds that rekindle their memories of combat.

Healing begins with the understanding that manipulating our physical characteristics or behaviors cannot fulfill a silent need of the Soul. Healing begins when we can accept the physical changes that occurs from combat. The destructive behaviors Warfighters, Veterans, and family members adopt in their physical lives might help them avoid facing reality. But healing comes from the understanding that our physical characteristics and behaviors do not create the healing -- they only reflect our healing.

Healing "PTSoulD" calls for coming to terms with the physical Self. Warfighters and Veterans with lost limbs and disfigurements learn to cope with these physical wounds. The behaviors and habits found in the personal characteristic of the whole person reveals the impact of the disorder of the Soul. Healing comes when we find meaning in the changes in our physical Self and choose to live lives of purpose devoted to a greater good in spite of the impact of combat trauma on our physical lives.

PERSONAL CHARACTERISTIC OF THE SELF: EMOTIONAL

"Everyone carries around his own monsters."[58]
Richard Pryor

LUKE

I just didn't know how to say what I felt. I was really scared inside and deeply embarrassed. Seemed like I was asked that question every other minute of every day of every week. The more I was asked how I felt the more embarrassed I got. There were times when I felt hatred and anger as cold as ice. Other times I felt like I was going a thousand miles an hour and I felt like I was born crazy. I hated roller coasters as a kid. Always did. I was out of control and always felt like I was going to be flung off into space and splattered on the ground like a bug. Yeah…you couldn't get me on a roller coaster if you paid me a million bucks. I felt like I was on that roller coaster. And I was scared to death. Like I was going to be splattered all over the ground. Like my legs and arms were going to fly off.

I knew I had lost my sanity. Just knew it. And my emotions were all over the map. I would cry at the slightest thought of the friends I lost. Just break down and sob. Jennifer would hold me tight when I did that. I wanted to hide. Then a car would backfire and I was hot as hell and ready to let loose on the nearest poor slob who happened to look like an insurgent.

The stuff we did in outpatient Psych sure didn't seem to help much. One day we just watched a movie. Another day we sat around in a group talking and all we could talk about was how we were yelling at people one minute and quiet as death the next. And how we lost our sanity in Iraq. One time a marine said he would rather have lost his arm than sit around like nothing was wrong. His buddies in physical therapy got all the attention. He was really pissed off that they got to see all kinds of cool people. They came by and visited. No one came by the Psych clinic. All we had was our anger. And that we usually turned in on ourselves...eating up our insides as surely as a cancer. Or worse we turned it on our closest friends and family...as I look back I wonder how Jennifer stuck with me... I don't have any friends anymore.

I reported to the outpatient ward every day. In my uniform. I was a walking time bomb. Angry that I had to be in the same space as the slob who couldn't cut it in basic. I had no patience for the Doc who never saw combat. I didn't think he understood that I lost my Soul. I had less respect for Soldiers who hadn't been there and were walking around feeling guilty. There were times when I was in-group and only two or three of us were in combat. The others talked a big game...but we had been there. And we really ripped them apart. One kid left crying. We laughed hysterically. The Doc wasn't happy with us that day. We ripped him also. What did he know about what we saw and did? How many had he killed? How many of his friends did he see get torn apart? What a bunch of crap. All I saw and heard and cared about was the movie that kept playing out in my head...in slow freakin' motion...

JENNIFER

Before Luke left for Iraq, he was my protector, my sense of security. It was terrifying to see him jump at the sound of a car outside backfiring or rant at people who just happened to be walking by. He had a look in his eyes that I had never seen before, a demeanor entirely uncharacteristic of the Luke I had known for years. I saw glimpses of Luke when tears filled his eyes and he told me about his buddies who hadn't made it back. It was as if he was slowly re-opening the door to his spirit, and little by little, letting me peer through the cracks. I knew better than to try to manipulate the door on my own. He was the gatekeeper to his own soul, and he was the only one who could open it completely. I was thankful for the hope I felt in his embrace when he latched on to me and sobbed openly. This was the therapy, the medication that I believed in.

After two weeks of camping out at a hotel near Walter Reed, I quit my job at the veterinary clinic. I couldn't manage caring for Sadie, visiting Luke daily, and maintaining my job back at home. Working at the clinic had always been my way to share my love for dogs with other people and their pets. Much of my job consisted of caring for hospitalized canines and explaining conditions and instructions to clients. I comforted dogs when they woke up from anesthesia. I hugged clients when their trusted canine friends breathed for the last time. I experienced new life in litters of puppies brought in for their first vaccinations and the simple, unrestricted joy in a child's eyes when she held her first puppy. Veterinary medicine was my thing, my passion, and it had suffered when Luke was in Iraq. It was a demanding job that demanded long hours. When Sadie was born I had to cut back my hours. I had just gotten back to working more hours when Luke was transferred back to Walter Reed. Sadie was just getting used to the daycare workers at the Methodist church in my town. She had stopped crying for me every time I dropped her off before work. She was finally getting used to our schedule, our routine, and so was I.

I would be lying if I said that I never resented Luke for the prolonged escape from reality that he was experiencing. Life hadn't stopped for me in the way that it stopped for Luke. He could visit with Sadie and me a few hours a day and watch us head out to the local hotel, without a thought for how our lives had changed or what we were going through. My dogs were on an extended stay with my parents, and my house sat vacant. I counted pennies and paid bills over the phone. I cared for our daughter completely on my own. I struggled to establish some semblance of a routine for the two of us—breakfast and play in the morning, a walk and a picnic at a nearby park, and a visit with daddy afterward. I had no time for anger or the luxury of tears— Sadie was watching my every move. I didn't have the option to stop and contemplate my sanity or emotionally break down. My child's life and Luke's healing depended on my ability to keep going and ignore the wounds that were building up within my own spirit. Some friends and family members expressed relief in the fact that my husband had come home from Iraq and escaped death, unlike many of the other Soldiers in his unit. I wasn't sure that he had.

§§§§

No other personal characteristic of the Self has such a clear line of connection to the Soul than emotions. A Warfighter's, Veteran's, or family member's feelings are neither right nor wrong, they just are. However, they choose how they feel in response to what they experience and as a reflection of their inner being. They choose to feel sad, or angry, or happy. Other persons, or events, or activities, or accidents of life do not make them feel. Warfighters, Veterans, and family members are in charge of their own emotions. When they act right, then they feel right. The path to healing is to change the behavior first then the feelings will change. "WVFMs" must start with the understanding that they can only change themselves.

The emotional core characteristic of the Self is the most dramatic. Warfighters, Veterans, and family members use emotions to express so much of what they think, how they feel, what they want, and how they see their inner being. Nothing reflects the trauma of war more clearly than our emotional stability. All our feelings however, are real and not to be judged. What we judge and examine is our behaviors and our attitudes. We choose our behavior and our behavior produces our feelings. We need to be aware of what we tell ourselves in our heads. We learn that how we feel is a reflection of our balanced healthy Self or a reflection of our silently wounded Souls. In the process of healing, "WVFMs" learn how their behaviors affect their feelings.

Emotions and feelings in themselves are neutral. For example, anger is a legitimate feeling and emotional expression. We can use anger to help and heal or we can use anger to manipulate and destroy. Anger can distance us from others. Anger can connect us to others. We can use anger to keep our closest loved ones away from our true inner feelings. In the case of "PTSoulD" as a result of the trauma of war, our feelings become dysfunctional and destructive to ourselves and to others.

The Soul, whether healthy or wounded, is transparent in

our emotions more than any other core characteristic. Silently wounded Veterans are emotionally unhealthy. It is the one area of life where the Soul has a clear opportunity to expose them and hold them accountable more than any other. Warfighter's and Veteran's extreme emotions display the silent wounds of the Soul. Wounded emotions can be manipulative and possessive, distancing and painful.

Warfighters and Veterans have deep emotional connections to what they witnessed and what they did in combat. The trauma of combat is an emotional trauma. "PTSoulD" is an emotional wounding. Combat and the acts of combat invoke such strong emotions as fear, anger, hate, uncertainty, and desperation among others. These emotions become so strongly embedded in the core of the person that they last a lifetime. The acts of combat feed a constant state of fear and anger. These emotions become constant companions for the Warfighter. They are not emotions they talk about openly or easily. When Warfighters become Veterans, they live with these emotions as much as they live with their memories. The acts of remembering and telling the stories bring with them the emotions.

Among the signature emotions of combat trauma are fear, anger, loss, and desperation. These emotions are formed during combat and become a source of "PTSoulD". Knowing that emotions in themselves are neutral, feelings are neither right nor wrong, they just are, Warfighters and Veterans can associate these signature emotions to the memories they hold of combat trauma. Family members develop the emotional connections to the stress and worry they endured while their spouses were deployed. As Warfighters, Veterans, and family members tell their stories they also learn to heal their emotions. Telling the stories reveals and uncovers the emotions. Revealing the emotions for what they are helps the "WVFM" begin to heal.

Many Warfighters, Veterans, and family members think of

their emotions of fear, anger, loss, and desperation as something that is wrong, a sign of weakness, or a source of shame. They bury their emotions deep inside. Others hold onto their emotions as not just a "silent" wound but a much more open and expressed wounding. In some cases the emotions become a crutch, or block that holds back the very painful memories of combat. They choose their feelings and emotions for the wrong reasons. The "WVFM" displays their "anger" in open and hostile ways through their behaviors to keep others at a distance and to avoid talking about or confronting their memories. Emotions are a phase of the grief process. Anger about the pain of grief and loss is an emotion displayed to avoid the agony of the loss. All of these emotions are real and cannot be questioned. It is what the "WVFM" does with the emotions that are the issue. The path of healing "PTSoulD" is a path that acknowledges the feelings and emotions. This acknowledgement then becomes a process of changing attitudes, changing behaviors that then change the feelings and emotions.

It is fair to suggest that even when the Warfighter, Veteran, and family member is on a path of healing this does not mean that their memories and thus their emotions will then "go away." They will live with the emotional response to combat trauma the rest of their lives. The hope in healing "PTSoulD" lies in the certainty that they can learn how to live with their memories and thus control their emotions. The fear becomes less controlling, the anger less real, and the desperation less interfering with their lives. In many cases, we know of Warfighters, Veterans, and family members who move to a state of spiritual forgiveness of themselves and their former enemies. We hear the stories of the WWII Veterans or the Vietnam Veterans who find and meet with former enemy Soldiers and find common ground of reconciliation and forgiveness. They find within their own sense of community and being a "Band of Brothers" the real path of healing. They find meaning in their pain, grief, loss, and desperation and then go to live lives of purpose.

Warfighters, Veterans, and family members who are silently

wounded always reflect their pain, grief, loss and desperation through their emotional responses. A hard self-examination of the emotions can help "WVFMs" understand their wounding. When they begin to understand they are responsible for their feelings and to change feelings they need to change behaviors, they can begin to heal.

PERSONAL CHARACTERISTIC OF THE SELF: MENTAL (INTELLECT)

"Knowledge is the food of the soul."[59]

Plato

LUKE

I know I had crazy thoughts. At the time, I know I was thinking crazy stuff. But I couldn't stop myself. I was so angry all the time. I was so scared all the time. I had myself convinced it was the fault of everything and everyone but me. It was the fault of that insurgent that jumped out in front of me. It was the fault of the IEDs that blew up my buddies. It was the fault of the Army, the Doc, the group, and the weather.

I didn't want to sleep. I did anyway because I was exhausted. And the drugs knocked me out all the time. Late at night, I would read stuff. One time I read a story by a Soldier who came back from combat and was trying to start living again at home. In one passage, he said: "I spent all of my time watching the rooftops, the side roads, the doorways, and looking into my rearview mirror to make sure no one was creeping up on my car from behind. I jumped from every person who came too close. I kicked open doors before I walked in. I wanted to yell at everyone walking around. Tell them what was happening. Tell them they were clueless. I was so angry at them all. It was all their fault."

By my fourth month as an outpatient on the Psych ward, I had learned a lot of stuff. Breathing techniques to use when the panic started. We read statements about ourselves in-group. Something about how we needed to love ourselves. Most of us lied. I actually learned to build a birdhouse in occupational therapy. But my anger never went away. Every time I met with my Doc, I got angry all over again. He could not understand why I was so angry all the time.

One day a buddy and me went and got a tattoo. I liked the ones about death. I wanted to honor my brother. I had a picture of him and the tattoo guy did a silhouette of him on my arm. Cool. Like a skull. Dead.

All through this long cold winter of my life, I still saw myself as a Soldier. I was called an Iraq Vet. I was called a warrior. Jennifer always wore my dog tags. That made me proud. But secretly I was terrified that I was going to end up like the worn out vagrants I saw on the streets…wrapped in old-field jackets…whacked out. With my nightmares and every muscle in my body wound tight and my anger I was terrified that no one would want me…no one…not even Jennifer… what would my daughter think of me in 30 years? I had convinced myself that I didn't think I was getting any better. My memory was shot. My gut burned. My head hurt. Every day I seemed like I was crawling inside myself more and more. I couldn't remember who I was before I deployed. Put me in a war for 12 months and my brain turns to crap. My brain is a deep black hole. Besides, that movie was still playing.

JENNIFER

During Luke's time in Iraq, I felt as though each day was a constant struggle to keep my head above water, to get up, and get on with the day. During Luke's stay at Walter Reed, it was as though someone was holding me beneath the water, and the light from the surface was fading with the passing of each moment. At some point, the water would completely fill my lungs, and the fight in me, the life in me, would be gone. I was near drowning.

Luke was angry most of the time. He was constantly re-enforcing his identity as a Soldier for everyone around him, and he was driving me insane. I didn't feel the need to incessantly reiterate to him the struggle of being an Army Guard wife. I didn't wail and complain or hurt others in anger. And I didn't blame the whole damn world for the pain in my gut that I was struggling to suppress. He didn't notice, much less acknowledge, what his time in Iraq and his subsequent descent from reality was putting me and Sadie through. Before the deployment and the baby, Luke and I would be ecstatic to see each other again after he'd been in the field or away training. We'd spend hours locked in our house, cooking food, snuggling, and enjoying each other's presence. Being back in each other's arms was an emotional and spiritual high. We spent days talking, giggling, and re-counting everything we'd both missed in each other's lives, no matter how insignificant. I never dreamed our reunion when he returned from Iraq would deviate so far from our well-known ritual. I knew it would be different with the baby, but I never thought Luke would be a totally different person.

When he got a skull tattooed on his arm and called it his brother, I was enraged that Luke thought that horrid image of death carved on his arm somehow honored Johnny. To me, it was a grave dishonor, and so was the way Luke was treating Sadie and me. We didn't matter anymore. All that mattered in his ridiculous mind was that everyone knew he was an Iraq War vet. He was somehow better than us because he had seen death. He was somehow above the rest of us non-veterans. He was far from pleased when I asked him if he thought there was something I could tattoo on my body to commemorate the loss of my husband's sanity and the man I knew as my best friend. He spouted back at me like a snotty teenager, "It's my body."

"That skull on your shoulder is not your brother. Johnny died and God forbid I say it, but he lived too." Unmoved, he stared me down. His eyes flicker, but he said nothing.

"I didn't die over in Iraq. And neither did Sadie. So maybe you should think about that and quit trying to get back to Iraq or fix something that can't be fixed. Johnny doesn't need you anymore, but we do." I was done putting my life on hold for a man that hardly cared if I was there. I was done waiting for him to acknowledge my struggle to maintain sanity, while continuing to function in everyday life. I needed normalcy. I needed stillness. I needed time away from Luke, and maybe for once, he needed to experience my absence.

What was the point of war? When had it ever solved anything and when were the results of war ever worth the cost? All war did was kill people. In one way or another war created death in everyone, it touched. And it touched more people than anyone ever realized. The focus was always on the Warfighters, the ones with missing limbs, or psychological disorders. The focus was their pain. Even at the FRG, I was coached on how to speak to Luke, how to be sensitive to what he had been through after he returned from the war. Did anyone ever sit the Warfighters down and counsel them on how to be sensitive to their families and friends—the ones that experienced deployment in a totally different way? Did anyone ever mention to them that their absence would at the very least, wound those waiting for them at home? Did Luke ever stop for a moment and consider the pain I was experiencing?

§§§§

It is said that "mTBI" is now a signature wound or injury of the Iraq and Afghanistan wars.[60] Brain injuries, as well as the silent wounds of the Soul, affect our mental capacities. The silently wounded Warfighters, Veterans, and family members need to know they are thinking, intelligent people. They have the ability to make their needs known to others. By no means does this mean that how smart they are is a reflection of the state of their Souls. How they use their smarts reflects the health of their Souls. "PTSoulD" has everything to do with the recurring behaviors and attitudes in the decision-making processes and how people think. The thought processes that go into decisions have a direct link to the Soul.

How Warfighters, Veterans, or family members think speaks about the Soul. What "WVFMs" think is often translated into what they do and how they then feel. What they think is also a self-perpetuating circle. Think bad thoughts and bad behavior results, along with feeling bad about themselves and about others.

When they think they are in pain, they are in pain. Perception is as real as any reality. People can literally "think" themselves sick. "WVFMs" are balanced, and healthy when what they think takes on the characteristics of healing and happiness. Warfighters, Veterans, and family members are no longer burdened by thoughts and behaviors of distrust, and they no longer see themselves as wounded persons. When they think that there is nothing left for them, they have misjudged life and begin to believe that nothing is left.

What Warfighters, Veterans, and family members tell themselves in their minds reflects the silent wounding in their Souls. For example, the memories of severe combat trauma can fill their thoughts and they can paralyze themselves with negative and fearful thinking. They tell themselves they are no good, they can't do this or that, they can't live, and no one loves them. It may sound silly when articulated in that manner. On the contrary, it is serious business when "WVFMs" feel useless and unloved because their wounding has changed how they think. This is why an honest examination of behaviors and attitudes is so critical to a lifetime of healing. Honest assessment of thought processes and decision-making activities can reveal less conviction and more stubbornness than the "WVFMs" previously admitted. New ways of thinking about things and seeing the world can be frightening, but the Soul thrives on fresh insights and new perspectives. A person's mental personal characteristics and intellectual life does not include mean, stagnated, angry, or deluded thoughts. These types of thoughts are signals of "PTSoulD."

For Warfighters, Veterans, and family members fear can be an overwhelming characteristic of combat. A Soul in fear is a Soul silently wounded. That wound often has the face of a child who is afraid of never seeing her Daddy again, or the face of the spouse who lives in fear that her Warfighter husband will not come home again. Fear is a neutral emotion. How Warfighters, Veterans, and family members respond to fear is something they can work on.

They combat fear by healing their Souls with a healthy nurturing of their basic needs.

Healing is about finding meaning in the silent wounds of our Souls and the life changes that result. Healing begins when we examine the pain, grief, and loss in our lives and come to the understanding that what we find reflects the disorder of the Soul. Healing is not about making the pain go away or undoing the changes in our lives to turn things back to what they used to be before combat. We cannot go backward. Healing is the result of making the choice to find meaning and purposeful living, to live with and control our pain and not allow the pain to control us, and to move forward to a future devoted to the greater good.

Warfighters, Veterans, and family members who are silently wounded actually victimize themselves by their thinking. The capacity to examine their thinking patterns (how they relate to their experiences) is important. Viktor Frankl suggests in his book, "<u>Man's Search for Meaning</u>," that how we think is our last refuge. That extremely traumatic events and experiences cannot take away our ability to choose what we think and how we react to the events we find ourselves a part of. Frankl's experiences brought him to realize that trauma can take away everything from us except our ability to choose our own thoughts.[61] Even the silent wounding of the Soul cannot take away "WVFMs" abilities to think for themselves about what they need and what they want for their lives.

The disorder of the Soul does affect how we think and what we think about. "PTSoulD" affects how we think about our choices and how we make our decisions. The thoughts about our behaviors, our feelings, and our memories of combat are all deeply affected by our pain, grief, loss, and silent desperation. The mental or intellectual characteristic affects all the other characteristics of the whole Self. Wounded thinking, for example, causes "WVFMs" to "think" they are no longer worthwhile individuals, that they have no hope, and that they are doomed to a life of despair. This wounded thinking can lead to pre-mature death through suicide if left untreated or without intervention. Wounded thinking is a signature characteristic of the disorder of the Soul. "PTSoulD" leads to wounded thinking and dysfunctional lives. Wounded thinking is reflected in exaggerated reactions, violent emotions, and wild mood swings.

Wounded thinking is a characteristic of "PTSoulD." Warfighters, Veterans, and family members hold traumatic memories that affect how they think about themselves, others, and their lives. The trauma of war changes how they think. How they think reflects who they are, how they behave, and how they feel. The path to healing begins by examining what "WVFMs" are thinking and what they tell themselves in their heads.

PERSONAL CHARACTERISTIC OF THE SELF: SOCIAL (RELATIONSHIPS)

"Hatred paralyzes life; love releases it. Hatred confuses life; love harmonizes it. Hatred darkens life; love illumines it."[62]

Martin Luther King, Jr.

LUKE

We could come and go off Walter Reed. I finally was getting more comfortable in my jeans and tee. I thought I was able to blend in with the scenery. Walking around I felt really creepy. As I look back, I am amazed that I didn't get myself in deep trouble and kill someone. Jennifer helped but at the time, she probably didn't think so...at the time, I didn't think so either. We would walk the baby around. But I was quiet and always angry. I jumped at everything. I was seething when I saw people laughing and joking as if they didn't have a clue that Soldiers were being killed every day. My friends were dying. My brother was in pieces. I was sullen and didn't carry on much of any conversation...not even with Jennifer. It seems like my thoughts were rattling around in that same old dark hole. The horror movie kept playing in my head.

Every now and again, I felt like I wanted to pull the trigger on people. If I had a weapon I would have probably let loose a dozen times at the loud sounds and at the person who walked out from behind something unexpectedly. Especially when they looked like the enemy, we faced in country. I was full of hate. I wanted to kill the things I hated. I walked around just waiting for a fight. If anyone even so much as looked at me wrong, I exploded. I was wound so tight I hurt.

It just seemed like I was reliving combat in everything that I did, or saw, or smelled, or heard. Everyone I bumped into was suspicious. Anyone who walked past was a threat. The fear seeped into my Soul. All I saw was the death of my friends and brother. Like my own private showing of a horror show. Sometimes what I remembered made me sick to my stomach and I would run off and barf in the bushes. That really scared Jennifer. She started walking a few steps away from me. Yeah, I noticed. I noticed a lot of little things like that. Like just how close things got. If they got too close, I stepped away.

One time it was a hot and humid day. An SUV drove by and the sun flashed just right on the windshield. For a moment, I could have sworn I was back in the heat and the sand of the villages outside our FOB and that an insurgent vehicle just triggered an IED. The memory made me sweat and shake and cower behind a tree. I looked at Jennifer and could see the fear in her eyes.

And there was the time I ripped apart the clerk at the quickie mart for making jokes about the war. I think he thought I was a crazed jerk. I probably was. One thing I remember from those dark days…people avoided me and I was lonely…very lonely…and angry…and the movie just kept playing along in my head.

JENNIFER

When I got home, I did everything I could to feel normal again. I worked some at the veterinary clinic. I brought the dogs home. I mowed the lawn. I watered the flowers. I did mounds of laundry. I attempted to rid my mind of that dead, soul-less look I'd seen in Luke's eyes. I pretended he was still deployed. I tried to forget that he was in the states at all and that I'd seen the man he was after war, a man I didn't know—a man I wasn't sure I'd ever be able to love. I missed Luke, and I would have grieved the loss of him if I hadn't convinced myself he was deployed and just hadn't made it home yet.

One evening some girls from work invited me over for wine and movies. My parents encouraged me to get out and be with my friends; hesitantly, I agreed and left Sadie at Mom and Dad's for the evening. The first movie they put in was about two brothers, drafted, and fighting in the Korean War. Their village was attacked by communists from North Korea, and they were separated from their family by the government and forced to fight. The movie was in Korean and the translation was far from perfect. The English voice-overs were hardly language that the typical American would use, and this had a comical effect for my friends. The more they snickered and giggled, the more uncomfortable I got. Someone's husband was drawn to the movie by the violent nature of the battles, and he was grunting and laughing as the arms and legs of Soldiers were blown off, bodies blown to pieces.

I stopped watching the movie. I tore at the edges of my shirt. I fought tears, hoping no one noticed. I wanted to yell SHUT UP. I wanted to stand up and ask everyone how any of the blood could be funny, even with the imperfect translation. Soldiers are in Iraq right now. Soldiers from our country. Dying, crying, and losing their minds. Spouses, daughters, sons, and parents are waiting for them at home and you can laugh when a guy gets his head blown off? What a privilege it is to be complacent American civilians who are hardly aware of the war being fought in the name of freedom, of the Soldiers dying to protect the land we live in freely. I said nothing. I wanted to feel normal.

I thought I was being over-emotional until I noticed one of the girls across the room. Her husband was in the air force and had spent five months in Iraq. He'd only been back a few weeks. Her eyes were on her kneecaps. She shuttered slightly at the battle scenes, but quietly maintained her composure. I left the room to get a glass of water in the host's kitchen. I fiddled around and put dishes in the dishwasher and started wiping down the counter. The air force wife walked in quietly and re-filled her glass. She gently made eye contact with me and said, "Don't you just love war movies?" "They're my favorite," I responded. Neither of us said anymore, and we both went back to the living room to finish the movie. But we understood each other and maybe we understood that nothing we said could change the thoughtless laughter and banter of our friends. Regardless, for a split second, I didn't feel so alone.

Towards the end of the movie, the main character's fiancé is shot in front of his eyes. Enemy Soldiers dump her body into a ditch with many others. It is a gruesome scene. No one laughed. No one spoke. Expressions were solemn, and eyes were teary. There's something about watching someone's family member or lover be brutalized before your eyes, even if only in a movie. No translation was necessary. The silence was deafening.

§§§§

Silently wounded Warfighters, Veterans, and family members can really mess up their relationships! The Social characteristic becomes severely damaged when the "WVFMs" are silently wounded. They tend to use their emotions to distance others. They use anger, for example, to keep others away from their inner pain, grief, loss, and desperation. "WVFMs" get angry with others as a way of keeping people at a distance. They think others do not understand their pain or do not want others to get close to their pain. The social characteristic of our whole person relates to our relationships. The acts of giving to others and receiving from others are a necessity for healthy balanced whole persons. When we are silently wounded, it becomes very difficult to fulfill this principle of the social Self. If left unchecked, the silently wounded Warfighters, Veterans, and family members will eventually alienate everyone and start living under a bridge, in a box, all alone and descend into suicidal behavior, meaning they can't live with anyone, especially others within family relationships, because no one can live with them.

The Warfighters', Veterans', and family members' social relationships tell the story of their Souls' silent wounding and healing. Their capacity to communicate, trust, share, and interact with other human beings equally, and sometimes lovingly, points out what is going on within the Soul. Good and healthy relationships are not primarily the result of learning, but an expression of the Soul. At best, "PTSoulD" is reflected by the "WVFMs" displaying socially acceptable, but distant behavior and polite conversation, but shallow facades of themselves. At worst "WVFMs" end up angry, bitter, cut off from friends and loved ones, and engage in destructive social behaviors. In short, other people soon can't stand being around those who display "PTSoulD." Friends disappear, marriages head for divorce, and they lose jobs because they emotionally attack their co-workers. All of their relationships are the reflection of their healing and wounding within the Soul. Warfighters, Veterans, and family members need to understand that how they relate to people reflects who they are and the silent wounding in their Souls. The same behaviors and attitudes are consistent with their loved ones at home, their friends, and the strangers they meet in their daily lives.

We like to think that the way we treat people in public is different from how we treat people in private. Warfighters and Veterans convince themselves that they treat strangers differently then they treat those with whom they have intimate relationships. That perspective both feeds their behavior and results in self-righteous denial. The truth is that they treat all people the same based on the silent wounds in their Soul. We cannot turn off what is in our Soul at will. We cannot decide when the Soul will or will not affect their attitudes and behaviors. Healing in the Soul begins when Warfighters, Veterans, and family members take ownership of this reality about themselves. They must also make deliberate choices to understand the hurt in the Soul that is causing or continuing their "PTSoulD" in order to heal the pain of loss and grief they still experience.

Warfighters, Veterans, and family members will do well to consider that the symptoms of "PTSoulD" often play out in their relationships. They choose to suppress and ignore the dysfunctional behaviors they display. Bad behavior becomes such a part of them that they soon cannot tell the difference and forget what healthy behavior is all about. Making an honest examination of what is going on in their social relationships with others is critical to their healing.

Others will try to give the Warfighters, Veterans, and family members feedback about their bad behavior in their relationships. Good friends and significant others will try to tell them that they are behaving badly. The "WVFMs" will hear them for a little while, but eventually they will shut them out. Anger takes over to create distance from those concerned about them, and they end up alone in their pain.

When silently wounded, the complexity of social and personal relationships can feel like a catastrophe. Often there are events in relationships that cause great pain, and all too often, the pain of the Soul continues to harm relationships. Breaking this cycle of "PTSoulD" is necessary to move toward healing the Soul.

The Warfighters', Veterans', and family members' social relationships in their work and their jobs are one reflection of the silent wounding that occurs within the Soul. What is happening in their Souls will come out in their workplace relationships. The silent wounds of the Soul go to work with the "WVFMs" every single day. The real "on-the-job training" for them is to examine their work experience and make an accounting of their behaviors and attitudes. While being employee of the month has its rewards, a lifetime of inner healing is infinitely more important.

The wounding or the healing of social relationships involves the level of honesty and integrity Warfighters, Veterans, and family members bring to the job when no one else is there to account directly for their performance. It involves the way in which they treat their peers and those who work for them. It includes their level of performance as a reflection of giving their best because their job is a reflection of their Soul. Personal laziness, dishonesty, and poor performance in the work place are a reflection of "PTSoulD." Cutting corners, cheating, and stealing from the workplace are not just bad work ethics; they are indicative of wounds in the Soul that have not been healed.

Combat trauma changes how Warfighters, Veterans, and their family members relate to others. The ways they change have to do with what is going on inside them. There are emotions and thoughts left over from deployments that can impact how they act around others. Whether they are parents, wives or husbands, children, co-workers, or people in general, their attitudes, words, and actions after deployments are affected. These feelings and thoughts can point to their emotional wounds. When emotionally wounded, Warfighters, Veterans, and family members can act in ways that damage relationships and can continue the difficult behavior they are working to overcome.

Silently wounded Warfighters and Veterans can experience conflict in loyalties. They have been through a life and death experience and created bonds with other Warfighters and Veterans that are not known to anyone outside the unit or the reunion group. There can be an internal struggle, as they must balance the relational needs of family members with the intense loyalties that remain with fellow Veterans and other Warfighters. Frustration can occur when family members seek information about the deployment to be met with "I don't want to talk about it" responses.

Warfighters and Veterans return from combat with the idea that everything will return to the way it was before they left. Disappointment begins when Warfighters, Veterans, and family members discover that not only have others changed in their absence, but that they themselves have changed. Combat trauma creates many conflicting ideas and emotions that hurt relationships.

Family members of Warfighters who deploy can feel betrayed and abandoned. There can be the emotional complaint that they didn't sign up for a part time marriage. Relationships require time together to grow and mature. Combat deployments disrupt that process. When Warfighters and Veterans redeploy and try to rejoin in their family relationships, they are met with anger, resentment, and suspicion.

Left unchecked, the perception of betrayal is taken out on the Warfighters and Veterans as they try to reintegrate back into their relationships. This resentment becomes payback to the Warfighters. Frustration can be heightened when the Warfighters are welcomed as the heroes in the public eye without recognizing the family members' contributions.

The people Warfighters, Veterans, and family members work with and even people in public places, may be finding them short-tempered, angry, or impatient at new levels. They may not even be detecting their own behaviors toward others. Healing the Soul involves understanding the impact of how they conduct their relationships in their life, to consider their attitudes, their words, and most importantly, their decisions to address what they see in themselves that needs healing.

PERSONAL CHARACTERISTIC OF THE SELF: SPIRITUAL

"People who pray for miracles usually don't get miracles.
. .but people who pray for courage, for strength to bear
the unbearable, for the grace to remember what they have
left instead of what they have lost, very often find their
prayers answered. . .Their prayers helped them tap hidden
reserves of faith and courage which were not available to
them before."[63]

Harold Kushner

LUKE

I felt like I was losing my mind a bit more each day. I was abandoned.
Even God left me. And I didn't think God had found me in the first
place. At least I wasn't all that sure. It was Jennifer that dragged me
off to the church.

I kept missing appointments. It was my meds and memory problems.
I had been too close to too many multiple bomb blasts in Iraq. There
are times when I would just zone out. I couldn't explain it. I was
just back in the sand and the heat. But no one seemed to care about
that. I didn't trust my Doc anymore. I didn't think he knew what he
was talking about. I didn't think he knew what I was talking about. I
stopped wearing my uniform. Shorts and tees.

One day the Doc I was seeing wasn't there. It was another new guy.
I went through a lot of Docs while in the Ward. We never saw the
same Doc more than three or four times. This latest Doc was different
than most. He seemed to really listen to me. At least I felt that he
really listened. He seemed to understand my fear and anger without
me having to tell him. He also told me that I did my job. No one had
ever told me I did my job. No one had ever told me that I was a good
Soldier. I always felt like I was a failure. And everyone around me
treated me like I was a failure. This Doc simply said that I did my job
and to be proud of that.

115

Something clicked for me then. But by then I was being boarded out. I had a new worry and that was how I was going to be rated by the VA and how I was going to survive at home. I remember one day a caseworker coming in saying that they needed a written statement that I actually had seen a traumatic event in combat. He couldn't find anyone in my unit to provide that statement. I couldn't believe what I was hearing. What was I doing these past months in and out of the Psych ward? Fishing. That was it. But my new Doc made a phone call and he got a statement the next day.

> "During a routine route clearance in August 2006, PFC Luke Smith's platoon was clearing a road and a suspected IED. PFC Smith was standing guard beside his M1114 when the suspected IED detonated 2X155 mm artillery shells. The detonation killed the platoon leader, 1LT John Smith and knocked the remaining soldiers to the ground causing additional wounded. PFC Smith saw his platoon leader killed by the IED device."

I would soon be going home. I was scared all over again. What was going to happen to me? I think that was the first time I thought about prayer in a long, long time…it was a simple prayer…"Help!"

JENNIFER

Luke's silence was killing me. When would he have the ability to talk to me and ask me about my day? When would he have the ability to become a part of my daily life and Sadie's? Hope came in small amounts, in his movement to hold my hand, or his suggestion to take the baby for a walk. At first, the idea of walking with Luke and our baby made me feel like we were approaching some level of normalcy again. The short fuse he carried with him made me feel otherwise. It was devastating to see him so fearful of every day sounds and cars passing by. Even when he didn't appear to be, he was always on the look out for something horrible. He had my nerves on edge. His paranoia scared me to death, and for the first time since I met Luke, I wasn't sure if he would be able to protect me. I wasn't sure if he had

116

the ability to differentiate between actual danger and a truck driving down the street. Chances were that he would stomp a cat to death if it grazed his shoe.

I was lonely when Luke was in Iraq, but in an entirely different way. The Luke I spoke to on the phone and messaged over the internet was the same Luke I had always known. After Luke returned to the U.S., I missed him when he was right beside me. I missed Luke when he jumped in fear or lashed out in anger. I wanted to talk to him and ask him what he thought I should do. I wanted to hear him tell me that things would be okay, that we should trust in us, and that we would get through anything, together, as we always had before. It was difficult to hope for the both us. It was difficult to maintain the faith that Luke and I would both come through this. Sadie was my driving force. She needed her mother and father. I wanted her so badly to experience her amazing father, the gentle, playful man he had been before war. I prayed for healing. I prayed that Luke would find his way and that I would have the strength to let go of my fear and pain. I prayed that the three of us would go home together in the end, that this part of our lives would one day be a distant memory.

When I found out Luke had been drinking, I wanted to kill him. I didn't understand why he was giving up, why he was so indifferent to what happened to him, and for that matter how his actions, or lack thereof, hurt Sadie and me. I kept coming back to the same question in my mind: Why do Soldiers fight? Soldiers don't kill people over ideals or politics. They don't even fight for freedom. And then it hit me: Soldiers fight for their families. Nothing more, nothing less. They fight because they must protect the man beside them. They fight because they must get home to their wives and children. Soldiers fight for the same reason military spouses and dependents fight to get through endless deployments. We fight to take care of our children and ourselves. We fight to deal with hardships and longing that most Americans will never experience, must less be aware of. We fight to see our husbands come home. We fight to see our daddies and our brothers come home. In Luke's mind, he had already lost the war. The man beside him was massacred. Johnny was dead. He didn't protect his brother, and his very reason for fighting was lost. Johnny was dead, and Luke was defeated.

§§§§

When Warfighters, Veterans, and family members begin the healing of their Souls, they experience spiritual growth. Spirituality teaches them to first love themselves before they can love others. This is a universal tenet in nearly every expression of spirituality in the world. The healing of Post Traumatic Soul Disorder (PTSoulD) first and foremost begins within the Self. The love experienced within can then overflow and touch others.

The concept of Soul is the essence of a person in character, personality, and the outcome of their experiences. Healing the Soul involves coming to terms with spirituality and determining how it is both empowering and enlightening or how it may in fact be a current source of wounding that keeps Warfighters, Veterans, and family members from healing in their Souls. The spirituality Warfighters, Veterans, and family members practice is unique to each of them. They see, hear, interpret, and act in different ways in their own understanding of having a personal spirituality.

Examining the spiritual characteristic of the Self is both critical and confusing. It is important to understand the terminology of different approaches. For Warfighters, Veterans, and family members, spirituality is the essence of their beliefs. Religion is the mechanism to organize, structure, and institutionalize spiritualities. Religion is one expression of the spiritual component in the Self and the lives of "WVFMs." When "WVFMs" examine their behaviors and attitudes that recur in this personal characteristic of the Self, they can understand how the development of their spirituality is a reflection of their Soul's silent wounding and healing. If they examine the spiritual practices that had their attention during their combat experiences, they will gain accurate insight into their Souls. When Warfighters, Veterans, and family members carry an open relationship with the pain associated with a disorder of the Soul, it will influence their spiritual characteristic.

By examining the spiritual personal characteristic of the Self, Warfighters, Veterans, and family members find insight into the healing and wounding that may be present within the Soul. For instance, if they see a pattern of exercising forgiveness with graciousness and love, then it becomes a clear signal that within the Soul there is a healthy balance in their sense of Self. If, on the other hand, "WVFMs" continue to practice a judgmental and condemning attitude or hypercriticism toward others or themselves, it indicates a silently wounded Soul still engaged in pain, grief, loss and desperation. Warfighters, Veterans, and family members remain in the deep pain that is the result of combat trauma and their anger over their sense of grief and loss. A lifetime of healing involves deliberate awareness of how the spiritual life is drawn from one's Soul.

An examination of the healthy attitudes and behaviors of the spiritual characteristic of the Self finds that the Warfighter, Veteran, and family member may foster forgiveness, love, honor, acceptance, and promotion of others, as well as themselves. The starting point of healthy beliefs and attitudes is from where they are and not where they think they should be. When the Soul is moving in the direction of healing, "WVFMs" discover that they no longer hold onto the beliefs that manipulate people, environments, or even God to make them happy. Rather, they will be at peace with a healthy Soul. Having completed and dismissed the pain of a silently wounded Soul, their spiritual lives will open them up to a whole new world of possible insights and discovery. When Warfighters, Veterans, and family members are willing to mature their spiritual characteristic, they discover a successful strategy for a lifetime of healing in their Souls.

Military deployments challenge the Warfighters', Veterans', and family members' spiritual beliefs and values. Combat trauma tests the very Souls of Warfighters. Deployed Warfighters not only question the meaning and purpose behind their enormous sense of pain, suffering, and loss, but also bring their personal beliefs into question. While it is healthy and necessary to question a belief system to allow movement toward growth and maturity, it can also be an unsettling time for the silently wounded. A silently wounded Soul is so full of pain, grief, loss, and desperation that once comforting spiritual values and beliefs are not always helpful or healing.

The silent pain of guilt and fear associated with combat can overshadow spiritual beliefs. Whether it is the guilt of leaving family or from certain acts carried out in the line of duty, guilt can paralyze the Warfighter. Fear from the constant trauma of combat can paralyze the Warfighter, Veteran, and family member into despair and disbelief in anything good in life.

Silently wounded spirituality creates excessive guilt that causes Warfighters, Veterans, and family members to punish themselves or put themselves down for what they have done in the line of duty. While having a conscience and remorse for possible acts committed in the line of duty is healthy and even necessary, holding onto overwhelming guilt and fear is not. Spiritually, Warfighters can feel that they need to be punished for what they have done. Some can feel that a higher power is angry toward them for how they have performed in the line of duty.

Silently wounded spirituality causes Warfighters, Veterans, and family members to adopt a set of spiritual beliefs that fosters an "us" against "them" outlook. Developing a spiritual value that suggests that somehow one class of people is more important or better than another and thus justifying words or actions that hurt others reflects "PTSoulD." The trauma of combat causes Warfighters to start believing and thinking in wounded terms.

Warfighters are faced with State sanctioned life and death issues. Seeing life taken, especially fellow Warfighters and taking life devastates the Warfighter's Soul. The emotional chaos of the loss of life and the horrors of combat can stir up the fundamental questions of life, death, and meaning in Warfighters. Memories can flood and haunt the redeployed Veteran and grief from such experiences continue to create emotional wounding. Sometimes the spiritual values Warfighters and Veterans possess are of great comfort to their silently wounded Souls. Sometimes the spiritual values they hold are actually harmful to them and do not support healing. Sometimes the trauma of combat destroys their sense of belief and their spiritual support.

The challenge to Warfighters is the conflict in values/ expressions of spirituality between what they have observed in other cultures during deployment versus what they grew up with at home. Global diversity in religion and spirituality can be either educational or deeply threatening.

Many Warfighters, Veterans, and family members go to religious services as part of their spiritual formation. This can be a potential area of conflict or growth for the family. Redeployed Warfighters may come away from a deployment with questions and intense feelings in how their religion addresses or doesn't address these things. The Warfighters, Veterans, and family members may withdraw or show disinterest in religious activities. This change in the family's set of rules for living creates doubt and concern in family members. It raises the subtle fear of what else the Warfighters or Veterans might give up after their experiences of combat.

CONCLUSION

"I suggest that the desire to become "somebody else" is not something to be encouraged and pandered to, but something we should recognize for what it is: a sickness of the soul, a refusal or inability to accept ourselves as we really are that keeps us ultimately from becoming the person we have it in us to become. Cosmetic psychopharmacology, like cosmetic surgery and cosmetics in general, is based on the popular delusion that it is actually possible to be somebody else, that the soul's sickness can be healed through a quick, superficial "fix." More generally, the entire modern biological approach to mental illness- the so-called Medical Model- fosters the same delusory hope, equating sickness of the soul with a neurological glitch, and promising patients an easy chemical normalization without their ever having to confront the existential crisis that is at the center of their pain. It is time we all recognized this delusion for what it is. There is no quick fix for the soul, no easy procedure for becoming somebody else through cosmetic alteration in brain chemistry. And it doesn't matter how many scientists and psychiatrists want to tell us otherwise. The science they are preaching is a religion just as unprovable as any other."[64]

Elio Frattaroli

The sight, sounds, smells, things touched, and memories of combat stay with those who have deployed. The impact of deployments and the painfulness of war deeply touch the human Soul. Very often Warfighters are silently wounded because they are not able to assign meaning to the events they have experienced. What they have seen, smelled, touched, tasted, and remembered does not make sense. Back home, in a completely different kind of environment, these combat experiences and their painfulness can create silent emotional wounding. Healing begins when the intellectual part of the Soul is able to reason and assign manageable meaning to the events experienced.

Family members are deeply concerned with how a deployment

changes the Warfighter. Warfighters and Veterans return changed by the trauma of combat. These changes emerge over time and affect everyone's lives. These changes reflect "PTSoulD." Warfighters and Veterans become cynical, bitter, and angry and family members become afraid, desperate and lost.

Family members can be frustrated that the person who left on the deployment is not the same person who returned. While there may be some degree of understanding that everybody changes as a result of such experiences, there may be such dramatic changes in personality and outlook that the family members feel like they are living with an entirely different person. And they may not like this "new" person. The enormous turmoil created by this experience can be painful and harbor loneliness in everyone concerned.

"PTSoulD" requires Veterans to perform an honest self-examination to understand how their beliefs, attitudes, and behaviors are impacted by the sense of meaning they give to the combat experience. Deployments not only require Warfighters to find meaning in their painful experiences, but they also require family members to arrive at a new sense of meaning of who they are as a family. Thus, the painful experience of combat can also claim the family as a victim. Family members are in the continued business of both holding onto the stable foundations that keep the family intact and continually changing to reflect the new. Giving new meaning and direction to the family who has a Veteran in it is exhausting and fragile work. It requires great emotional energy from every family member.

We are responsible for ourselves. The degree to which we assume this responsibility is the measure of our happiness. We are whole persons. Responsibility for ourselves is:

> <u>Physical:</u> we must provide food, clothing, and shelter for ourselves.

<u>Emotional:</u> we are in charge of our own emotions; no one can make us feel a particular way.

<u>Mental:</u> we have the ability to make our needs known to others.

<u>Social:</u> giving to others and receiving from others is a necessity for whole persons.

<u>Spiritual:</u> we decide to believe that we are loved and that we need to love ourselves in order to love others.

These core characteristics of the whole person are not new but take them and make them yours. There is no easy solution. Examining our attitudes and behaviors that make up a healthy balanced Self or a silently wounded Soul takes courage and hard work.

Part Three.
Finding Meaning --
Finding Self

"The ultimate mystery is one's own self."[65]
Sammy Davis, Jr.

INTRODUCTION

"A true war story is never moral. It does not instruct, nor encourage virtue, nor suggest models of human behavior, nor restrain men from doing the things that men have always done. If a story seems moral, do not believe it. If at the end of a war story, you feel uplifted, or if you feel that, some bit of rectitude has been salvaged from the larger waste, then you have been the victim of a very old and terrible lie. There is no rectitude whatsoever. There is no virtue. As a first rule of thumb, therefore, you can tell a true war story by its absolute and uncompromising allegiance to obscenity and evil.... You can tell a true war story if it embarrasses you."[66]

Tim O'Brien

Post Traumatic Soul Disorder (PTSoulD) is a wounding of the whole person. The healing process discovers the hidden wounds caused by the pain, hurts, trauma, grief, and loss experienced in combat. The healing process is also about a rediscovery of who the Warfighters, Veterans, and family members have become. Healing is a process of finding meaning in the pain, loss, and grief that results from combat trauma. This discovery often takes place within one's own private time and place. The objective of finding one's Self is to provide a process for the healing of the grief, pain, loss, and trauma that silently wounds the Soul through self-reflection, personal growth, and self-awareness. This is a process of self-examination and finding meaning that will lead to purposeful living. The silently wounded "WVFMs" must seek to find meaning in their lives. In finding meaning, they find themselves. Upon coming to an understanding that Warfighters, Veterans, and family members are silently wounded in their Souls, they can also begin a healing process by calling upon their own inner strengths and resources. The road back is a road of finding connection, finding Self, discovering meaning in life, and turning to purposeful living.

THE ROAD BACK

"The journey of a thousand miles begins with one step."[67]

Lao-Tse

LUKE

To say that was a rough time would be like spittin' in the wind. It seemed like everything was moving in slow motion and at the same time changes were coming faster than light. Anyway, I got word the Board was acting on my case and I was looking at being discharged and sent home. As I recall that was the second, no, third most scary time in my life. The first was when I got married, and the second was when I saw my brother blown up. I know I was not acting right. Didn't feel right either. That movie kept going in my head. But I noticed it wasn't in such slow motion anymore. I still woke up in the middle of the night in a cold sweat.

As I was waiting for the Board results and discharge, I heard a lot about some of my friends. One of my best friends already made it home. He wrote me and said he was having a hard time adjusting again. His head was still on the streets of the combat zone. He told me how he had a lot of anger. I could relate to that one. He said he was really scared at night. I never knew him to admit to being sacred. He finally went out and bought a nine-mil and put it under his pillow. He said that helped him feel more secure. One day he was strung out tight when he went to a coffee shop. Some kids were arguing about the war saying how it was bad and everything. He said he went into a rage and blew up at them. The shop owner called the cops and threw him out. He managed to make his way home before he was arrested, but he admitted that scared him a lot.

I spent a lot of time just hanging around. I didn't feel comfortable around anyone. Towards the end, I started skipping the group sessions. Then I just started hanging out in front of Malone house smoking. I remember thinking that I never smoked until I got to Walter Reed. That was strange. After Walter Reed, I smoked all the time. It was a nervous habit, a distraction; it passed the time. I couldn't stand still for more than two seconds.

JENNIFER

I didn't have time to watch my husband pretend life didn't matter anymore. I had to mow the lawn and keep the house clean, so my baby could crawl on the floor. I had to prepare bottles, feed dogs, visit Luke, and attempt to maintain my own sanity. When more tattoos appeared on Luke's body and he began pounding down beers for survival, I felt like he was giving up on me. I felt like he was giving up on the "us" that began back in high school. So where did that leave me?

When I cracked open my old journal, I hardly knew what to write. I flipped through the pages and read the sparse scribbling from the time Luke was in Iraq. When Luke was gone, I had spent all my energy emailing and writing him. My journal was almost never opened. It was one of the many things I lost hold of during Luke's deployment and then his time at Walter Reed. Pen in hand, Sadie asleep in the other room, I closed my eyes and let my pen glide across the page…

> Sometimes you have to keep on fighting, even when you want to give up. Sometimes quitting is not an option. There comes a time though, when you have to stop, when you have to just slow down and just breathe—to just be still.
>
> Survivors get tired of surviving. Fighters lose the will to fight. I am tired of being strong. I'm tired of fighting. I'm tired of keeping on. I don't feel like it. Is that a good enough reason? I don't have the energy, or the will, or the passion, or the resilience that I used to have.
>
> I just want to lie within the warmth of our bed. I just want to hold my love again; I want to feel his arms around me. I want to feel comforted and quieted. I just want to breathe again. I don't want to fight anyone or anything. I'm not asking for elation; I just

want peace. I just want to be OK.

Going to church was my way of searching for an inner stillness. I needed to find a place of peace within my own gut; I couldn't depend on Luke for that anymore. The phrase "Be Still and know I am God" kept echoing through my mind. I knew it was from the Bible, but I couldn't place which book it was from. It didn't matter. That seven-word phrase was the beginning of my journey back to peace. "Be still and know I am God." I wasn't as alone as I thought I was. I felt a deep sense of peace when those words echoed in my mind, and I silently recited them whenever I needed to.

§§§§

The most important question to ask ourselves about the disorder of the Soul is "What can Warfighters, Veterans, and family members do to nurture healing in their own Souls?" At first glance, the idea of healing the Soul appears to be the domain of religion by default. When healing the Soul is only an act of religion, then healing is in danger of remaining a very private and personal matter seldom discussed for lack of understanding or embarrassment. If the silently wounded Soul is to experience healing, one must engage many different options for understanding and healing. Certainly religion and spirituality are one of those options. But we cannot rely only upon traditional patterns of healing. Healing the disorder of the Soul requires the application of every effort in a life-long journey of finding meaning and living a life of purpose. We suggest that healing the disorder of the Soul takes place in an intentional and deliberate encounter with one's silent wounds and in developing personal life-style choices to mitigate them. Healing "PTSoulD" does not have a quick fix nor is it the domain of any one discipline or institution. Healing the disorder of the Soul is nonetheless the critical need of this time.[68]

"You are your own best therapist!" That quote by Sigmund Freud[69] points out the impact our own determination to find meaning and healing can have in our lives. One of the most difficult concepts for us to understand is the capability we have in our Souls to heal, find meaning, and live lives full of purpose. We do choose how we want to feel. We all know the core premise of healing is the desire to want to heal. Ultimately, the "WVFMs'" decision to change their behavior or to grow in some area of their lives is up to them. This does not suggest that healing is simply a matter of will power. Healing may need the assistance of many factors to include therapy, medications, support, or a lifetime of struggle. What we are suggesting is that the journey of healing is a journey we each must want to take. Other people may give us suggestions and guide us in our thinking just as this book does, but when it comes down to it, the Warfighter, Veteran, and family member makes their own choices. They determine how they will live. They are their own best therapists.

Warfighters, Veterans, and family members have the capability within them to seek healing. It becomes a matter of making the decision to act. Nobody can do that for them. We recognize that sometimes we think that there are things too painful, too deep to discuss with others, or to even expose to the light of day. This reflects the disorder of the Soul.

Healing the disorder of the Soul is not accomplished by any quick checklist type of process or by following a simplistic program or how-to outline. Healing the Soul is about a life long process of self-examination and seeking meaning in our suffering. Warfighters, Veterans, and family members have the enduring capacity to survive difficult and traumatic events in life and carry on. They have the inner strength and capacity to seek control over "PTSoulD."

The most exciting thing about developing a lifetime of successful healing is that it is an altogether possible goal. The critical first step to healing is the "WVFMs'" decision to move in that direction. It is not an easy decision or we would not sense the need to write this book. And the journey is not complete with a few quick steps. "WVFMs" have to make the truly important life changing decisions in their lives in small steps. Sometimes the decisions are so overwhelming to understand that the only way they can make them is in small portions. "WVFMs" will find that once they are resolved to move toward a lifetime of healing that the first small step will be easier than they imagined. They will also find that having taken that first step, there is just a little bit more clarity about the second step. And they take it. Before they know it, Warfighters, Veterans, and family members are moving into a whole lifetime of successful steps toward their healing.

SELF-EXAMINATION AND THE PERSONAL CHARACTERISTICS OF SELF

"The life that is unexamined is not worth living."[70]

Plato

LUKE

As I think back on those days, I remember I felt most comfortable around other Veterans. Didn't matter who. I remember going to a VFW meeting around the corner one night and felt relaxed and comfortable for the first time in months. They were WWII Vets and a few Vietnam Vets. I listened to their stories. I remember thinking that in a strange way they were my stories. Maybe a change of time and place but what they saw I saw. I could understand. I knew what they were talking about. For the first time I began to think that, I might make it past the next week. For a long time I thought I wasn't going to make it…that I wasn't going to find myself again. When I went to that meeting, I felt like I wasn't alone. I don't know why I never went back. Maybe I was scared I would find myself, and I wouldn't be able to live with who I had become.

I got to know a few fellow Vets. But we were the silent wounded. We were the ones that walked around like nothing happened. We didn't have missing legs or scars on our heads. We were the crazies. When we went by the physical therapy ward we were surprised at all the energy of the patients. Those guys were getting topnotch new legs and a lot of attention. The day I went by to find a friend there were some football players from DC there. And a lot of reporters. I slipped out the door. I never saw my friend and no one paid a rat's- ass bit of attention to me.

One of the things I remember doing was skipping meds. At first, it made me feel like I was going to crawl out of my skin; so I would start again. But I really didn't like the fog they put me in. I couldn't think. They did quiet the movie in my head, but they damped out everything else too. It wasn't long before I preferred the horror show in my head than being doped up all the time. So I started skipping meds. I also started thinking about things. Jennifer was by my side, and I started to think about how much of a butt-head I was. At the same time I was still on edge and angry. I hated being that way around Jen.

JENNIFER

In a Sunday sermon, the minister said that we need to trust God for everything. The idea of God's presence helped me find some peace, but I wasn't ready to trust God. When Sadie went down for a nap that afternoon, I opened up my old journal again...

> I need to trust You for everything, yet I don't trust anyone or anything anymore. I don't know what to trust in anymore. I don't even know how to trust. Don't fear? How? How do I rest in You? Find peace in You? Calm in You? Where the hell were you? Was that stuff supposed to happen to Luke? To Johnny? Was my family supposed to fall apart? Did you plan that? Or did the war cause it? Or did it just happen? Was Luke's descent into insanity your work? Was Johnny's death? Am I supposed to trust you had a plan and that fit into it? Wrong questions, right? But if I very well can't get them to go away, then what? Are you really listening? I mean for REAL? Or do we just make you up to make ourselves feel better? I'm supposed to be grateful, right? For all the positive in my life— my baby is healthy, and my husband is alive. Gratefulness is not bringing me peace.
>
> I don't know where to go or what to do; I don't know if I believe in you. And yet I'm sitting here talking to you. Or to myself? Or to no one?
>
> If you aren't real, then how did Luke survive over in Iraq, and how am I making it through? If you are real, then what were you thinking? Are you powerless in some things? HELP? You did send it; Luke is finally

138

starting to come around, and I'm finding peace, even if only for moments at a time. But, don't you think you waited a little long? No, I waited too long. Help came when I made the decision to find peace. You are helping me follow through, sending me what I need to survive.

Is that what you are doing? Giving me what I need? Time to be confused and scribble words that make no sense? Or is this my mind failing? Are you here? I mean really. Always? God is still here. Are you sure? Are you? Am I too blind to see you or are you not here at all? Have you been with me the whole time, saving me in my agony over and over again?

I want to breathe. I want to laugh. I want to feel warmth and pleasure. I want to dance and dream again. I want to stop looking back to what my life was before deployment, to who I was before deployment, but I don't know how. I don't know if I'm there yet, and I don't know if that's okay. How do I move forward? By writing? By trying to dream? By just giving another hour, another day, another shot at happiness, and maybe someday attempting to feel joy? I'm still me. I'm a broken version of Jennifer, damaged, but not beyond repair.

§§§§

The five personal characteristics of the Self reflect how healthy or unhealthy we are. Each of the personal characteristics of the Self form and develop the key parts and experiences of our lives, reflect who we are, and who we want to be. When Warfighters, Veterans, and family members experience life-changing pain, grief, and trauma, the wounds are deep and affect the very core of their Self and their Soul. How they respond to the pain, grief, and trauma is actually their choice to make. The examinations of their personal characteristics of Self allow Warfighters, Veterans, and family members to review their choices and begin a path to healing their Self and their Soul.

Warfighters, Veterans, and family members must take seriously the premise that they are responsible for themselves. This is a positive direction suggesting that we are all survivors and not helpless victims. Healing the disorder of the Soul is reflected in the personal characteristics of the Self. Healing begins by taking responsibility for the Self, examining our lives, finding meaning in our pain, and making the decisions to change behavior.

Healing the Soul involves the examination of the personal characteristics that can lead Warfighters, Veterans, and family members to connecting to their sense of who they are now. Not who they think they are or who they were before the combat experience, but who they are now, with their silently wounded Souls. When we examine our sense of Self, we begin making different choices to change our behaviors. This examination works because it allows "WVFMs" to understand who they have become on their own terms, in their own time and space. It focuses on what is unique to them through their own reflection and understanding. They then make the decision to heal their Souls.

Self-examination allows Warfighters, Veterans, and family members a private, individual, and non-judgmental means to examine very sensitive and painful experiences and thoughts. Such an approach allows them to work on their own time schedule and at their own individual pace. Self-examination allows "WVFMs" a personal reflection that in turn creates or sustains the changes in Self and behaviors in their personal characteristics.

"WVFMs" begin to heal when they come to understand that they can control how they react to combat trauma. Healing is making different choices in response to the pain, grief, loss, and desperation in their lives. Healing "PTSoulD" begins in our acknowledgement that the silent wounds indeed exist and that change is necessary in our lives.[71]

ACKNOWLEDGING THE SILENT WOUNDING

"Today, in our age of weapons of mass destruction, unpredictable terrorism, and up to the minute news, the battlefield is everywhere. . .The result is massive trauma, not just for combatants but also for civilians, who can suffer equally deep emotional and spiritual wounds from their losses."[72]

Edward Tick

LUKE

It wasn't long before I couldn't tell what was real and what was fantasy. It sounds crazy when I think about it now. But the movie in my head soon blended in with my day-to-day boredom. Maybe I was seeing myself years later like those Vietnam Vets sitting around in their groups with their anger and their pain. Was I going to be like that the rest of my life? I couldn't tell which nightmare in my head I was trying to forget. But I had gotten to the point where the anti-nightmare meds made me feel like a dead person all day. Especially in the mornings. For a long time when I tried to stop the meds, I would get an anxiety attack and end up in the ER again. I think after awhile I was written off by the Docs. It was my fault, but it didn't feel like it at the time. I missed too many appointments. I blamed the meds. It seems like towards the end I was only seeing someone once a day for a half hour or so. I was still in the Army, and I still thought of myself as a Soldier, but I couldn't remember what a Soldier was. I spent too much time picking up trash. Too much time blaming everything and everyone except myself. I wasn't ready to blame myself. Not yet.

One night, bored, and full of meds that were supposed to make me sleep; I dug around in my ruck again and found my green pocket notebook. It had all kinds of notes including Arabic phrases to use. I remember repeating them a few dozen times. All I could think of was killing a few more insurgents. Sweet lovin' revenge. Hooah! I was still sucking on gummi bears by the handful. The mini-PX by the main cafeteria had the big bags. Seems like I got a bag a day. Then I started taking notes. Ended up writing down a few of my thoughts. I

143

still have that notebook and now when I look back there were some very bitter and angry thoughts. That started a routine. Not every night at first. In fact, it took me a week before I did it again. But I left the notebook on the table and started writing my thoughts.

The Board finally acted on my case. They had me down for chronic combat trauma "PTSD." They gave me a 30 percent disability but said it was temporary, and I had to be reevaluated every year. Temporary. I remember seeing that word and laughing. I wished. I hoped. If it could only be true. I thought that I would never be me again, the me that I was before I hit the streets in Iraq. The exhaustion. The sleepless nights. The constant sound of gunfire. The strings of deaths. My brother. How long would I remember? Today I still gag over certain smells. I think the smells stayed with me the longest. How many days would go by when I felt sick just thinking about tomorrow? Crap…just thinking about the next hour!

I was discharged and had to report to the VA hospital back home. My records said that I showed some improvement over the time I was in the Ward. But I remember how I saw myself, not how others saw me. My family and friends later told me how shocked they were by my mood swings. My Uncle was a WWII Vet. He said I was like a grenade rolling across the floor, and everyone was holding their breaths waiting for the explosion.

Jennifer helped me pack. How she stuck with me, I will never know. But I felt grateful deep inside. I regret now that I didn't tell her at the time. All I remember was looking over my shoulder all the time, avoiding any open spaces, and wondered what home would be like. I was scared that it would not be like I remembered. It took me a lot longer to realize that I was not like I remembered. On the outside, I was the bad-ass Vet with the tats. And it took a long time to admit to Jennifer that I was scared shitless inside all the time. Then I remember crying my eyes out on the ride home. Just crying the whole freaking ten-hour trip. I felt so sad. I felt like I had lost everything I knew to be me and what I remembered as home. I wanted home to be everything I remembered it was before I left.

JENNIFER

When I helped Luke pack up his stuff to come home, he told me that he'd been writing his feelings down on paper. "Me too." We didn't talk about what we wrote down, but we felt connected in the fact that we were both journaling. Maybe we weren't ready to sort our feelings out in our marriage, but at least we were acknowledging that we both had feelings we needed to work through.

My parents had Sadie and the dogs for the weekend; they had suggested I pick up Luke on my own, without the stress of the baby. A strange sort of hope snuck into my gut that afternoon. For the first time in a long time, Luke and I were alone. He was oddly quiet, yet his eyes flickered with thought. His expression was soft again, the way I remember it before Iraq. He looked almost okay, like he had just woken up from a very long dream. My heart wasn't racing; I couldn't hear my pulse pounding beneath my temples. I was still. My husband was finally coming home.

An hour or two into the drive home, Luke started crying. He didn't say anything; he just cried. Once he started, he couldn't regain composure. I suggested pulling over, but he insisted I keep heading home. I was relieved. Finally, Luke was FEELING something besides anger and rage. The pain of Johnny's death and our separation welled up from his soul. Tears streamed down my face, and for the first time in a long time, I knew we were both going to be okay.

§§§§

A successful healing strategy engages us in taking an inventory of the health and balance of the personal characteristics of the Self. As Warfighters, Veterans, and family members examine their behaviors and attitudes in each of these personal characteristics, they begin to realize that they reflect the deeper health and balance of the Soul. Whether the health and balance of the Soul reflects wounding or healing, it is certain that the way that one thinks and acts are mirrors to the Soul. Such examinations, if honestly conducted on a regular basis, allow the Soul to heal to return the Self to a balanced and healthy whole.

GRIEF

"Grief drives men [to] serious reflection, sharpens the understanding and softens the heart."[73]

John Adams

Grief is a good thing. To grieve is to heal. Grief and loss are the critical emotions displayed by Warfighters and Veterans, after their combat experiences. The central issue around healing the Soul for Warfighters and Veterans is dealing with grief that results from combat trauma. The sense of loss is profound and finds its source in many events. There is loss of innocence, loss of life, loss of the familiar, loss of relationships, and loss of their sense of Self. "PTSoulD" creates a deep sense of grief.

Working through deep and profound grief by Warfighters, Veterans, or family members is progress toward a new reality. Problems arise when they have a delayed confrontation with reality of their grief. There are many responses to grief. Grief is a natural response and Warfighters and Veterans need to understand it in terms of ongoing cycles. Every Warfighter and Veteran sets their own healing pace for dealing with their grief and loss. Warfighters and Veterans need to remember that they are their own best therapists. However, they also find it helpful to understand what is going on and to understand that there are unique dynamics when death occurs in a military environment. Grief can be understood as uncomplicated, normal grief or complicated grief, the result of a silently wounded Soul.[74]

Normal, or uncomplicated, grief reactions are those that, though painful, move the Warfighters and Veterans toward an acceptance of their loss and an ability to carry on with their lives. Warfighters, Veterans, and family members with uncomplicated grief may feel very saddened by the death of a fellow Warfighter, friend, or just the loss of life in general during combat operations, but they, nevertheless, are able feel that life still holds meaning and the potential for fulfillment. Warfighters and Veterans with uncomplicated grief are also able to maintain a sense of Self and trust in others and their identity remains intact. They maintain positive life attitudes and positive behaviors alien to those with complicated grief. "WVFMs" with uncomplicated grief reactions are willing and able to reinvest in interpersonal relationships and activities, and though affected, perhaps deeply, by the loss, they find that they are willing to explore new roles and relationships and derive new or renewed sources of satisfaction in their lives. Uncomplicated grief remains when "WVFMs" are on a path of healing the silent wounds of the Soul.

In contrast with the uncomplicated grief reactions described above, Warfighters and Veterans experiencing complicated grief reactions question who they are, how they will survive, and their prospects of future fulfillment in the face of their combat trauma. Combat trauma produces a profound sense of loss. Warfighters and Veterans with complicated grief feel acute separation distress from their fellow Warfighters, with intense pangs of yearning or longing for the Warfighters killed, the general sense of loss of life, and the loss of Self in the chaotic trauma of combat. They experience a sense of emptiness and lack of purpose, a disturbing sense of feeling detached from others and a numbness, sometimes feeling like a part of them died along with everything and everyone else. The trauma of combat in a real sense "kills" a part of their Self and Soul and understanding the grief and loss that result is critical for finding a path to healing.

Warfighters and Veterans live with unresolved grief. That is a part of the silent wounding of the Soul. There is no definite point in time or list of symptoms that define unresolved grief. How Warfighters, Veterans, and family members express their grief varies. Some act as if nothing has changed. They refuse to talk about the loss, become preoccupied with their memories, or they may not be able to talk or think about anything else. To escape they become overly involved in work, hobbies, or drink more, smoke more cigarettes, get into drugs, or take more prescription drugs. "WVFMs" neglect their health or become overly obsessed with their health and see their health care professionals compulsively. Others become progressively depressed, or isolate themselves from others.

Family members show unresolved grief in many of the same ways. Teens for example become involved in illegal drugs, illegal activities, (such as stealing), destructive behaviors, (such as cutting), or unprotected and excessive sex. Family members may have more accidents, become distant and distracted, avoid their friends, forget their homework, and have difficulty completing schoolwork, or develop absenteeism. Very young children exhibit behavior problems, excessive fears, night terrors, aggressive behaviors, and tantrums. All are expressions of the grief and loss that occurs as the result of indirect exposure to combat trauma and "PTSoulD."

THE GRIEF PROCESS

"There are no mistakes, no coincidences. All events are blessings given to us to learn from."[75]

Elisabeth Kübler-Ross

The Kübler-Ross grief model describes, in five stages, the process by which Warfighters, Veterans, and family members deal with their pain, grief, loss, tragedy, and combat trauma. The model was introduced by Elisabeth Kübler-Ross in her 1969 book, "<u>On Death and Dying</u>."[76] The stages have become well known, and are called the Five Stages of Grief.

The stages as applied to Warfighters, Veterans, and family members are:

<u>Denial</u>: This initial stage finds the Warfighters shocked at what they experience in combat. They cannot begin to assimilate this new reality. The trauma and chaos of combat becomes life changing. Warfighters express disbelief over what they experience and are soon paralyzed in their Souls by trauma, grief, pain, loss, and fear. Warfighters and Veterans repeat this stage when they return home and try to reconnect with life as they remember it. They soon discover they are changed by the combat trauma. Family members experience denial in the face of the fear and worry that invades every aspect of their lives as their Warfighter spouse is deployed.

<u>Anger</u>: A common symptom of combat trauma is a deep lingering anger. Warfighters, Veterans, and family members become deeply angry about their experiences and the changes they sense in themselves. That anger lingers far beyond the end of the combat experience and may define the Warfighters or Veterans for years to come. Anger takes over the Veterans as they discover that their lives are no longer the same. They express their sense of deep loss and pain through ongoing anger. Family members become

deeply angry over the changes that take place and the loss they experience.

Bargaining: This stage may occur at different times during the grief process for Warfighters, Veterans, and family members. Warfighters will begin to bargain with their experiences of grief while still on the battlefield. Their deep sense of fear and grief will bring them to a point of profound anger and prolific bargaining. The bargaining will occur again as "WVFMs" begin to cope with reintegration into their home life. Family members bargain as a coping measure while they endure the deep fear that pervades their lives. Bargaining can become an interwoven cycle with the anger stage.

Depression: Depression is a common experience with Warfighters, Veterans, and family members alike. Depression can take many forms. Clinical or medical depression needs medical and clinical intervention. Warfighters and Veterans must not be afraid to seek out medical help for depression. It is depression that is often treated as a behavioral mental illness. Depression mixes with anger and bargaining to form the new reality of the "WVFMs." All of the classic symptoms of combat trauma appear along with this volatile mix of anger and depression.

Acceptance: This stage is the stage of healing. When Warfighters, Veterans, and family members can begin to see past their anger and deal with their depression, they can begin to heal. Acceptance is a process of discovering meaning and purposeful living. The silently wounded Soul is a Soul in pain, full of anger, and deeply depressed. Healing occurs when the Soul breaks into the realization that acceptance and change can occur. Healing occurs when "WVFMs" find meaning in their pain.

Kübler-Ross originally applied these stages to any form of catastrophic personal loss or trauma. Warfighters and Veterans can apply an understanding of these stages to combat trauma, the

152

silent wounding of their Soul, and their path of healing. These steps do not always occur in order, nor are they always isolated events. Not every Warfighter or Veteran will experience each step. Nevertheless, healing "PTSoulD" and dealing with unresolved grief and loss from combat trauma can be understood through these stages of the grief process and the behaviors that take place in each stage.

Grief and loss create deep changes in Warfighters', Veterans', and family members' senses of Self. These stages can help describe and understand the changes in each of the five personal characteristics of Self. No matter what the "WVFMs" experience, healing can only take place when they reach the acceptance stage.

Combat trauma creates a deep and complicated grief where the story of their sense of pain and loss is difficult to tell. They can not find meaning in their experiences. Combat death, trauma, chaos, are all difficult memories for Veterans. Combat trauma leaves Warfighters in such shock that they have difficulty understanding and absorbing what happened. Combat seems unreal…what is real is what is back home. When Warfighters return home they discover that combat trauma has taken over their sense of Self and they can no longer understand the former reality of "home."

Warfighters and Veterans simply have a great deal of difficulty integrating their story of combat into the story of their lives. This is why storytelling and finding meaning in their pain is such an important path to healing. Warfighters and Veterans with silently wounded Souls from combat trauma must be able to integrate the story of their grief and loss from combat into their lives and who they have become as whole persons. Their story is now a part of who they are. Their story holds meaning for their lives. Warfighters and Veterans can go for years without integrating their stories of combat into their stories of their lives. That integration through storytelling and finding meaning is a critical path to healing.

SUICIDE

Vietnam – "U.S. forces: KIA 58,178, wounded 300,000 +
(includes 74,000 quadriplegics/multiple amputees,) MIAs
2,000 +, PTSD 1.5 million, Suicides 100,000 +, Homeless
150,000 nightly, total cost to U.S. $925 Billion."[78]

Desert Storm – "the Gulf War (90-91) was lauded as
an operation causing little loss to U.S. forces. During
hostilities, the U.S. suffered 148 combat deaths, 235 other
deaths, and 467 wounded. However, this low casualty rate
comprised only what was immediately suffered during the
short period of active combat. As of May 2002, more than
a decade later, the VA had recognized a total of 262,586
veterans disabled due to Gulf War duties and 10,617 dead
of combat related injuries and illnesses since. That raises
the casualty rate of American forces in the Gulf War to the
rather substantial figure of 30.8 percent."[79]

The hidden costs of war include the post-combat premature
deaths from many causes that can be linked to combat to include
premature deaths due to disease, cancers, wounds, and death by
suicide. When the cause is not physical in nature, (such as diseases
and cancers), the lingering trauma of combat is at the root of these
post-combat casualties. We suggest that premature death as a result
of combat trauma is the end-state of Post Traumatic Soul Disorder
(PTSoulD) that is not treated. The psychological motivations for
suicide include the sense of pain, grief, loss, and quiet desperation
that is a signature of combat trauma. Warfighters, Veterans, and
family members want to escape from the unbearable pain and
grief, the quiet pervasive desperation that they live with everyday.
Suicide occurs when "PTSoulD" remains without intervention and
Veterans seek release from the pain and despair that overwhelms
them.

The conditions for suicidal behavior lie in the memories of combat that remain with Warfighters and Veterans. For family members it is the memories of the dysfunctional post-combat behaviors displayed by Warfighters and Veterans as they try to resume their family relations. The anger, distance, fear, stress, anxiety, desperation, and other behaviors are displaced onto the family members and they suffer their own "PTSoulD." "PTSoulD" includes the traumatic memories of combat and the specific events or acts of horror that haunt the Warfighter and Veteran. Many attempts to heal the wounds may fail. Other self-help attempts, such as illegal drugs or alcohol, simply mask the pain. When all else fails to erase those memories, they seek death as an acceptable solution.

There are common misunderstandings about post-combat suicide. Some think that Warfighters, Veterans, and family members who commit suicide are "crazy" as a result of a pre-existing personality disorder. Or that once Warfighters and Veterans return home they are now in a good and positive environment that will prevent suicide. People are surprised when the "WVFM" who is the "good" neighbor, the father, businessperson or woman, and in all outward appearances successful Veteran, commits suicide. Others think that Veterans who talk about suicide as an option will not actually go through with the act, or if they do, and it is unsuccessful, that they are no longer at risk.

Another misunderstanding is many think that talking about suicide to Warfighters, Veterans, and family members who are upset will put the idea into their heads. Or those Veterans who are deeply depressed do not have the energy to commit suicide. Depression as the result of "PTSoulD" is not the issue and in itself is not the suicidal risk.

> "It is a well-known but poorly understood fact that the risk of suicide becomes greater when a depressed patient begins to recover. This doesn't fit well with the usual

assumption that the symptom of depression itself is what makes the person suicidal. Rather it suggests that the biological shutdown of depression may actually protect against suicide- by making it more difficult for the patient to take any action- and that reactivating the patient with medication may then increase the risk of suicide unless adequate attention is paid to the patient's underlying reasons for hopelessness."[80]

Elio Frattaroli

There are many indicators or predictors of suicide such as alcoholism, drug abuse, suicide talk or preparation, prior attempts, isolation, living alone, loss of support, hopelessness, rigid thinking, work or relationship problems, debt, career problems, marital problems, mental illness, stress, life events, anger, aggression, irritability, or physical illness. It's a long list. All of these indicators also reflect a silently wounded Soul and represent the dysfunctional behaviors resulting from untreated combat trauma.

Intervention is critical for Warfighters, Veterans, and family members who are suicidal. This is a crisis intervention. The assessment of suicide risk is a complex process and consultation with mental health and medical professionals is always advisable. "WVFMs" who are at risk fear losing themselves and look at suicide as a solution to avoid the pain, grief, loss, and desperation of combat trauma. They hold an unbearable guilt and develop profound feelings of hopelessness, helplessness, and worthlessness. They are ashamed of what they did or saw. They are profoundly alone in their lives. These are reflections again of the untreated "PTSoulD."

Healing the Soul and preventing suicide can be mutual goals. They are lifelong goals. Be alert to the warning signs and reach out to the wounded Soul. Understand why combat trauma creates a silently wounded Soul. Understand the signs of hopelessness, helplessness, and worthlessness. Pay attention to verbal warnings and behavior warnings. Combat trauma is a breeding ground for suicidal situations to include guilt, physical trauma such as the loss of limbs, grief over the death of fellow Warfighters, and other life changes in our core personal characteristics that are linked to combat trauma and the silently wounded Soul.

Dysfunctional behavior from combat trauma and a silently wounded Soul also signal suicide warnings. Warfighters and Veterans are haunted by the memories of their combat experiences. The pain, grief, loss, and desperation from combat trauma is profound and left untreated can fill Warfighters and Veterans with despair. Warfighters, Veterans, and family members silently wounded in their Souls are at far greater risk of post-combat death by suicide, especially Warfighters who lost friends in combat.

Our response to the suicide risk of our Warfighters, Veterans, and family members is critical. We all need to remember to answer the cries for help from our "WVFMs." Let them know that we care. Get professional help and take threats seriously. Don't keep it a deep dark secret. Get help. And remember, it's okay to talk about it! It may save a life!

> "The majority of us lead quiet, unheralded lives as we pass through this world. There will most likely be no ticker tape parades for us, no monuments created in our honor. But that does not lessen our possible impact, for there are scores of people waiting for someone like us to come along . . . someone who will live a happier life merely because we took the time to share what we have to give. Too often we under estimate the power of a touch, a smile, a kind word . . . all of which have the potential to turn a life around. It's overwhelming to consider the continuous opportunities there are to make our love felt."[81]
>
> Leo Buscaglia

TELLING THE STORIES OF COMBAT

"According to author and healer Deena Metzger, a story is a 'map for the soul.' It is a 'living thing, a divine gift.' When we tell our own stories and listen to those of others, we come in touch with all three: life, divinity, and soul ... Storytelling also knits the community together."[82]

Edward Tick

Story telling asks a Veteran to consider for a few moments what the values most important to them are and how committed they are to developing life solutions. Namely, what matters to a Warfighter, Veteran, and family member helps in part to define how the healing will take place -- how quickly and how deeply.

Healing begins with Warfighters, Veterans, and family members telling their stories. It is like taking an account of their Soul's experiences with the trauma of combat. Each "WVFM" has a unique story and yet every Warfighters', Veterans', and family member's story has common elements. "WVFMs'" stories capture both the triumphs and failures of their experiences. Warfighters, Veterans, and family members account in their telling, writing, or saying of their stories the places that were fearful, dark, and lonely. Their stories reveal their "PTSoulD." Their stories also include healing, healthiness, and peace. This combination of experiences for the Soul is a treasure of great value. When "WVFMs" give their stories to others, it is a gift. It is the greatest gift they will ever give because it is about their silently wounded Souls. To give the story of their Souls to another human being is to entrust them with the most precious, delicate, and important part of their lives.

Warfighters', Veterans', and family members' stories have depth and characteristics, resolve and triumph. When they come together, tell, and listen to their collective stories, they learn and gain insight into their world and their pain, grief, loss, and desperation. "WVFMs" find woven in and throughout their collective stories recurring themes of healing and hope. In their collective stories, "WVFMs" find that they, as human beings, are really not very different from one another. Their collective stories teach them history, show them new things they may never experience individually, and confirm that the Soul within each of them has an enormous capacity to heal. A Veteran's story of combat trauma contributes character and depth to everyone's life story.

It is peculiar that a society that has such passionate viewpoints about the value of life rarely makes time to let Warfighters, Veterans, and family members tell their stories, let alone listen to them. "WVFMs" need to tell us their stories. What else in life is of more supreme value or is worth our time than listening to and entering into the Soul of another person?

The most important thing that Warfighters and Veterans can do in their grief and loss is immediately take out the photo albums, memorabilia, trophies, plaques, and special possessions and tell the story of their experiences. Those memorabilia are pages in the story of past experiences that are still alive in memory. They are momentary glimpses into a Soul. The memories Warfighters and Veterans are collecting within them through storytelling may not appear to have dramatic revelations or be novel-like in details, but they are small embers of light, warmth, and life that get tucked away and add just a little bit of goodness and texture to their Souls. Their stories then become part of everyone's story by adding an extra little bit to everyone's Souls.

Warfighters and Veterans can begin their healing by telling their stories of combat. Once they begin, it is something they can work on the rest of their lives. Warfighters, Veterans, and family members first tell their stories for themselves and their own self-understanding and self-improvement. To heal they must focus on their own Soul's story. As "WVFMs" write their story (for personal insight), they focus on the events that have emotional significance for them, events that influenced their behavior, feelings, and values.

It is important for them to be frank and to give details.

Warfighters, Veterans, and family members should also build and maintain their stories of healing. They can understand their Self through writing using such techniques as writing their life stories, or keeping diaries or journals. In their writing they record significant experiences, causes of problems, progress in self-improvement, and what self-help methods work. "WVFMs" alike can use their writing to connect with the deepest processes guiding their lives.

STORYTELLING THROUGH WRITING

"Make it thy business to know they self, which is the most difficult lesson in the world."[83]

Miguel de Cervantes

Writing in general can help the Warfighters, Veterans, and family members begin to tell their own stories and reflect upon who they are as whole persons. Writing exposes the silent wounding in the Soul. Writing helps "WVFMs" start a path of healing. There are many forms of writing including diaries, narrative stories, poems, autobiographies, lists, journals, and books. The art of writing is the art of self-examination. Writing does not need to be formal or even accomplished. Writing is for the individual "WVFM." While it may be true that some "WVFMs" turn into accomplished authors and tell their stories in bestselling books, most must only concern themselves with being honest with themselves. Read the books by accomplished authors for their insight and for their stories. Warfighters, Veterans, and family members should accomplish their own writing for themselves.

One form of writing is writing the story of the Warfighter or Veteran's life. It is amazing how often a "WVFMs'" problems are rooted in the problems and traumas of their lives, their families, or their lifelong experiences. Warfighters, Veterans, and family members can only know themselves by knowing their own histories. The writing of an autobiography, incorporating their life history, greatly increases their awareness of the events underlying their combat trauma and "PTSoulD." Writing out their story can be fascinating and healing. The knowledge can also be a wonderful legacy for them.

Many writers of autobiographies have commented about the powerful emotions, insights, and finally personal relief from re-living stressful periods of their lives. Warfighters, Veterans, and family members writing down their stories are self-healing by writing

163

their way through their trauma. Keeping a daily diary while in combat is another method of writing. Self-examination and healing begin when the "WVFMs" can put their emotional and physical trauma into words. "WVFMs" are openly willing to write about their experiences. The process of Warfighters, Veterans, and family members writing their deepest thoughts and feelings translates the trauma into language that tells a story. This storytelling process is the key to gaining healing for "PTSoulD." The written "story" changes how the "WVFMs" think about the combat experience and trauma. The more the Warfighters and Veterans write, the more insightful and understandable their stories become. This form of self-treatment takes little or no professional time and is something the Warfighters, Veterans, and family members can do at any time.[84]

Writing is not an instant cure. It takes a long time for Warfighters and Veterans to learn to cope with their combat trauma and silently wounded Souls through writing. In some cases the memories are too vivid and the trauma still too real to commit to detailed writing. Writing can make Warfighters and Veterans remember very traumatic experiences. For some Veterans, especially those whose experiences have not been believed before, an especially important part may be sharing the traumatic memory with someone who will listen carefully, care, be supportive, and reassure the Warfighters or Veterans that their story is understood and believed. That is why "WVFMs" gravitate to unit and family member support groups, organizations, and reunion groups. They can share their stories with other Warfighters, Veterans, and family members that understand and believe. All this learning takes time.

"WVFMs" can write their own autobiographies. They can decide what psychological mysteries they would like to solve and what self-improvements they would like to make. Many Warfighters and Veterans say their life is dull and ordinary and writing their autobiography is embarrassing at best. The only criteria for the

Warfighters, Veterans, and family members is the willingness to honestly share their Souls and the details and depth, the joy and the pain, of the Self.

Writing an autobiography will be healing for the Warfighters and Veterans. However, keep in mind that writing a history for others is a very different process than writing privately for self-understanding and self-improvement.

Warfighters' and Veterans' writing will be more profitable if they have some specific self-understanding or self-change goals in mind, perhaps only three, or four. Thus, this method of healing begins with an autobiographical review of their life, which will help "WVFMs" decide where they want to go with their writing. "WVFMs" can begin with a tentative list of some things they might want to understand better about themselves and make another list of things they might want to change about themselves. In their writing, they can pay particular attention to these areas (and others that occur to them) as they write their stories. For each "mystery" and each "problem" make up a work sheet for ideas, books to read, possible explanations, and possible self-improvement approaches and so on.

When writing their stories, Warfighters, Veterans, and family members should first try to focus on the events that have emotional significance for them, events that influenced their behavior, feelings, and values. It is important to be frank and to give details.

Writing the autobiography, a major undertaking, should put Warfighters', Veterans', and family members' lives in perspective and help them see the major directions they are moving in, or where they are not making much movement. Throughout the writing process, "WVFMs" alike will probably find some other areas of their lives they would like to understand better. They should add them to their list of mysteries.

STORYTELLING THROUGH JOURNALING

"The great art of writing is the art of making people real
to themselves with words."[85]

Logan Smith

Journals are excellent ways for Warfighters, Veterans, and family members to record their progress in their healing, which may not be obvious otherwise. They record, or "Journal," their daily successes and their failures. Recordings done immediately following a self-improvement effort are also good places to figure out what "WVFMs" did right or wrong, what self-instructions worked well, and what self-defeating thoughts undermined their healing efforts. Insight into the causes of a behavior or feeling can be gained by using a journal for self-examination of their behaviors. The "WVFMs'" journal focuses on self-help efforts and goals, relationships, and feelings. Journal writing in which "WVFMs" pour out their anger, fears, frustrations, disappointments, has been found to reduce anxiety and depression as well as improve their healing. It is best that Warfighters, Veterans, and family members write in their journals every day, getting their pent up feelings out as soon as possible.

Journal keeping is a self-examination activity and a solitary ritual. Journaling is not just keeping a diary. A diary gives a ledger of one's external activities and events. A journal gives a ledger of one's internal activities and events. Journals tend to be very personal and may include interpretations of meaning. The primary interaction is internal. The activity of journaling and documenting one's thoughts, feelings, wounding and healing allows Warfighters, Veterans, and family members to expose a part of their Soul. This exposure allows them to look at themselves perhaps from a slightly new perspective. Journaling lets "WVFMs" look at themselves from outside their inner lives. When "WVFMs" read the words or listen to the recorded voice, they can be caught off guard. Did I really think that? Did I say that? Yes. Journaling is a healthy ritual for "WVFMs" and a useful mechanism for putting their experiences and thoughts into perspective. Journaling is an excellent ritual of self-discovery. This vehicle of reflection lets Warfighters, Veterans, and family members read their stories and appreciate the progress that healing Souls make over time.

Some Warfighters, Veterans, and family members, by personality, will never be comfortable with disclosing themselves to other people. Some "WVFMs" are very private people or they simply may be shy. For a variety of reasons, they keep their biggest emotions and highest thoughts locked inside. The ritual of journaling can be the catalyst to something tremendous and brilliant waiting to be born from inside of their Souls. Journaling becomes a vehicle for reflection for some "WVFMs" who may never express themselves to others directly. Journaling then becomes a means to enter into their inner worlds to find their paths to healing.

Journaling serves Warfighters, Veterans, and family members as an intermediate way to be heard until they have resolved to connect to others so that they may hear what the pages of their journaling have expressed about their Souls. The ritual of journaling leads "WVFMs" to open expression, a healthy product of the Soul. Journaling not only gives them a portal of entry into the outside world but also simultaneously gives the rest of the word a portal of entry into their Souls. It can be a new and quite frightening experience for some to open up and reveal their innermost lives. It can be difficult for some "WVFMs" to negotiate how they will meet and what that place of shared vulnerability will look like or where it will end up. Journaling can be a controlled mechanism to move slowly into this new dynamic of life. There are tremendous stories within each Warfighter, Veteran, and family member. The ritual of journaling can be a vehicle of expression to nurture the life of their stories.

A journal serves as a key self-examination tool. A journal allows Warfighters, Veterans, and family members to consider their thoughts in depth and detail the attitudes and behaviors attributed to their sense of Self. Journaling is not simply keeping a diary of the events as they occur like a newspaper reporter. Rather, journaling is capturing, organizing, and giving "WVFMs" a path forward with what they are learning, what they have discovered in their experiences, and what they plan to do with these lessons and experiences to implement their own healing goals.

When Warfighters, Veterans, and family members write down their insights and ideas and especially their challenges and problems, they put a new perspective on both the facts and feelings they have in each situation. Journaling affords "WVFMs" the opportunity to clarify and focus facts while giving an opportunity to have a fresh perspective upon feelings from the event. From this, they have a critical foundation to begin to organize their personal solutions for healing and accomplishment.

Journaling is writing. It is the action of committing to paper what is in Warfighters', Veterans', and family members' minds and spirits. "WVFMs" capture personal revelations, plans, issues, insights, and possibilities that in turn give a set of building blocks to clarify and act upon their personal solutions and goals. Journaling should be a natural extension of their thinking and feelings. It is a blueprint for positive behavior change and thus healing for the Soul.

Warfighters, Veterans, and family members should always begin with what is easiest to write down. This may be the immediate thought or the issue for which they have a lot of energy. They need to write spontaneously. Journaling is not a final exam booklet. Journaling is by the individual, for the individual. It is for no one else unless they decide it is.

Warfighters, Veterans, and family members need to always be honest and candid with themselves. They need not simply write what sounds good, but the depth of experiences and thoughts and reactions to the interactions in their self-examinations. "WVFMs" write as the thoughts come. They should not preplan and outline thoughts before writing them down. Being spontaneous in this way allows better understanding of patterns of response and reaction if written as they come.

Journaling can act as a series of building blocks for moving from basic to more in-depth consideration in a given subject. Journaling allows "WVFMs" to have a tool that intentionally invites them to consider and respond to subjects that they may not normally consider or intentionally avoid in each of the personal characteristics of the Self.

STORYTELLING THROUGH TECHNOLOGY MEDIA

"Virtual reality, as the name suggests, is simply the creation of an entirely artificial environment whose sole purpose is to precisely imitate a real environment."[86]

Gillian Koenig

Introducing technology into the world of storytelling to help Warfighters, Veterans, and family members conduct and continue their deepest and innermost healing is new territory. Yet, the virtual world is helping "WVFMs" tell their stories in many new and interesting ways. Technology is the full range of personal computers and interactive experiences primarily in software design, the use of media including television, movies, and radio. It can include radios, IPods, MP3 players, cell phones, and the vast array of gadgets that set the conditions for communication, collaboration, community, and information exchange. The desired outcome behind the potential use of technology to enhance healing in Warfighters and Veterans is that the interactive experience can set the conditions for telling their stories. "WVFMs" can tell their story in their own personal time and space with a sense of openness, willingness, self-initiation, and vulnerability sufficient to allow them to develop a greater and perhaps more rapid level of personal healing. The use of such technologies can serve as a stand-alone means to allow "WVFMs" to conduct some level of self-examination of the conditions and possible insights that allow them to move forward in their healing.

Considering the number of hours a day the average American spends in front of a screen, whether it is television, computer, or film, it can be understood that a key route to who Warfighters and Veterans are as human beings is through visual media. Technology provides a unique opportunity to focus "WVFMs" on self-examination in how they interface and interact with television, film, music videos, recorded music, video games, and the Internet, all which constitutes the world of imagined, constructed, or "virtual" reality. Popular culture media is a central part of how the average individual today accesses, understands, and interprets their worldview, constructs their values for living, and orients their models of healing. Being able to bridge the constructed worldview that has been developed in a world of digits to the world that exists in everyday needs and problems is the new challenge of today's Warfighters, Veterans, and family members.

In an increasingly high-tech world, more and more Warfighters, Veterans, and family members are going online. The extraordinary discoveries and advancements in communication technologies and information exchange will no longer allow any segment of society or social exchange to live in an isolated or uninvolved parallel existence. As these advancements continue to become mainstreamed in day-to-day activities, the very cultural fabric of our society will also change. Computer based activities and interactions are becoming mainstream in today's society. Emerging computer interactive games and simulations have unlimited potential not only for teaching behavior change but also assessing the condition of the Soul![87]

Blogging has become a mainstream method of expression. Warfighters and Veterans are connecting at unprecedented rates through Internet blogs. Storytelling becomes the critical subject of on-line blogs helping Warfighters, Veterans, and family members alike tell about their experiences. The Cyberspace community of the Internet has millions of members gathering each day in community in a technological virtual reality where relationships are formed, information is freely exchanged, and services obtained. Warfighters and Veterans are telling their stories, finding connection, and healing together.[88]

CONCLUSION

"In my discomfort, I'd forgotten what it can mean to simply bear witness. Having your story heard, not only by those who were with you but by those who weren't, and who otherwise would never understand, and therefore never understand you, validates it."[89]

Lee Alley

Warfighters, Veterans, and family members are silently wounded and in pain as a result of combat trauma. The path to healing is a path of self-examination and self-discovery. "WVFMs" need to know and understand who they are. That process involves several techniques such as understanding grief, storytelling, writing, and engaging in the search for meaning. Self-examination and self-discovery are the search for meaning. When Souls are silently wounded, healing begins when meaning is discovered and "WVFMs" attain a sense of purposeful living.

Grief is the normal response to pain, loss, and tragedy. Grief is the critical emotion of combat trauma. Grief affects every part of the whole person, each of the five personal characteristics. Grief has physical, social, intellectual, emotional, and spiritual dimensions. Common to every Veteran of combat is the pain, loss, and trauma that irrevocably changes the individual and silently wounds the Soul. Although Warfighters and Veterans can understand the process of grief through the Kübler-Ross model, in reality they will have a variety of responses that are influenced by their culture, experiences, background, family, and spiritual awareness.

The silent wounding of the Soul and the variety of responses to the whole person that results are symptoms of grief. The trauma of combat creates silent and profound grief in Warfighters, Veterans, and family members. The path to healing is also a path of understanding and embracing one's deep pain of grief and loss.

It is important to tell stories, and equally important that these stories be heard. Stories evoke the power of experience. They remind "WVFMs" that unknown forces are at work in each and every one of them, no matter how ordinary they may appear to be. Stories remind "WVFMs" that no one gets by with a perfect, unscarred life, and now and then, everyone shines with the divine. Stories inform them of resources they otherwise would not know to look for. Stories tell Warfighters, Veterans, and family members that, however the details differ, they all feel the same emotions. This reminds them that they are not alone in their own private pain, that they all belong to the same human family.

Stories connect Warfighters, Veterans, and family members one to another. They provide pathways and solutions. They give courage. Healing begins when "WVFMs" find the courage to reason and assign manageable meaning to the events they experience. The silent wounding of the Soul by combat trauma requires "WVFMs" to perform an honest self-examination to understand how their beliefs, attitudes, and behaviors are impacted by the sense of meaning they give to the combat experience.

Deployments not only require Warfighters to find meaning in their painful experience, but they also require family members to arrive at a new sense of meaning of who they are now as a family. Thus, the painful experience of combat can also claim the family as a victim. Family members are in the business of both holding onto the stable foundations that keep the family together and at the same time working the constant changes necessary to reflect what is now happening to everyone. Giving new meaning and direction to the family who has a Warfighter or Veteran in it is exhausting and fragile work. It requires great emotional energy from every family member.

Self-examination helps move Warfighters, Veterans, and family members toward healing their Souls as they discover how to sustain and heal the personal characteristics of the Self or personhood. Self-examination takes many forms including telling the stories, journaling, and finding meaning.

Every Warfighter, Veteran, and family member has attitudes and behaviors reflected and exercised in their personal characteristics of the Self. What they think creates attitudes. Attitudes influence behaviors. When the personal characteristics of personhood are unhealthy and not balanced, "WVFMs" develop unhealthy attitudes and behaviors. By learning how to meet, heal, and sustain Self, Warfighters, Veterans, and family members rediscover healthy attitudes and behaviors. This is a discovery of meaning. This moves them toward healing the Soul.

Part Four.
Finding Community –
Finding Connection

"I can honestly say the Web page has changed my life . . . We always felt so alone in our grieving for my dad. We discovered there was someone who had thought about him everyday. Thank God, all of this happened because of the web page."[90]

Lee Alley

INTRODUCTION

"As Odysseus, the archetypical warrior, made his way home, he narrated his journey, setting off to war, waging the long war, coming home, listener after listener. The story grew until, finally home, he could tell the whole tale and become whole. We tell stories and we listen to stories in order to live. To stay conscious. To connect one with another. To understand consequences. To keep history. To rebuild civilization."[91]

Maxine Hone Kingston

Warfighters, Veterans, and family members with silently wounded Souls can find meaning, healing, and purposeful living within community. Community takes many forms. There are support groups, organizations, social groups, unit organizations, reunion organizations, Veterans organizations, family support groups, religious groups and organizations, and many others. Communities are formed in both the non-traditional virtual world as well as in the traditional real world. The ability to discover meaning in suffering and to regain purposeful living through working to the greater good and giving to others happens best within community. Warfighters, Veterans, and family members should seek out a connection with community to begin their path to healing.

The virtual community consists of the Internet or World Wide Web and is a vast world with unlimited potential for finding and building community to help Warfighters, Veterans, and family members develop self-awareness, do self-examination, find meaning, and achieve purposeful living.

Traditional community abounds around "WVFMs." The silently wounded Soul tends to hide and seek shelter in the grief, loss, and pain. Individuals think that only their pain is real. To expose their pain to others takes a great deal of personal courage. The support provided in community groups is that the individual

Warfighter, Veteran, or family member discovers that there are others who have stories of pain, grief, and loss. The sharing that takes place are stories of healing.

Sharing their stories within community, "WVFMs" discover the rich diversity of backgrounds and experiences they have. This discovery can significantly enhance their healing. Community interaction helps Warfighters, Veterans, and family members find insightful and interactive diversity for self-examination and self-care.

The Warfighters, Veterans, and family members emerging today are technologically sophisticated, globally connected, and fast-paced. They will be comfortable in joining virtual communities. The virtual world is a rich resource finding the tools necessary to succeed in their mission of healing and seeking purposeful living.

Every community, both traditional and non-traditional, must be trusted and secure. The virtual community is becoming a trusted agent of information and source of assistance in addition to traditional support groups and communities. With the rise of virtual communities, virtual support has become a reality for "WVFMs." Warfighters and Veterans are finding significant healing and support within virtual communities.

Warfighters and Veterans must exercise their healing within community. Healing is not achieved in isolation. Isolation breeds depression, bad thinking, and a deepening of "PTSoulD." Warfighters and Veterans are often reluctant to share their innermost thoughts in traditional counseling. The traditional, as well as the virtual community, is becoming a safe haven for telling their stories and finding support, acceptance, and healing. Today, both the traditional and the virtual communities are real, alive, and fulfilling legitimate needs for maintaining connections among "WVFMs." Making a connection with others is a critical step to healing whether it is in the traditional community groups or the virtual communities found in the Internet world.

LUKE

More than two weeks at home had passed when I realized that things just weren't going to be the same. Nothing was like I remembered it. Being home wasn't going to change things around in my head. Everything I did was different. I didn't feel safe anywhere. I was always looking over my shoulder. Every stranger was the enemy, and as I look back, I am ashamed to admit that everyone who looked Iraqi was an insurgent ready to kill me. I felt unprotected even in my own bedroom. Jennifer couldn't understand why I was always locking the bedroom door at night. She was frustrated because she had to tend to the baby. We eventually moved her into our bedroom with us.

I remember one night being startled awake by some loud noise and falling out of bed yelling. As I look back, it was kind of weird. Something you read about or that happens in the movies. I was really embarrassed when I woke myself up hitting the floor. Anyway, Jennifer was about scared out of her wits wondering what happened and the baby was awake and crying. It was a mess. I was in a cold sweat and shaking and scared and yelling. That was the night that I went out into the kitchen and started surfing the net just to divert my head and for something to do. My Dad had gotten me this laptop computer. I came across web sites by Veterans. The first one was about WWII. I remember the stories they told.

As the weeks passed I was on-line more and more. I discovered more sites and more stories. I was writing more. I was also reporting to the VA hospital. I can't remember when I was actually feeling better about things. It was like getting old…just crept up on me until one day I thought I was doing OK. I ended up in a group. Used to be my worst nightmare. But this one was OK. It was a group of combat Vets like me. The group counselor was a Vietnam Vet who had lost his leg when he stepped on a land mine. The first few sessions of the group, I was really suspicious and angry. Didn't talk much and was really nasty. The bad-ass Vet with the tats. What took me by surprise is they didn't start bugging me right off, about how I was feeling and stuff. I think that was the only reason I went back the second and third times. No pressure. In fact, it was the group counselor that really got things going for me. He just told pieces and parts of his own story each time. And the others told pieces and parts of their stories. All I did was listen. About the fifth session in, I just came out with my story about seeing my first dead insurgent on the side street of a village we were patrolling. What shocked me afterwards was the fact that I said anything and that every eye was on me. I felt like they were inside my head and knew exactly what I was seeing and what I was feeling. For the first time in over a year, I felt the knot in my stomach start to unravel. Just a bit.

Jennifer kept urging me to go with her to church. I was never much for church since, well, Sunday school when I was a kid. I didn't go for a long time. Jen took the baby and went every Sunday. She said she started when I left for Iraq. She had friends, and they helped her cope. It took awhile, but it wasn't soon after the night I made such a fuss thinking a bomb had gone off in our bedroom that I went with her. The whole time my head was on the streets of the villages. To this day, I don't know why I didn't come unglued that day.

Later that same day we went over to her parents for a BBQ. Of all the memories that stick with me the most, it is smells. The smell of the cold well-used BBQ hit me hard. It smelled like death. And all I could see was the movie in my head. That time I did come unglued and had to go home early. Jen was angry, and I think her parents were upset. There were a lot of rough times like that before there were fewer.

JENNIFER

When I was a teenager, I liked watching war movies. I didn't enjoy the death scenes or the violence, but my tears ended when the movie ended. I stopped watching war movies or any military-related films once Luke deployed. I thought I'd be able to watch them again once he returned home safely. But, the deployment and the Iraq war changed me. My boycott of war movies extended to films and television shows with any form of violence.

182

Luke's appreciation for war movies increased after he returned from Iraq; I didn't want violent films in my home. I didn't want my innocent child to experience the cruel, evil side of the human species. I didn't want to experience it any more than I had to. How could people find violence entertaining? How could people watch Soldiers suffer and die while stuffing buttered-up popcorn down their throats? I could barely handle the sound of a war film playing in the opposite side of my house.

I had a lot of questions for God. I felt overwhelmed with the concept that humans could inflict so much violence and so much pain on one another. I felt like a child who was learning what it feels like to be a victim of a lie for the first time. I grew up believing in the compassion and goodness of human beings. I grew up believing in a loving Creator. How could I mesh a God of peace with the brutality of the human species? Not knowing who or what to turn to, I opened that old journal again...

> Find peace. Find solace. I cannot seem to find anything. I'm tired. I feel so crazy. How did I get here? Have I always been this insane? Confused? Whatever the hell I am. I'm not sure of anything, and nothing seems to bring solace. Anxiety disorder or something? Write, just keep writing. Something will come. Something always does.

> I find something here. Something comforting in scratching words on to dead trees. Something in writing. Something I find nowhere else. In nothing else. In no one. Pen to paper—what could it possibly be that brings me inevitably back to the written word— to books written and not yet written. To writing with no clue what I'm going to write, or what I'm writing, or if I'm even going to write about anything or why—

> Something draws me to the page—something— something indefinable. Something lost to words— something lost to expression. Something that just

IS. Something within me—something I cannot bring words or sense to. Something that is not articulated.

I'm going to write and keep writing. Keep going. Write Jen. It's just you. This is you if nothing else is or ever will be. Fill up the pages—overcome the pain that devours your spirit. Don't think. Just write. Enter the peace—the solace—the pen and the paper and nothing else. No one else. No stress. No deadlines. No rules. No inadequacies or strengths or faults or names or reasons...

I am going to keep writing. I don't have to— it's not a must—but my soul longs—something pulls my hand to the pen, the pen to the page again—to write about nothing and everything—to get to the point or to come to no point whatsoever. To contemplate or to just be. To do nothing. To find nothing and everything. To keep hoping and to give up entirely. To be me and to be someone else. To just exist. No guilt. No remorse. To be alive and dead altogether.

There must be more. I thirst. I thirst for what I do not know. I yearn to go out, but also to sit here and do nothing—to escape the world—to rejoin it—to do both and to do neither. This limbo I'm experiencing is better than real-life, but so much worse. Maybe this is real-life. And the other way of existing is a joke. This is raw. This is real. This is different. This is a breath of fresh air. This is not being able to breathe at all. This is not caring and caring too much. This is wanting to be understood, but really, really wanting to understand myself.

This is a rebellion and a submission. This is getting back to my core—if such even exists. It's learning to trust myself and simultaneously depending on the help of others. Pushed by a divine being? Part of a plan or simply life—unplanned? Controlled or predicted? And yet we always ask "Why?" We bang our head against the wall waiting for blood. We give in. We push back. We "let go." For what? To what?

We must torture ourselves with "Why?" We must lose ourselves in contemplation and theorizing and giving credit, drawing patterns and conclusions—searching and searching—programmed to search—programmed to find a certain something. But some of us are not satisfied. Some of us find no satisfaction, and in the lack of satisfaction, we devise theories and patterns of our own...

What would I have said months ago? Would my self of last year recognize this current self? Would I even know me? Do I even know me now? Do we ever truly know anything? How can anything be absolute? We have no control—such seems absolute, but yet, not always. "Something" calls me to keep going—to get through one more day, to live completely on hope.

§§§§

IN COMMUNITY -- LISTENING TO THE STORIES

"She searched the internet and found the most beautiful web site, the Virtual Wall, with a page in his memory and honor. I will never forget the day my sister Laurel, Kirsten's mother, began to forward e-mails from men who knew and loved David."[92]

Lee Alley

Old sayings remain in our oral traditions because they speak universal truths. The expression that a "picture is worth a thousand words" was recognized as a profound insight. Who knows how much people are really learning about themselves and how deeply they are impacted when they are watching a television show, attending a movie, listening to music, or interacting with a computer game, program, or simulation. Today's generation is a generation glued to image technology. That phenomenon is not likely to change in the foreseeable future. Today's rich technologies are an abundant resource to intentionally address the deepest of human pain and serve as a sophisticated means to assist Warfighters, Veterans, and family members in finding meaning, healing, and achieving purposeful living. "WVFMs" find healing in telling their stories. They find meaning and purposeful living in knowing that their stories are heard and believed. One of the greatest contributions of community is the capacity for the whole to listen to each and every story. Community becomes the healing haven for "WVFMs," a place where they tell their stories to a group that holds them sacred.

The virtual world displays images as well as sanctuary for listening to one's story. Just as the sights, sounds, and smells of combat wound the Soul, the sights and sounds of the virtual world can also lead the Warfighter and Veteran in a path of healing. The virtual world allows Warfighters, Veterans, and family members to tell their stories in images, sights, and sounds as well as words.

Imagery is an immensely powerful storytelling method. It is even more powerful to "see" the stories through images, sights, and sounds. That is an aspect of virtual community that is not shared well by the traditional community.

Visual storytelling in the virtual community stirs up within "WVFMs" a connection to the traumatic experiences in their lives, the wounds from combat, and the painful events for which they may still possess intense feelings and deep emotions.

It is easy to understand how quickly and consistently "WVFMs" can be brought to an emotional involvement in this type of setting when compared to sitting in a caregiver's office or participating in traditional community groups. The pictures, sounds, and the interaction they experience with the stories portrayed in the virtual community touch them in ways that simple exchanges of words cannot. The sights, sounds, and even smells touch the very Soul, and when that vulnerable window is open, Warfighters and Veterans are more open to healing, finding meaning, and returning to purposeful living.

Traditional community settings are different than the traditional counseling and care giving settings. Warfighters, Veterans, and family members find healing within community settings of fellow "WVFMs." The emphasis for healing is to discover acceptance within the community. Too often, the deep and painful needs of Warfighters and Veterans are very difficult to uncover and unravel in traditional care giving settings where conversation, or talk therapy, is the primary means of uncovering painfulness and deep hurt. Traditional care giving methods and institutional settings rely heavily upon talk therapies at the one to one or one to many (group) levels. It is a reason-based approach that does not give equal space to the other parts of the whole person that ultimately affect constructive behavior changes. It does not take into account the Soul itself, the very place where the deepest pain abides.

Warfighters, Veterans, and family members are complex and unique. They each receive and process information at different levels and experience different results. Traditional and virtual communities support this complexity and uniqueness. Professional caregivers are coming to understand that using community, both traditional and virtual, to supplement and extend their methods for reaching Warfighters and Veterans has vast potential.

Today the virtual community is becoming the single most effective use of technology for Warfighters, Veterans, and family members to find connection and healing. The desired outcome of the virtual community is to set the conditions of openness, willingness, self-initiation, and vulnerability sufficient to allow "WVFMs" to affect a greater and perhaps more rapid level of personal healing. They can safely tell their stories and know that they are being heard, understood, and believed. Participation in the virtual community serves as a stand-alone means to allow Warfighters and Veterans to conduct some level of self-examination of the conditions and possible insights that allow them to move forward in their personal healing.

The virtual community is flexible enough to address many issues of grief and loss and assist Warfighters and Veterans in addressing specific concerns with specific skills.

The virtual world presents a new way of relating to people. It becomes a counseling model, a mentoring model, and a learning model to support a larger group of Warfighters and Veterans that currently seek assistance only through traditional and institutional settings. The application of the virtual community to healing and helping Warfighters and Veterans is about being able to leverage the stories provided by each individual in assisting everyone in the healing process. Warfighters, Veterans, and family members have the opportunity to determine if and how the stories in the virtual community relate to their own personal experiences. It is a mechanism of self-examination that uses the community to initiate the healing process.

Warfighters and Veterans live in a culture that utilizes the virtual world to gather information, manage knowledge, and solve problems. Warfighters, Veterans, and their families communicate within the virtual community. Warfighters and their families suffer physical, psychological, and spiritual trauma as the result of the acts of war. Addressing the spiritual and emotional trauma is as critical to healing the whole person as addressing physical and psychological trauma. Veterans today have discovered that they can connect through both traditional communities and the virtual community.

Warfighters can connect instantly from the war zone with their families back home through the Internet. Warfighters, Veterans and family members build their own virtual family connections in the midst of combat. In a sense, the virtual world creates a source of combat trauma for everyone that is connected together. So not only is the virtual world a source of healing, it is also a source of wounding. The unique aspect of the current Global War on Terrorism is that the family, local community, and the Nation as a whole is wounded through mutual exposure to combat trauma in the virtual world.

Today the number of Warfighters, Veterans and family members finding healing and support within community is increasing exponentially. This marked increase in membership in communities of all sorts reaches literally every facet of life. It not only continues to flourish in global exposure but also more importantly, it is becoming a part of mainstream culture. "WVFMs" alike are witnessing the evolution of traditional and virtual communities, places where they find connection and support in their profound sense of grief.

Support and healing with community allows self-examination of those personal qualities and beliefs needed to sustain Warfighters and Veterans in times of stress, hardship, and tragedy. These qualities come from religious, philosophical, or human values, and form the basis for character, disposition, decision-making, and integrity. Beliefs are convictions held as true; they are based on one's upbringing, culture, heritage, families, and diverse religious traditions. Warfighters and Veterans are free to choose their own beliefs and the basis for those beliefs. America's strength comes from that diversity. Self-examination plays a role in preparing Warfighters for battle and healing Veterans upon their return. When both traditional and virtual communities reflect their stories, Warfighters and Veterans find support for their self-examination disciplines.

Within the foundation of self-examination, there is the proposition that one cannot heal what they do not understand. Moreover, one cannot understand until they are aware. An important part of healing involves self-examination and self-awareness. Self-awareness is acknowledging that one is in pain, suffering profound grief and loss. How Warfighters and Veterans see their wounds and their Souls is vital. Accurate self-examination begins with the acknowledgement and awareness that Warfighters' and Veterans' needs are real and have an impact upon their subsequent healing. Self-examination helps direct Veterans toward healing their Souls. Healing the Soul involves leveraging or even challenging current behaviors, understandings of Self, and cultural habits and belief systems that contribute to either the healing or wounding of the Soul.

Margaret Kornfeld, in her work, "Cultivating Wholeness,"[93] points out that the medieval mystic Julian of Norwich uses the metaphor of "gardening" as an expression of [caring for the Soul]. A gardener, like any caregiver, has a twofold task. A gardener tends to the ground and cultivates the plants growing in the ground. The gardener does not make the plants grow; nature does. The gardener attends to their growth, as the plants become what they are meant to be. The care and counseling of Warfighters, Veterans and family members grow out of their participation with others in the natural events of life: marriage, birth, coming of age, death, illness, and all the normal life crises. This occurs within community.

Involvement in community allows Warfighters, Veterans and family members to do storytelling. The community's part is "story listening." Story listening is the activity of merging individual stories into the story of the community. Within community, the essence of the individual's story can often be presented in ways that do not tell the level of the pain or wounding in an immediately straightforward way. Veterans, Warfighters, and family members often use images and metaphors to describe their own pain and respond to the metaphors of the stories within the community. Story listening is the means by which the individual's pain, grief, loss, and desperation are explored, and the story is unveiled to discover the issues of deepest concerns. The problem the individual initially presents is most often in the form of a metaphor, symbolizing the deep pain within the Soul. The story of the silently wounded Soul can be discovered within the stories of the group. It is critical to understand that the issue of trust is a critical concern for the storyteller. The lower the trust level, the more abstract the story. In these incidences, the community becomes a trusted group. If the community is not trusted, Warfighters, Veterans and family members must seek out another community where they sense trust and support.

The community, as story listener, should be aware of the common story that connects them all together. The group hears the same themes of grief, pain, and loss in each individual's story. The community, as story listener, can only listen and reflect on member's stories as deeply as they are able to enter their own pain.

Community, traditional or virtual, allows individuals to express their story and become a part of it through an interactive response. The virtual community story listener provides a means of non-judgmental, consistent, unbiased reactions to the individual stories. This is the strength of community to help Warfighters, Veterans and family members heal and recover.

The community as story listener is always aware that Warfighters, Veterans, and family members' pain is not the group's pain. Individual pain can trigger a response from the community in the form of supportive empathy. The community must then avoid shutting down an individual's story and engage the most critical skill of all the members: listen, listen, and listen. A story is the vehicle that carries deep truth about an individual or community. Story listening is hearing what lies deep within the lives of people and their Souls.

IN COMMUNITY -- FINDING THE SELF

"There are some men whom a staggering emotional shock, so far from making them mental invalids for life, seems, on the other hand, to awaken, to galvanize, to arouse into an almost incredible activity of soul."[94]

William McFee

The virtual community is rapidly being applied to the capacity to develop, self-assess, and learn life skills for effective and consistent behavior change. The virtual world now has a central and practical use in every home, and military families rely upon it for many facets of their lives. Traditional approaches to address these problems have, up until this point, relied upon traditional methods and institutional models to educate and provide venues of therapy and assistance. The reality of today's Warfighters and Veterans is that such a limited scope of options is no longer fully or consistently meeting their ever-increasing demand for healing. Too often institutions and traditional helping resources are overrun, unresourced, and unable to fully assist the Warfighter, Veteran, or family member. Today's virtual world extends the possibilities for reaching Veterans. Warfighters and family members find help in the virtual community that they trust and willingly open themselves to.

"PTSoulD" causes Warfighters and Veterans to disregard what is going on around them and encourages them to use an excessive amount of manipulation, plotting, and maneuvering to get away from their problems. Warfighters' and Veterans' healing is deeply impaired when they are not clearly aware of the complex and conflicting feelings they hold. A critical step toward Warfighters', Veterans', and family members' healing is regaining an awareness of their Self, their behaviors, and their environment. Awareness is not easy to gain, however.

The virtual communities are a superb source for trusted groups. The formal trusted group is a powerful vehicle of expression to help with maturing and growing a healthy Soul. Warfighters and Veterans find healing within groups of other Warfighters and Veterans. Family members find support and healing from family support groups, groups of other family members, teen groups, and even groups set up for children of Warfighters and Veterans (under parental supervision). More and more this is occurring in the virtual community. Whatever benefit Warfighters, Veterans, and family members gain from their one-on-one encounters is multiplied several times over in a group setting. This is a result of not only the direct feedback to the Warfighters and Veterans, but also the interaction that occurs between other members that adds layers of richness to what they learn and experience. Trusted groups are larger settings that extend the capacity for "WVFMs" to express themselves.

In a traditional group setting Warfighters, Veterans, and family members need to know what each person contributes to the members of the group. They need to know what progress will look like and how they will measure and account for their personal progress and the progress of other group members. They need to know if there are any limits about discussion topics. They also need to understand group dynamics.

The ritual of accountability in a trusted group builds community. Community interaction is a symbol of the healthy state of the Soul. When the five personal characteristics are out of balance and the silent wounding that caused that imbalance is energized with pain, community suffers. The trusted group setting is in place to nurture, mature, grow and heal. Trusted groups need to be aware of the danger in focusing primarily on the common wounding of members; trusted groups can deteriorate into support groups that focus on wounds. When the focus is on wounding and not healing, it causes people to dwell on their pain. When Warfighters, Veterans, and family members choose their trust group, they should be careful to select a group that focuses on healing.

Souls must consider whether or not they are more energized after participating in a formal trusted group setting. There will, hopefully, be times they come away exhausted because they have done intense work and experienced personal growth. If, however, they come away feeling drained or empty, Warfighters, Veterans, and family members need to raise their concern. They have probably moved more into an emphasis upon wounding rather than sustained healing. The Soul can sense this.

Trusted groups are good in helping heal the silently wounded Soul. Participants' individual stories collectively form a new story, and everyone is a part of it. Regular contact with people, exchanges of insights and ideas, and regular accountability in a wider setting are all benefits of this experience. In trusted groups, what Warfighters, Veterans, and family members learn about others is really what they are learning about themselves. What they gain from the collective whole is as important as what they gather from each individual. Both the individual stories and the emerging collective story enrich them, and in so doing, bring the community to life.

IN COMMUNITY -- FINDING MEANING

"Man need only divert his attention from searching for the solution to external questions and pose the one, true inner question of how he should lead his life, and all the external questions will be resolved in the best possible way."[95]

Leo Tolstoy

Finding meaning in suffering is not a new concept but it is a concept that we struggle over with each new encounter. We know of American Prisoners of War (POW) from WWII, Korea, and Vietnam who told their stories of survival in the face of extreme suffering. Viktor Frankl provides his story of survival from the Nazi death camps where he suggests in his book, "<u>Man's Search for Meaning</u>," that it is possible to find in our suffering the possibility to change who we are. We grow and learn from the experience. He suggests that we have the opportunity to choose our path to grow, learn, and change or to lose the opportunity to move forward. We have the opportunity to decide for ourselves if our suffering has moral value for us or if we are indeed of worthy character to survive the trauma.[96] Frankl tells us that when we find ourselves in an experience that causes us great trauma that is our task in our lives. The traumatic event is ours to experience. We cannot escape that. We have to walk our path and travel our valley of death alone and no one can take that walk for us. The opportunity lies in how we accept and accomplish that walk. We can walk in dignity and triumph or we can stumble, fall, and lose the opportunity to prevail to a deeper meaning and a greater good.[97]

How do Warfighters, Veterans, and family members discover meaningful purposes for their lives, and once discovered, how do they live purposefully so they can accomplish their goals? Many traditional care giving methods for "WVFMs" focus primarily on symptom reduction - how can they help the person to feel better? But preoccupation with feeling better often distracts them from accomplishing the important purposes of their lives. Finding meaning within pain, grief, loss, and desperation and the trauma of combat helps "WVFMs" move forward and take action, even in the face of fear or uncertainty.

Finding meaning is a process that helps Warfighters, Veterans, and family members discover purpose, particularly during the healing times of their lives. Living purposefully means staying focused on what's important and not being distracted by silently wounded Souls. This is more and more difficult when combat trauma diverts the "WVFMs'" attention from healing to their pain, grief, loss, and desperation. Combat trauma is one obstacle to a purposeful life. Another obstacle can be the desire for life to be the way it was before the combat experience. Both stumbling blocks lead "WVFMs" away from a life which offers fulfillment and meaning - a life they can look back on without regrets.

Warfighters, Veterans, and family members should ask themselves each day if they are willing to take on the responsibilities of the transformation and healing of the Soul. Are they willing to be that which they have never been before? Did they seek to find meaning in their grief, pain, and loss today? Did it hurt? Will they push against the old destructive behaviors again today? Do they commit to doing so tomorrow?

When they find meaning Warfighters', Veterans', and family members' most important questions -- Is there more to life? What is my purpose? Why am I here? -- can be addressed and answered.

Finding meaning is an effective tool for peeling away the pain, grief, loss, and desperation to heal the Soul. When Veterans take personal responsibility for their actions they are learning to examine their thoughts, words, and behaviors objectively and seeing them for what they really are: reflections of their silently wounded Souls. This provides Warfighters, Veterans, and family members with opportunities to make conscious choices to change or eliminate those thoughts, words, and behaviors that continue to wound the Soul.

Warfighters, Veterans, and family members find meaning in their work and what they accomplish in their lives. When consumed by the grief and loss from combat trauma, they need to turn to meaningful deeds and find that something to accomplish that gives satisfaction in their Souls and confirms meaning in their lives.

Warfighters, Veterans, and family members find meaning in the experiences and encounters they have with others. Whether those encounters are with loved ones or with friends or occasional strangers, they seek and find meaning from others. Love expressed and acted upon at many levels involves meaning. Love in marriage, family, and friendship provides the silently wounded Soul with meaning.

When Warfighters, Veterans, and family members are changed in their lives, Self, and Souls due to the trauma of combat, they can become so wounded that all they see in themselves is the pain, grief, loss, and desperation. This embitters their attitudes and causes dysfunctional behavior. To find new meaning in their lives, "WVFMs" should seek to change their attitudes and climb out of the deep black hole of pain, grief, loss, and desperation. Changing their attitudes changes their behaviors and how they feel. Feeling positive, happy, satisfied, and alive about themselves and their lives is a source of meaning and healing.

Warfighters, Veterans, and family members have different windows into their Souls. For some, it is spoken words. For others the most effective in-road to the Soul may be visual. For a growing number, interaction is critical to learn, grow, and heal. Such interactions can prove helpful finding meaning in their pain.

The visual images found in the virtual world are powerful vehicles to communicate, interpret, and represent both painful wounding and the healing that occur in Warfighters', Veterans', and family members' Souls. Virtual communities have a profound influence on today's generation. Today's new Warfighters and Veterans identify with characters, themes, and ideologies in the virtual world. This vehicle can open them to explore, discuss, journal, and reflect upon their lives through such themes found in the virtual community. This gives them another tool of expression free of the difficulty of expressing experiences in words alone. In this way, the virtual community helps "WVFMs" find meaning in their pain.

Warfighters' and Veterans' stories help them find meaning and allow them to interact with the virtual community to add meaningful insights that contribute to their growth and healing. Warfighters, Veterans, and family members find meaning in what they watch, especially if they are watching the most interesting character of all -- themselves! The use of the virtual community to find meaning is a method to help "WVFMs" in an environment that is both familiar and safe to them. The visual images found in the virtual world can do two things. First, they can give "WVFMs" interacting with the virtual community an opportunity to tell their story representing their wounding. Secondly, the virtual community can add meaning to the stories through insights that allow the Warfighter, Veteran, and family member to discover healing.

IN COMMUNITY -- FINDING HEALING

"Enter by the narrow gate; for the gate is wide and the way is easy, that leads to destruction, and those who enter by it are many. For the gate is narrow and the way is hard, that leads to life, and those who find it are few." [98]

Jesus Christ

Warfighters, Veterans, and family members seek connection in their grief, pain, and loss. The traditional and virtual communities help them connect with others who share the same pain and trauma from their combat experiences. The consideration of connection is appearing as a rising mitigating factor for Warfighters and Veterans seeking to find healing from the wounds of combat trauma. For many "WVFMs," finding trusted connections equates to finding healing. The lack of connection from many traditional care-giving sources inhibits many "WVFMs" from seeking traditional and institutional assistance. Connection equates to trust, and the lack of trust in traditional care giving sources is a major barrier for Warfighters, Veterans, and family members seeking healing. In a study published in the New England Journal of Medicine, Volume 351: July 1, 2004, "Combat Duty in Iraq and Afghanistan, Mental Health Problems, and Barriers to Care" the following is observed:

"This finding has immediate public health implications. Efforts to address the problem of stigma and other barriers to seeking mental health care in the military should take into consideration outreach, education, and changes in the models of health care delivery, such as increases in the allocation of mental health services in primary care clinics and in the provision of confidential counseling by means of employee-assistance programs. Screening for major depression is becoming routine in military primary care settings, but our study suggests that it should be expanded to include screening for PTSD. Many of these considerations are being addressed in new military programs. Reducing the perception of stigma and the barriers to care among military personnel is a priority for research and a priority for the policymakers, clinicians, and leaders who are involved in providing care to those who have served in the armed forces."[99]

Warfighters, Veterans, and family members interact with and utilize the virtual world in their daily lives and decision-making. This includes the use of virtual knowledge to gather information and to make decisions. Warfighters and Veterans use and interact with the virtual world on a consistent basis as a part of how they conduct their lives, find meaning in their suffering, and find the courage to move to purposeful living.

Warfighters, Veterans, and family members see gathering information from the virtual world as relevant and consistent to their healing process. Warfighters and Veterans tend to trust in the information they receive. The capability to gather information in a sense of privacy without being pressured and pursued is a critical factor in the use of the virtual community.

Similar trust is sometimes found in traditional communities that are trusted groups where the group members share the same stories of grief, pain, and loss. But the openness and trust is slow to build and embarrassing ideas, thoughts, and questions often are not asked or explored. Warfighters, Veterans, and family members quickly learn from virtual community interaction and support to address, interact, and problem solve increasingly complex personal issues.

"WVFMs" increasingly turn to the Internet to find support and sustain healing. They do not see any significant difference between information gathered online and information gathered in person or through traditional communities. Individual contact or in-person interaction is not a primary concern for gathering sufficient and accurate information.

Many Warfighters, Veterans, and family members find a higher degree of credibility in on-line information being more current and up to date than the information they were able to gather through traditional caregiving and institutional means. The capability to more instantly seek out, gather, and amass information from the virtual world is a critical issue for the current generation of "WVFMs." Both Warfighters and family members use the Internet and the virtual community to complete the same tasks as they previously sought assistance for in the traditional care giving sources. The virtual community is perceived as non-judgmental, non-invasive, and does not pressure individuals seeking help and support. The capability to remain anonymous in the virtual community precludes the issues of personality and social stigma.

Warfighters, Veterans, and family members have a positive level of commitment to and belief in using the virtual community to examine themselves. There is a general awareness among "WVFMs" that in today's culture many personal and professional transactions requiring the posting of personal and sensitive information on web-based sites is a normal part of daily living. They find the posting of very sensitive personal information in the virtual community less of an issue of concern than finding support and understanding.

Warfighters, Veterans, and family members participate heavily in the area of the virtual community that includes blogging, instant messaging, and chat rooms to conduct inquiries and to discover relevant information and insights into their issues and problems. Most "WVFMs" today have exposure and experience in one or more of these interactive areas of the virtual community. "WVFMs" benefit and find healing in the virtual community. They derive a sense of connection while retaining safety and anonymity, and they have a global resource for information exchange and insight gathering unlike traditional care giving and limited one to one contacts.

The unique sense of community derived in the chat room environment has a very relevant place for the stories of Warfighters, Veterans, and family members. While "WVFMs" generally agree that the people with whom they discussed their lives online were essentially strangers, there were unique bonds of community established and personal trust even greater than what they had experienced with in person, face-to-face, communities. This unique dynamic appears to give more permission to "WVFMs" to disclose their inner wounding than in person-to-person counseling.

Within the virtual community environment, Warfighters, Veterans, and family members can in fact assign any personality that they envision to the co-users. This unique feature allows them to project their pain, grief, loss, and desperation without being inhibited by personality, time, or being self-conscious of their physical presence. In other words, in a virtual community the issues presented are the only concern. There is no consideration of environment, physical capabilities or limitations, rank, or unit of assignment, etc. "WVFMs" find a never before attained level of support and healing in the communities they establish in the virtual world. They find that their approaches to problem solving, the expanse of relevant information they gathered to address their healing, and the factors involved in their decision making processes results from the input of individuals from vastly different cultures, religions, economic and social backgrounds. This unique input allowed them to think at levels they would not attain in traditional and localized environments. In summary, good health, higher productivity, improved quality of life, and a higher level of wellness may be achieved by participating in the virtual community.

CONCLUSION

"The happiness which brings enduring worth to life is not the superficial happiness that is dependent upon circumstances. It is the happiness and contentment that fills the soul even in the midst of the most distressing of circumstances, and most bitter environment. It is the kind of happiness that grins when things go wrong and smiles through tears. The happiness for which our souls ache is one undisturbed by success or failure, one which will root deeply inside us and gain inward relaxation, peace, and contentment no matter what the surface problems may be. That kind of happiness stands in need of no outward stimulus."[100]

Billy Graham

Healing "PTSoulD" occurs when Warfighters, Veterans, and family members form intentions, develop strategies, and reinforce what they have learned. Reflection and self-awareness helps "WVFMs" examine belief systems and values, deal with strong feelings, make difficult decisions, and resolve interpersonal conflict. Active participation in the virtual community fosters self-awareness and is perceived as generally credible, transferable, dependable, confirmable, and essentially private. "WVFMs" find that virtual communities appear to have a capacity for critical self-reflection that pervades all aspects of traditional care giving, including being present with a caregiver, solving problems, eliciting and transmitting information, making evidence-based decisions, performing technical skills, and defining their own values. This process of critical self-reflection leading to accurate self-examination depends on the belief in the ability of the virtual community to effect accurate information and relevant assistance.

Silently wounded Warfighters, Veterans, and family members should begin right now to inventory their lives. They should consider their behaviors and attitudes. They will find that their behaviors and attitudes reflect the health or wounding of their Souls. They then should consider the activities that will sustain the healing of their Souls and move them toward finding meaning and renewed and purposeful living. Their Souls are anxious to explore and discover these things.

Warfighters, Veterans, and family members should invite themselves to begin collecting the stories of their Souls. Telling their story and listening to the stories of others is a powerful healing agent. Stories are the transparent pathway to their inner lives and to the life of the Soul. Continue in the maturing and growth of the health of the Soul by innovative and consistent activities of self-awareness. The exercise of our special activities confirms the consistency of the healing that is going on in their Souls. Finally, "WVFMs" should engage in community.

Part Five.
Purposeful Living –
Healing the Silent Wounds

"What was really needed was a fundamental change in our attitude toward life. We had to learn ourselves and, furthermore, we had to teach the despairing men, that it did not really matter what we expected from life, but rather what life expected from us. We needed to stop asking about the meaning of life, and instead to think of ourselves as those who were being questioned by life - daily and hourly. Our answer must consist, not in talk and meditation, but in right action and in right conduct. Life ultimately means taking the responsibility to find the right answer to its problems and to fulfill the tasks which it constantly sets for each individual."[101]

Viktor Frankl

LUKE

The pastor of the church was a retired Army chaplain. I didn't know that for a long time. It kind of slipped out one day when he asked me how I was doing. I was in one of my zones…cold sweats and a panic attack coming on. The breathing lessons I learned back in the Ward helped. At the time, I thought they were a joke. Bunch of namby-pamby crap. I was sucking air and trying to calm down, when the pastor came up and asked if I was all right. I just blurted out that I was remembering some stuff from combat and that I would be OK soon. He told me he was an Army chaplain and was in 'Nam with the First Cav. It was like his eyes saw right into my brain and was watching the movie that was scrolling along about that day on the road and the IED going off. I saw pain in his eyes, and I am sure he saw it in mine.

He asked me if I was willing to help him with a project, he was working on. I didn't have a quick enough excuse to say no so I sort of said OK. He wanted help working with some homeless guys. At first, I thought they were do-nothing bums. Why didn't they just go get jobs? The chaplain, he was chaplain now and not a pastor, just started quietly telling me about who they were. I found out many of them were Vets. They were living with their demons. Their demons got the best of them and they could no longer survive the day. So here I was, the bad-ass Vet with the tats helping these guys who were at the end of their luck. I sure didn't feel very bad-ass anymore. What scared me most was they could easily be me. There were times back in the Ward and soon after getting home when I couldn't think my way past my own misery. I sat around and did nothing. It wouldn't have taken too much of a shove to end up here, no home, no family, drunk, and at the end of the rope.

Anyway, I started helping the chaplain several times a month. We also started talking. Not about much at first. But after awhile we were talking about our experiences in combat. He started telling me about his trips out to the firebases and the nightmares he had of seeing Soldiers shot up. One story he told me was the day they hit the Vietcong over in Cambodia. He jumped the sixth skid to take off with a bunch of the grunts. He never really said much after that. Just

211

sort of stared off into space. Another time he told me about coming under sniper fire while working with some of the troops in his unit out at another firebase. It took them by surprise. The sniper got one of the guys and he had crawled out to try to drag him back. The sniper started shooting at him and all he could do was lie on top of the troop he was trying to help while the rest of the squad worked to take out the sniper. It took twenty minutes to do it. All he said was that he was never so scared in his life as bullets kept spitting around him every few minutes. The guys finally got the sniper and brought the rifle he was using to him. He said he kept it and brought it home. It is in his closet at home as a reminder of how close things got. I remember his story to this day like it was this morning. And I remember listening without saying a word. And I remember when we first met all I knew was that he was the pastor of this small town church. And of all the people in the world, this guy would never in this lifetime understand what I had gone through in combat. And he was surviving his own memories, his own movie playing out in his head. Maybe I could too.

JENNIFER

At some point, we find stillness in the lack of answers to life's greatest mysteries. We find a place of awe— and we are humbled by the fragile, yet resilient nature of life itself. Before deployment, I thought little of missing the opportunity to have dinner with Luke or taking our time for granted. It never quite occurred to me that our time together was always temporary and never guaranteed.

Deployment was devastating and maybe, in some way, it was also a gift. Civilians told me countless times that they couldn't imagine a weekend without their spouses, much less a year. But how meaningful is the time you spend with someone when you consistently take that person and that time for granted? I was changed in ways I could hardly articulate in spoken or written words. I found peace, and I lost it. But, slowly, my spirit headed for its center— to the only thing that has ever truly mattered— my love for Luke and my family.

I am almost done with this journal. It may be the first journal that I fill down to the very last page. It's a strange feeling—to have written all that is going to be written in this book.

Today I looked through an old journal from my senior year in high school. My life changes so rapidly, and it seems that I change rapidly too. It's crazy that I can look back on my own words and have a difficult time recognizing myself. It can be confusing or enlightening. It adds even more mystery to life. How much life changes—when I don't expect it—how things change and mold—gradually and yet startlingly fast at times. It shows me how much life is going to continue to change and amaze me in ways I never considered…

I wonder what I will be writing about this time next year, or in the next few months. I rest my efforts— Life does its own thing it seems. And things have a way of… of? Well, of continuing, growing, changing, evolving. A search for security in rules and absolutes seems pointless now. Almost nothing is clear-cut and dry—not anything, I can identify in life.

I don't know what I will have tomorrow or next year. I don't know what life or even my own health will be. I only know what I have right now, for this moment, for this day, and I think that is what I must learn to find peace in—the right now—the place I am in, the emotions I feel, the dogs that I love, my family, and the people that are a part of my life. Life isn't black and white. It can change in any moment in any way, without prediction. You can lose all you have and gain so much more. What you thought was real can appear false and deceiving. Any one you love can be lost—it can even be your own spirit that takes a turn for the worst or for the best.

So do we plant roots? And build life on what? Hold those we love close, in every moment possible—

believe in ourselves—maybe waste less time and concern ourselves more with what our hearts desire. We only have right now.

My life feels more right than it has in quite some time. I have come to a quiet place. I am finally experiencing a time of rest. I have finally found peace within myself. I fear life less. And in knowing less about what I want, I actually know more. I think I have learned how to enjoy life at the present, accepting its changes and accepting myself.

Something is coming; I just don't know what that something is yet…

§§§§

INTRODUCTION

"The only ones. . .who will be really happy are those who have sought and found how to serve."[102]

Albert Schweitzer

Purposeful living in the face of trauma often seems like an impossible goal. When Warfighters, Veterans, and family members are in the midst of their pain, grief, loss, and desperation no other option in life seems available. When in the middle of a horrific experience, one cannot imagine life beyond the trauma. The stories of prisoners of war for example, are stories of amazing personal horror, loss of Self, grief, and anger. When a person is tortured and held captive for what seems an endless number of lifetimes, it is hard to imagine survival and recovery. And yet these same stories are amazing stories of hope, perseverance, and recovery. Victor Frankl's example of survival from the trauma of the death camps is an example for everyone. What makes the difference between survival and recovery and despair and death lie within the person themselves.

Frankl suggested that the difference between survival and death was a sense of purpose and meaning. He said that we find meaning in something or someone we value. We survive through a sustaining love, or faith, or connection to family and friends that we deeply value. Through this connection to something or someone outside of ourselves, we develop meaning, and healing, for ourselves. This has implications about our spirituality. Faith is something we can deeply value.[103]

Frankl suggests finding meaning through doing something that creates value.[104] We find meaning by doing something for the greater good. If we are in a position where we cannot do something immediately, the desire to seek the greater good later in life remains a key to survival. Seeking the greater good is enhanced by a healthy spiritual life.

We also find meaning through the value created in our attitude or life behaviors. If we feel and think positive thoughts we often live with a positive demeanor and survive our trauma. If we descend into despair, anger, and hate, we often do not survive a traumatic event that fills us with even more anger and despair. What we think about ourselves has a powerful consequence for our lives, either good or bad. It is often said we can "think" ourselves sick. We can imagine ourselves to failure. We can feel our way into despair. What we think, feel, and imagine can become self-fulfilling. The opposite is also true. We can think, feel, and imagine our way into healing, meaning, and purpose.

We all have those unique aspects of our personal characteristics that become our gifts, our dreams, and our capabilities. Finding meaning and purposeful living unlocks our highest potential for living and serving with meaning and purpose. Healing is an aspiration to expand our capacity to serve a greater good and to uncover meaning and purpose in our lives. We find purpose and meaning within our connections with community. The process of healing Post Traumatic Soul Disorder (PTSoulD) means changing our perspective and our behaviors from being victims to taking responsibility for our lives. Through their commitment, selfless sacrifice to the greater good, and dedication to purposeful living, Warfighters, Veterans, and family members are transforming their lives.

It's time to answer the call from our Souls. We have a knowing inner voice that is gently calling to us. Within each Warfighter, Veteran, and family member is the ability to connect not only to their own personal guidance system, but also to the greater community. Through awareness, and self-examination, we allow the wisdom of our body, our thoughts, our emotions, our relationships with others, and our spirits to guide our personal journey of healing.

Warfighters, Veterans, and family members have sacrificed their lives, their spirits, and their Souls to serve their families, friends, communities, and their Nation in war. It is now their time to excel and love the life they have chosen to live. They deserve to experience joy, peace, and authentic love. Our personal inner voices of healing will help us move through our pain, grief, loss, and desperation to a life grounded in meaning and purpose; a life we all want to live. Warfighters, Veterans, and family members have painful stories to tell of their journey of pain, grief, loss, and desperation from combat trauma. Their healing journeys are courageous. Theirs is a journey of spirituality.

HEALING THE SOUL - SPIRITUALITY

"It is better to allow our lives to speak for us than our words. God did not bear the cross only two thousand years ago. He bears it today, and he dies and is resurrected from day to day. It would be a poor comfort to the world if it had to depend on a historical God who died two thousand years ago. Do not, then, preach the God of history, but show him as he lives today through you."[105]

Mahatma Gandhi

Spirituality is that which gives us hope, faith, and love in something other then ourselves. It is what ultimately connects us to others, to community, to God or something greater, something bigger, something more then us. It is all about what is good, what is beautiful, what is meaningful, and what is true. We are Self and Soul, and if either part goes wrong, the other part is affected. We find spirituality in our connections with others. Many Veterans today make those connections in the virtual community. The virtual world is as alive and real as any traditional community can be. Many Warfighters, Veterans, and family members can connect quicker in the virtual world than they can in traditional settings. The virtual world allows them initial anonymity. Many times, it is in the dark of a sleepless night when connections are made. Many "WVFMs" can describe finding their Souls online in the dark hours of the night when they can't sleep because of their dreams.

Spirituality refers to the vitality and power within our lives. To speak of spirituality is to speak of our Soul and the power of life that is within us. Spirituality is a recipe for healing the feelings of hopelessness, helplessness, and worthlessness— the utter despair from combat trauma. Spirituality is found in the stories we share— the stories of fear, despair, and horror. Sharing our stories and hearing the stories of others heals our Souls and helps us find our spirituality. We post our stories online for others to read and find healing. The virtual community is a powerful healing force in our lives.

Spirituality is not a belief system, not based on morals and values, but more on the understanding and consciousness of our existence. Spirituality is a way of living. Being spiritual is basically living for the greater good, which heals our Soul. We can belong to any religion, or no religion, while still being spiritual. Spirituality is the next step up for the healing of the Soul, which puts Warfighters, Veterans, and family members on their path of meaning and purposeful living. Being associated with other silently wounded Souls on our spiritual path means that we find spiritual strength in our connection to go forward in our own personal healing. We walk our spiritual paths together in both the traditional community and the virtual community.

Spirituality offers healing in times of suffering and provides a message of hope to a silently wounded Soul. We describe the trauma of combat as an unbearable guilt and feelings of hopelessness, helplessness, and worthlessness. Spirituality provides faith, hope, and love. Spirituality helps those with "PTSoulD" find meaning in the pain, grief, loss, and desperation.

Spirituality helps Warfighters, Veterans, and family members overcome their emotional suffering. Spirituality is in itself meaning. Even in despair, spirituality helps "WVFMs" live for a greater good and find purposeful living.

Spirituality involves taking part in life. Spirituality guides us to reach out to that which is greater than our Selves, reach out to others, or reach to serve a greater good as reflections of healing the silently wounded Soul. Healing the silently wounded Soul means actively participating within community and becoming involved in life activities.

Warfighters, Veterans, and family members find meaning, personal growth, mental well-being, positive relationships, and purpose in their spirituality. Healing the Soul is spiritual healing. Healing is taking responsibility for our own lives. Spiritual healing is finding happiness, satisfaction, and meaning in our lives.

Fear is a signature of combat trauma. Spirituality can help Warfighters, Veterans, and family members overcome fear. We can't expect to be protected from every evil of the world during this life. But we can have confidence that in our spirituality we will find faith, hope, and love. That knowledge should provide us with reassurance and healing.

Warfighters, Veterans, and family members find healing by staying grounded in their spirituality, where they find direction for their lives. "WVFMs" should nurture their spiritual life. It will help them through the difficult moments in their lives when the memories of combat return to haunt them. They need to nurture their spirituality through acts that include service to the greater good. Being strong spiritually means that we have meaning and purpose in our lives.

Spirituality takes place within community. Warfighters, Veterans, and family members with silently wounded Souls are called to participate in community. Communities can provide "WVFMs" opportunities for mutual cooperation, support, and healing. Community is an important element of our spiritual lives. We can do much to allay our fears and discover healing when we connect with other silently wounded Souls and share our stories of pain, grief, loss, and desperation. We then live for the greater good and find purposeful living within our communities.

A spiritual community, both traditional and virtual, can provide more than support when we are in need of help. The members of a spiritual community, especially in the virtual world, can strengthen our resolve to heal, can link their stories to ours, and can restore us to health. Telling our stories with a community alters us. Often when life hurts, we linger by ourselves and assume that we are alone in our pain. When we enter a community to share our stories we understand and find connection. Warfighters, Veterans, and family members find real connection in the virtual world today. They connect and find they are not alone in their pain—there are others who suffer too. Through the virtual world, we all realize that we are not alone in the world; we connect to others and their stories, extending our spiritual strength to help. Suddenly the nature of our silently wounded Souls begins to change. We stop drowning in self-pity. We stop thinking about ourselves alone. Before long, we become aware of others. We become aware of our world. We begin to see our own pain, grief, loss, and desperation in a new light. We find healing in connection. Sometimes, connection to a spiritual community, even a virtual spiritual community, can literally save a life.

Spirituality is a powerful force when Warfighters, Veterans, and family members embrace it. It shows the way to healing when it seems there is no way. Spirituality heals our inner silently wounded Souls. With spirituality, we know that we can live with the trauma of combat and the changed persons we have become. We can overcome the pain, grief, loss, and desperation that mark a silently wounded Soul. Spirituality enables us to find happiness. Simply put, an active spirituality brings us joy.

Spirituality is shown to have a profound effect on our silently wounded Souls. Research has shown that spirituality can provide healing from the trauma of combat. It can reconnect us to our Self and the healing of our Souls. Spirituality can effect enduring physical, emotional, mental, social, and spiritual healing.

We are often asked how spirituality is related to combat. It is not such a strange question to ask. When we examine the history of war, we find that nearly every war that has ever been fought has had a spiritual implication in the causes and has been supported by at least one spiritual expression. The Global War on Terrorism is no different. The spiritual implications may be radical or a shadow of mainline beliefs, but there is spiritual fervor regardless. Warfighters of both sides of a war go into combat confident that their spirituality is on their side and theirs is the righteous cause. Their spirituality strengthens their courage and convictions. Spiritual influences have also created moral confusion, political conflicts, atrocities, and extreme acts of violence. One side might consider the same act of violence a sacred duty while the other side sees it as a violation of spiritual teachings. The side that is victorious believes that their spirituality was with them and their faith carried the day, while defeat might be interpreted as divine punishment for their failures.

Warfighters are violently wrenched away from their sense of spirituality by the trauma of combat. Their beliefs, traditions, and experiences are questioned by what they saw and what they did in combat. They seek reconnection with something greater than themselves. They seek revalidation in their spirituality from the perspective of reaching out to that sense of a greater "other" beyond themselves that creates meaning, hope, purpose, and healing. In telling their stories, Warfighters are not always seeking out others who shared a common experience of combat. But rather, they seek others who can help them reconnect to their spirituality.

Therefore, aside from the horror of the acts of combat, the experience of combat often leads Warfighters to search for meaning and purpose. They seek answers to their loss of innocence and seek purpose and meaning in their grief, pain, and loss. Spirituality certainly cannot be on both sides at once. Warfighters faced with the trauma of combat question the painful realities of combat and resulting value of life, culture, and humanity. Combat trauma can shatter Warfighters' and Veterans' traditional sense of spirituality. Warfighters who are unable to resolve the challenges to their moral and spiritual beliefs find themselves silently wounded in their Souls.

Most Warfighters and Veterans who experience direct combat believe that their cause was just. Some held firm in their belief throughout the combat experiences. They saw their spirituality as a source of strength to help them endure their pain and suffering.

Others had their spirituality shattered when faced with the trauma of combat. They questioned their spirituality and came to believe that their spirituality failed them. Military chaplains who counsel Warfighters in the field and after a war find that many Warfighters have difficulty making sense of combat situations that did not fit with their moral or spiritual beliefs. However, we must also note that some Veterans have experienced spiritual growth as a result of their combat experiences. They found a path to healing their silently wounded Souls early on in their combat experience.

Warfighters, Veterans, and family members must come to understand that spirituality leads to healing "PTSoulD." Their ability to find meaning in the grief, loss, pain, and desperation of combat trauma through their spirituality leads to healing and purposeful living. Combat Veterans who are able to find meaning and purpose in their traumatic experiences are less likely to succumb to "PTSoulD."

Spirituality pervades the survivor of combat trauma. Spirituality keeps Warfighters and Veterans alive in the face of unspeakable experiences. Their grief, loss, pain, and desperation can be overwhelming. Spirituality infuses them with new courage and commitment. Spirituality helps Warfighters, Veterans, and family members cope with their grief and loss. Combat trauma assaults their spirituality. The experiences of combat force Warfighters and Veterans to ask questions about themselves and their beliefs. The trauma of combat hurts "WVFMs'" understanding of themselves, others, and their beliefs about their lives and the world they live in. Regaining an active and alive spirituality helps "WVFMs" connect to the healing of hope, faith, and love. Finding our spirituality is finding meaning in our suffering. Spirituality is the inner search for ultimate meaning and purpose in life.[106]

HEALING THE SOUL - PURPOSEFUL LIVING

"You nourish your Soul by fulfilling your destiny."[107]
Harold Kushner

In developing their successful strategies for a lifetime of healing, Warfighters, Veterans, and family members can adopt and use their daily activities to help them heal their Souls. What they "do" can mirror the wounded or the healed Soul. Since all behavior is representative of the state of their Souls, life activities can represent the goodness in the Soul. The legions of volunteers in this world who serve out of pure sacrifice and love are representatives of this point. They show up in hospitals, nursing homes, orphanages, animal sanctuaries, committees and clubs and give of themselves with no connection to personal gain. Volunteers are usually more faithful and show up to work with more consistency than paid workers do. They give themselves to others without asking in return. Doing so is a truly healing process. There is something very nurturing to the Soul when "WVFMs" volunteer their time, talents, and money. The power of these special activities called volunteering can help keep Souls healthy for a lifetime. This turns the silently wounded Soul to finding meaning, healing, and turning to purposeful living again.

"You gain strength, courage, and confidence by every experience in which you really stop to look fear in the face. You are able to say to yourself, "I lived through this horror. I can take the next thing that comes along."[108]
Eleanor Roosevelt

Warfighters, Veterans, and family members can transform their lives through a life of service to the greater good. Seeking the greater good is for persons who aspire to expand their capacity to serve and uncover meaning and purpose in their lives. Every "WVFM" has inherent gifts, unrealized dreams, and hidden capabilities. Seeking a life of purposeful living and working for the greater good unlocks their hidden capacities, their highest potential for living purposefully and serving from their Souls. A life of purposeful living supports meaning and healing in "WVFMs" who seek to make a positive difference in the world.

Warfighters, Veterans, and family members often find purpose within their traditional and virtual communities that they transform into cooperative and purposeful communities. They find lives of creative service, continuing growth, and ever-expanding meaning and purpose.

When Warfighters, Veterans, and family members find meaning and seek purposeful living this represents a fundamental shift in the way they view their lives and choose their attitudes. Purposeful living is about consciously choosing to change their behaviors from serving Self to serving others. Purposeful living changes how "WVFMs" feel. They change from being angry and bitter to being happy. Purposeful living takes "WVFMs" from selfishness to selflessness and self-centeredness to service to others. Warfighters, Veterans, and family members find healing and meaning in purposeful living through their commitment, selfless sacrifice for the greater good, and dedication to humanitarian values.

Warfighters, Veterans, and family members with silently wounded Souls can achieve happiness in their lives. Happiness is not a tangible thing that exists in the physical world as something that can be bought or sold, eaten, or achieved through physical exercise. Happiness depends on Warfighters and Veterans changing their attitudes and behaviors and choosing to interpret their lives for the greater good. Happiness is achieved when "WVFMs" achieve purposeful living. They can be happy about achieving their goals, and loving, caring people support them. "WVFMs" living lives for the greater good acknowledge their feelings of happiness. Purposeful living is living a balanced and healthy life and feeling happiness within the Soul.

To be happy Warfighters, Veterans, and family members must live for something outside themselves. They must live for the greater good, another person, a cause, a belief, or a purpose to achieve. To live only for themselves, wrapped in grief, loss, pain, and desperation of their silently wounded Souls, is to exist in a world of misery. To be happy silently wounded "WVFMs" must have hope, which is their commitment of time and energy to purposeful living. Without purpose, they have no hope, and to have no hope is to have no reason to live.

Warfighters, Veterans, and family members must answer the call from their Souls. They have a knowing inner voice that is gently calling them to lives of health and happiness. Within them is the ability to heal, find meaning, and seek purposeful living. Through self-awareness and self-examination, they allow the wisdom of their Self, their thoughts, their emotions, and their spirits to guide their personal journeys of healing. "WVFMs" deserve to experience joy, peace, and happiness.

Throughout the ages, there have been exemplary Veterans who have uncovered their Souls. They all have something in common: leading lives of service in their chosen field. They are the known and unknown Warfighters, Veterans, and family members we see every day.

Their example calls every "WVFM" that suffers from the trauma of combat to higher possibilities and speaks directly to their purpose in their lives. Their example suggests that the more Warfighters, Veterans, and family members seek to serve the greater good the more the Soul finds meaning and healing. Furthermore, purposeful living calls "WVFMs" to change their behaviors and their attitudes. When they serve as selflessly as possible, they heal the Self and find meaning in their Souls. What remains is the healthy Soul.

Examples abound of Warfighters and Veterans who suffer

trauma and "PTSoulD" and yet maintain a fierce will for meaning. Among them is the blind Soldier skiing on a downhill slope (with an assistant skiing before him with a sign: "Attention, a blind Soldier skiing!"), or a smiling and excited young woman Veteran with paralyzed legs, being helped by two volunteers in loading her sled to a ski lift on the same mountain; later she is "skiing" down a difficult slope. There are also Warfighters with missing arms that learn to fly fish with their artificial limbs.

There is the story of the Vet who lost both legs to go on and lead a life of public service and the Vet who overcame the trauma of being a POW to become a member of the Senate. The NCO who overcame the loss of a leg to re-join the Golden Knights parachute team and the NCO who overcame the loss of both legs to jog with a President.

They are examples of Warfighters and Veterans who have won over their disabilities and turned tragedy into human triumph. While the inhuman ordeal of an extreme handicap is the fate of many Warfighters and Veterans, others suffer silently wounded Souls that are the reality of "normal" life. They are the fathers, mothers, sisters, brothers, husbands, and wives who go on to live their lives in normal settings. They are the housekeepers, the storeowners, the businesspersons and women, the contractors, the laborers, the doctors, bankers, lawyers of our communities that have found healing, meaning, and are working for the greater good. They still have the sights, sounds, and smells of their combat trauma running through their memories like a movie on continuous playback. They still have silently wounded Souls. But they have learned to adjust, find meaning, and seek purposeful living.

Allen B. Clark[109] who was a West Point graduate and was wounded in Vietnam, resulting in the loss of both his legs, went on to become the director of our national cemeteries. He got involved in politics to help Vets. He worked at the VA for a short stint. Allen Clark's journey of recovery and finding meaning, following the physical tragedy of his wounding, led him to his calling of service to other wounded Vets through his Combat Faith Ministry. The list of people taking adversity and turning it into good is endless.

Viktor Frankl gives us many examples of people surviving deeply traumatic events and experiences. He suggests that we can grow and learn from our suffering. Finding meaning and seeking purposeful living from our experiences is an act of growing and changing. Finding meaning helps us to explain what occurred in our life journey and how it affected us. To understand what happened and to give meaning to it helps us to learn how to heal, move on, and find purpose in our lives.[110]

HEALING THE SOUL – A SELF-GUIDE TO OUR OWN HEALING

> "One of the bitter legacies of Vietnam was the inadequate treatment of troops when they came back. Tens of thousands endured psychological disorders in silence, and too many ended up homeless, alcoholic, drug-addicted, imprisoned, or dead before the government acknowledged their conditions and in 1980 officially recognized PTSD as a medical diagnosis. Yet nearly three decades later, the government still has not mastered the basics: how best to detect the disorder, the most effective ways to treat it, and the fairest means of compensating young men and women who served their country and returned unable to lead normal lives."[111]
>
> Dana Priest and Anne Hull

Self-examination has been a theme throughout this book. We focused on the use of technology and the virtual world as sources of support and healing. We have provided insights as to the impact and affects of combat trauma on the whole person and established what the healthy Soul might be like. Now we must actually walk the path to meaning, purposeful living, and a life dedicated to a greater good. We would like to leave you with a practical tool that you could use to start you on your own path of healing. The tool is called "Healing the Soul – A Self-Guide to Our Own Healing." Here is the way it works.

"Healing the Soul: A Self-Guide to Our Own Healing" is a two part tool. It consists of creative media computer software and a Guidebook-Journal. It is an educational interactive experience; based on the adult-learning model that suggests when adult learners initiate their own learning they can achieve and sustain changes in their own behavior. The assessment software is not a therapeutic substitute or counseling process. Rather, it is a self-guided learning tool to do self-examination and develop your own plan of personal growth and healing.

"Healing the Soul" is a self-examination system to help you become more aware of the impact that your silent wounds caused by combat trauma has on your life. It is a self-guided tool for you to work on your own time and at your own pace without the assistance or oversight of a counselor or caregiver. The program is repeatable. The objective of the program is to provide a process for the assessment of the affects of the pain, grief, loss, and desperation on your silently wounded Soul. This is a process of the self-examination of your behaviors. The first step is to understand that you are silently wounded and this wounding has changed your life and is the source and cause of dysfunctional behaviors and poor life-style choices. The second step calls you to begin a healing process by calling upon your own inner strengths and resources, and/or you may decide to seek out the additional support from a counselor or caregiver.

"Healing the Soul" examines your behaviors and attitudes that are demonstrated in seven life experience areas that complement the core personal characteristics of the whole person. These seven life experience areas are: Relationships, Finances, Work and Jobs, Recreation, Personal Image, Spiritual Beliefs and Meaning, and Intellectual. The behavior patterns that you discover for yourself in these life experience areas reflect how healthy or unhealthy you are. The results of your self-examination in each of these life experience areas reflect who you are and who you want to be. When you experience the life-changing pain, grief, loss, and quiet desperation from combat trauma, the resulting "PTSoulD" changes the way you think, act, and feel. This silent wounding reflects in your day-to-day behaviors and lifestyle choices. We suggest that how you respond to the pain, grief, loss, and quiet desperation is actually your choice to make even if that choice is not a conscious deliberate decision. Self-examination brings these choices into your awareness. Once aware, you can make different choices. The "Healing the Soul" system develops each of the life experience areas into self-guided assessment modules that will help you understand the changes in your life from the trauma of combat.

The premise of "Healing the Soul" is that you are responsible for yourself. The degree to which you assume this responsibility is the measure of your happiness. The degree to which you take responsibility for the healthy balance in the core characteristics of your whole person reflect in your behaviors in the seven areas of life experiences. Healing begins by taking responsibility for your Self by examining your life experiences and making the decisions to change ugly and harmful behavior. Changing your behavior changes how you feel and is the path to healing.

You hold the inner strength to resolve the problems that confront you in your life. "Healing the Soul" begins when you accept and control your sense of Self and empower the resources and strength you have as a person to affect your own healing.

The self-guided assessments within each of the seven modules highlight some of the common behaviors that either reflect the painfulness of your silently wounded Souls or contribute to the quiet desperation you feel. Only by honest, close, and thoughtful examination of the behaviors in each of these areas of your life will you be on your way to lasting happiness and healing.

The self-examination of life experiences that leads you to connecting to your sense of Self-works because it allows you to understand who you are on your own terms and in your own time and space. It focuses on what is unique to you through your own reflection and understanding. You then make your own decision to heal your Soul.

The "Healing the Soul" system allows you a private, individual, and non-judgmental means to examine very sensitive and painful experiences and thoughts. Such an approach allows you to work on your own time schedule and at your individual pace. This self-guided tool is an interactive, virtual computer media experience that allows you to practice a new technique or skill at your own convenience. It also provides practice for life choices without concern of being observed, corrected, or embarrassed. The tool helps you to look at sensitive issues in your life and interact with a non-judgmental scenario that parallels common life themes and issues in the life experience area studied and thus see your own behavior in the acted-out examples. Through this model, you receive experience with different choices, reinforce new behavior concepts, receive instant feedback that shows the levels of strength of your personal resources, and receive objective overall performance feedback that is confidential and private. In short, the program lets you experiment with life changes until you find the right mix that works for you.

You have ultimate accountability for your response to life events with successful life solutions. You make the choices and you adapt and live with the consequences and benefits of those choices.

Self-assessment coaches you to understand that a series of events do not define who you are. It is how you react and the choices you make in response to events that define you. This self-assessment tool is based upon the concept that examples of similar experiences, as portrayed in video stories, games, and other interactive experiences, will allow you to "see yourself" and thus determine and evaluate your own beliefs, attitudes, and behaviors in each of the seven illustrative areas of life. These life examples represent issues of healing and allow you to interact with the media to discover the insights that contribute to your growth and healing. The goal of these assessments is to determine, for yourself, your own values, beliefs, and goals that allow you to meet your deepest needs of fulfillment and healing. In so doing, you start the process of moving toward healing your Soul.

This interactive media tool allows you to engage in self-paced self-assessment. The life solutions, which you discover, verify, and apply, are your own. Self-assessment is more honest, non-judgmental, and reinforces your own decisions. When you discover your own solutions to help heal the soul, you are more likely to carry them out and sustain them in your life.

We each learn in different ways. Not everyone can learn effectively through an interactive computer based media experience. This tool provides you with many different opportunities to gain insight and self-assessment to include the non-computer based Guidebook-Journal. It is our hope that you will find one or more ways to find healing through this program.

This is a self-assessment program designed for you, the individual, to use by yourself and in your own time and space. This model relies heavily upon journaling for continuity between your sessions and to reflect on your progress and growth. The Guidebook-Journal is a primary focal point of your reflection. It is a mechanism of accountability to yourself and, if necessary, with a caregiver and becomes a blueprint for constructive behavior change.

The Guidebook-Journal is a self-guiding tool to conduct more in-depth examination and consideration of the material presented in each interactive-media module. It allows you to consider at more depth and detail the areas covered in the audio-visual portion of the tool. It approaches each subject area with presenting a number of open-ended questions. These questions allow you to conduct self-reflection of your assessments. It is designed in such a way as to allow you to write down your personal insights. The emphasis of this activity is to then scan the entered data and look for patterns and themes in the recorded attitudes, beliefs, and behaviors.

The Journal portion of the Guidebook-Journal concentrates on Focused Journaling. Focused Journaling is designed as a series of building blocks to move from basic to more in-depth consideration in a given subject. This system allows you to have a tool that intentionally invites you to consider and respond to subjects that you may not normally consider or intentionally avoid in each of the seven areas of assessments.

The Journal questions are posed in a way that asks for more than yes or no answers. The questions are designed for you to wrestle with and more importantly serve as a blueprint for designing your personal solution for healing and happiness. Asking and answering questions is a timeless mechanism to gain fresh perspectives and useful insights into your experiences. Asking and answering questions for yourself is non-threatening and will challenge and invite you to healing and growth on your own terms and when the time is right for you.

The "Healing the Soul" system is based on the research and concepts developed in this book. It addresses the changes in your life as a result of "PTSoulD." The self-examination that takes place allows you the opportunity to discover what you do not like about your life and then how to make different choices. It is one thing to understand that you are silently wounded, full of pain and anger, and living a life of quiet desperation. It is another to make the decision to change. It takes great courage to live a life of quiet desperation. It takes greater courage to make the decision to heal your wounded Soul.

A NEW BEGINNING

"The tragedy of life is what dies inside a man while he lives."[112]

Albert Schweitzer

A final story of wounding and healing: the story of a Veteran. The Veteran was a father and lived and passed away as a man silently wounded. His family cannot say if in the latter part or end of his life he ever found an abiding healing for his wounding. They shared some twinkling moments of love and joy in the later years of his life that looked very much like moments of healing for him. However, his life forced his family to come face-to-face with their own wounding and allow them to begin paths toward their own healing.

His family was never able to separate the Vet's alcoholism from him as a person. The two were completely woven together in their increasingly angry opinion of him. Wounding will do that to a family. The pain they experience with their wounding cannot be contained, and it spills over into how they see everything else. That is the sad thing about a silently wounded Soul. A silently wounded Soul tends to spread out, infect, and rob lives of love, relationships, and happiness. It even fogs a family's thinking to the point of disorientation from a reasonable perspective. It clouds their Souls' judgment. Worst of all they will never begin to heal their Souls if they can no longer separate the pain itself from the wounding experience.

It was during their later years that the family members came to understand for the first time that the honest path to love of Self had everything to do with how healthy or how wounded their own Souls truly were. In addition, as long as the wounding within them continued to condemn their father bitterly, they could not find healing in their Souls. They eventually found the way to say to their husband and father what they had never been able to say through years of pain, "I love you." Despite the wounding, they needed to say it and he certainly needed to hear it. That moment, for the first time, they knew that both the family and the Veteran, as a husband and a father, experienced true healing within their Souls. It opened up a lifetime of healing.

The memory of the wounding remains a part of the lives of Warfighters, Veterans, and family members and a part of their life stories. The relationships they have with each other, their families, their spouses, and their friends continue until the last days of their lives.

We cannot pretend to tell Warfighters, Veterans, and family members when, if, or how healing will finally occur for them. We can suggest that it is a lifetime process. It is not a quick fix or a "steps to a healthy Soul" formula. Healing the Silent Wounds is about finding meaning and discovering purposeful living in our lives. We also suggest that healing begins with a deliberate choice. If we make the choice to heal or not, one thing is very certain. Life will continue to move ahead and we will move with it, either silently wounded or on a path toward healing. We have a lifetime to do either.

EPILOGUE

"We can't solve problems by using the same kind of thinking we used when we created them."[113]

Albert Einstein

LUKE

I have come to be proud that I am a Veteran. But it is still a private pride. I don't share it much except online. Iraq put us through hell. When I left for Iraq, Jennifer and I said farewells as if it might be our last. We didn't see it at the time but that is what we both thought. I remember that we put our lives on hold because of the long ramp-up prior to deployment. This is why Jennifer and I got married before I left. Our lives didn't start up again until after we got home that day from Walter Reed.

I have been getting better at telling my story. It was hard at first. But it is my story. Those thoughts ran through my mind as I left the group this evening. When I got home I got online with a chat group that started up soon after I got home from the Ward. It was almost by accident. I remember surfing around the net one night when sleeping was more of an effort than staying awake. I came across a site for Iraq and Afghanistan Vets. At first I didn't pay any attention but I recognized one of the names. Hey, that was my friend! I know him! What is he doing on this site? That all ran through my head in a flash. He was telling his story. My freakin lord it was the same as my story. As I look back that seemed like a turning point for me. I must have read that story twenty times that night. For the first time I understood that we were Soldiers and we had done our job. We weren't members of the sick, lame, and lazy squad.

I have been in my job now for eight months. For a while, soon after I got home I couldn't keep a job more than a few weeks. I would blow up at someone and get canned. Drank too much. I still have to watch that. If I start remembering, I can start drinking to drown it out. But I wear a shirt and tie now. Jennifer and I also bought a small house in town with the help of her parents. Our daughter is walking and we found out that Jen is pregnant again. She must be four or five months along now.

The only time I talk about the war is with my group, and online. So our neighbors and new friends probably don't even know my story. For all they know I am Mr. Normal. Now that is a freakin joke. Maybe I will tell them someday. For now, I still survive from day to day. And my note taking that I started centuries ago while at Walter Reed has now grown into several journal books. Yeah, go figure, me who nearly flunked English in high school keeping a freakin journal. I laugh. But I can also write down my thoughts and feelings and somehow that seems to help.

Maybe I can survive. The days before the deployment are days I can't even remember anymore. It seems my life, who I am now, began on a road in an unnamed village in Iraq when an IED took my brother apart.

Well, I am home now. I can hear my daughter giggling in the house and Jennifer saying something about ice cream. Another day. Survived another day. When I stepped through the door, Jen was there with a hug. My daughter was hanging on my pants leg. Maybe I can do it another day. But I am still scared of the dark. One day at a time.

JENNIFER

It's amazing how sneaky hope can be, how it finds its way into your life without you ever being the wiser. I'm five months pregnant with Sadie's little brother. She's skipping in the front yard, chasing a butterfly in her "I'm the Big Sister" t-shirt. She's fascinated with Mommy's belly. "Mommy chubby," she says as she wriggles her pinky finger into my belly button. She already loves her baby brother, and she hasn't even met him yet. Luke is elated that he is having a son. I'm grateful to be so blessed, to live each day being loved by my family, knowing of no other home than the warmth of Luke and our baby girl.

I found a picture of Luke from his senior year in high school. His face is smooth, round, and young. He is laughing in the photo; he is innocent. I placed the photo next to one of him taken a few weeks ago. Only five or six years have gone by, but it appears as though he's aged at least ten. I stared at the photos, side by side, the photo of my high school sweetheart and the photo of my husband, the Iraq War Veteran. Did he have any idea of what was to come? How his innocent eyes would change into eyes that will never be able to forget?

He's doing better though. He's gentler, quieter, goofier, more like the Luke I fell in love with, but still hardly the same at all. He still gets that distant look of horror in his eyes from time to time. Sometimes he wakes up in the middle of the night so abruptly that he startles me and gets the dogs to barking. But I see a glimpse of peace, a sign that he's healing, when he tickles Sadie or falls asleep with her on the couch. In those moments he becomes that same kid I fell in love with so long ago...

§§§§

The stories of our Warfighters, Veterans, and family members are sacred ground. Stories have been with us throughout time. Storytelling for much of human history was the only way to communicate and pass on history. Stories are the teachers that guide us through the challenges in our lives. They enable us to dream, to be inspired, and to digest the mysteries of the universe. They inform, they guide, they teach, they inspire, and they heal. Through stories, we become a part of something larger than ourselves. Through stories, we are awakened to our potential as whole persons.

With the information explosion of the Internet, we are constantly on the threshold of new awareness about our world and ourselves. Through this information explosion Warfighters, Veterans, and family members form a new sense of connection and community. Through the stories we witness on the Internet we can believe that we are not alone. Through our collective stories, we reconnect with the Self. The concept of Self is a growing understanding that at the center of each of us lays a core of Self and Soul out of which emerges our true being. The Self is the core of who we are which connects us to our spirituality.

This Self contains what we are in our feelings and emotions. The Self is all that makes up our core personal characteristics. This true center of our being connects us to our Soul, the spiritual companion of the Self. Our Soul is our connection to the spiritual. Our Soul takes on our personal characteristics. Expressing that which we know as our Self strengthens us in our search for our Soul. Self and Soul work together to maintain our connection to the world and to our spirituality.

Our core personal characteristics, our core Self, is the spiritual essence of our Souls. Our Self waits to be discovered. To live life more fully, a life that is purposeful, we first need to know who we are and make choices based on this inner awareness. Then, we can begin to experience healing in our Souls, happiness, meaning, and purpose in our lives. We can heal our lives. Healing is a process that happens naturally when we are connected to our spirituality. This takes place when we are in balance with who we are.

In our journeys with Warfighters, Veterans, and family members, we discovered two basic issues. One was that our Veterans were seeking forgiveness from their families, friends, communities and their Nation for the things they saw and did in combat. The second issue was the increasing instances of dysfunctional behaviors and lifestyles that included suicide as a symptom of combat trauma and a delayed casualty of war. We understood immediately that we needed to do something about this. Our role exists within the realm of forgiveness and the protection and sanctity of life.

Our Warfighters and Veterans need our forgiveness for what they saw and what they did in combat. They need our help and support to find healing, meaning, and purposeful living. We must not abandon them to their pain, grief, loss, and desperation. Left untreated and without intervention, their pain, grief, loss, and desperation escalate into death by suicide.

Our concern is about healing our Warfighters and Veterans as they return from combat. Combat trauma irrevocably changes the person. We call this trauma Post Traumatic Soul Disorder (PTSoulD). Thus, this is a story of the silent wounding from the trauma of war and of healing. This is also a story of preventing additional post-combat casualties through suicide.

Warfighters, Veterans, and family members are different than "before" and forever changed. This is a story of learning how to heal and how to live with the changes. This is a story of remembering, understanding the Self, finding meaning in the wounding, telling the stories, and finding healing through connection within a community of relationships. Warfighters and Veterans cannot return to life as it was before combat. They will never forget. They will endure the changes for the rest of their lives. Warfighters and Veterans lose their innocence in combat and that innocence is forever lost.

This is a story of the whole community. It is only within the connections of the whole community that healing is possible. Warfighters, Veterans, and family members seek connection within community. The community then bears witness to their stories, their trauma, and their pain, grief, loss, and desperation. We all, then, accept responsibility for the silent wounding of the Souls of Warfighters, Veterans, and their family members.

Healing the Soul is about connecting again to life, family, and community through purposeful living. The Soul becomes wounded when the sights, sounds, and smells of combat create a deep pain and leaves Warfighters feeling profound loss and grief. For Warfighters and Veterans to remove the pain in their spirits and the wounds of their Souls they need to reach deep within themselves and examine what is taking place in their lives. This takes a great deal of personal courage. It takes as much courage to heal as it does to face the fears of combat in the first place.

> "This story shall the good man teach his son; And Crispin Crispian shall ne'er go by, From this day to the ending of the world, But we in it shall be remembered - We few, we happy few, we band of brothers."[114]
>
> William Shakespeare

What Warfighters, Veterans, and Family Members are saying about "Healing the Soul - A Self-Guide to Our Own Healing."

"I have reviewed Healing the Soul and find the interactive software and work book most useful. We have ordered copies for all of our endorsed deploying, deployed and recently returned military chaplains. We are providing this resource for their personal healing and as a tool for the service members they serve. I only wish there had been a similar resource when I returned from the two combat tours I served in Viet Nam. We are blessed to have Healing the Soul and other programs to assist service members and their families today."

Chaplain (COL) Tom Carter, U.S. Army, Retired
Director of Endorsement
United Methodist Endorsing Agency

"I received and reviewed the program "Healing the Soul." I am impressed. The interactive reflective process engages. I expected more presentation. But the heart of the work is with the individual; this material keeps the focus with the individual while assuming some community responsibility for the concerns. I hope that the material is well supported."

Dr. Martha Ann Rutland
Director of Clinical Pastoral Education
VITAS: Innovative Hospice Care

"I was a member of the initial invasion into Iraq. I was introduced to "Healing the Soul" after returning home from the war in Iraq and found it to be very helpful in dealing with personal issues. The interactive exercise on my financial habits was particularly enlightening. The "Healing the Soul" program is easy to use on your personal computer. It can help anyone preparing to deploy and returning from combat. I recommend this great product to anyone who is going to war or coming home from war."

Richard Rios, Iraq Combat Vet

"Wow! What an innovative educational tool. And it works. I should know. As the recently retired, Deputy Chief of Chaplains, I spent a lifetime dedicated to the care of the human soul. What's more, I have found it very helpful personally. Any of us can, and often do, experience very stressful and traumatic circumstances that leave deep emotional scars. This tool guides you effectively through seven critical areas of life assisting with healing of your soul. It is self-paced and can be done in the privacy of your own home at your convenience. This wonderful program allows you to take care of yourself by helping you discover both your strengths and areas where you may need healing. It doesn't stop there. It guides you in finding that healing. This tool should be put in the hands of all soldiers, military family members, department of defense civilians, police, firefighters, EMT personnel and all who face high stresses and tragic events daily. In fact, it will assist anyone interested in doing a meaningful self assessment."

Monsignor Jerome Haberek, Brigadier General (retired)

To:
Subject: R'cvd "Healing the Soul"
Classification: Unclassified

Just wanted you to know that I received the "Healing the Soul" resources last week. It is very timely since the Department of Army is now mandating a "chain teach" on the PTSD to every soldier by mid-October. It looks to be a great resource, thanks for sending it my way. If I require additional copies, what is the best way I can order more? Thanks for remembering the silent wounded...

Chaplain (LTC)

ENDNOTES

1 David Canada, biography sent to the author, 26 October 2007.

"David Canada is a native of Charlotte County, Virginia. He is an Elder in the Virginia Annual Conference of the United Methodist Church. He attended Ferrum Junior College, North Carolina Wesleyan College (Bachelor of Arts, 1969), Candler School of Theology at Emory University (Master of Divinity, 1971), and Wesley Theological Seminary (Doctor of Ministry, 1996). Much of his interest and training are in the areas of pastoral care and health care ministries. David's Clinical Pastoral Education includes units at the Georgia Association of Pastoral Care, the University of Virginia Medical Center, and the Fort Carson Clinical Pastoral Education Center. He also completed advanced and supervisory residencies in Clinical Pastoral Education at the Medical College of Virginia and Walter Reed Army Medical Center. David has also been a licensed nursing home administrator and served in administration at Virginia United Methodist Homes. His other pastoral appointments have been as a church pastor in both the Virginia and North Carolina Annual Conferences of the United Methodist Church.

David served as a United States Army Chaplain for 24 years. His assignments included Fort Carson Colorado; Augsburg, Germany; Fort Lesley J. McNair and Walter Reed Army Medical Center in Washington, D.C.; Youngsan, Korea; and William Beaumont Army Medical Center. During those assignments, he was assigned to Armor, Field Artillery, Combat Engineers, and hospitals. He is a retired Lieutenant Colonel. His awards include the Legion of Merit and Honorary Membership in the Army's Society of Medical Merit. His military education includes the Basic and Advanced Chaplain Officer Courses, the Instillation Chaplain's Course, the Army's Advanced Drug and Alcohol Counselor Course, and the Command and General Staff

College.

David is the author of <u>Spiritual Leadership in the Small Membership Church</u>, published in 2005 by the Abingdon Press. He also serves on the Editorial Advisory Board for Circuit Rider Magazine. He is currently a member of the Virginia Annual Conference Board of Ordained Ministry.

David is retired. He continues to write and serve as a spiritual director. His hobbies include reading, playing the drums, and baseball.

His wife Judy is from Rocky Mount, North Carolina. They have been married for 40 years. They live in Chesterfield, Virginia. They have a son named Mike, a daughter-in-law named Tina, and a granddaughter named Evelyn Rose."

2 Maxine Hone Kingston, ed., <u>Veterans of War, Veterans of Peace</u> (Koa Books, 2006) 19.

Shepherd Bliss, a Vietnam Veteran, is an ordained United Methodist Clergyman.

3 The Department of Defense Health Board Task Force on Mental Health. "An Achievable Vision: Report of the Department of Defense Task on Mental Health." June 15, 2007.

The group highlighted the urgent need for action to address two "signature injuries" from the current conflicts - Post Traumatic Stress Disorder (PTSD) and Traumatic Brain Injury (TBI).

James Risen, "Back From Iraq, Contractors Face Combat-Related Stress," <u>New York Times</u>, 5 July 5, 2007: P1.

See this newspaper article for a discussion on the issues of contractors returning from the battlefield suffering from PTSD.

4 Edward Tick, <u>War and The Soul</u> (Quest Books, 2005) 72-73.

See Chapter Four "Ancient Myth Modern War" for a detailed discussion of the hidden cost of America's Wars. Dr. Tick provides a thorough discussion of the cost of WWI, Vietnam, The Cold War, and The Gulf War. Research shows that a large percentage of the casualties from wars actually occur long after the trauma of combat and hostilities cease. The data reflects that Veterans live the rest of their lives with these silent wounds. p 70.

5 Ibid. p.72-73. One of the alarming hidden costs of war is the high percentage of Veterans and family members that commit suicide.

Kimberly Hefling, "Iraq, Afghan Vets at Risk of Suicide," Associated Press Writer, 31 October 2007 (Yahoo.com). "The ongoing research reveals that at least 283 combat veterans who left the military between the start of the war in Afghanistan on Oct. 7, 2001, and the end of 2005 took their own lives. . . .A total of 147 troops have killed themselves in Iraq and Afghanistan since the wars began. . . And that doesn't include those who committed suicide after their combat tour ended and while still in the military — a number the Pentagon says it doesn't track."

Kaplan Mark S., Huguet Nathalie, McFarland Bentson H., and Newsom Jason T., "Suicide among male veterans: a prospective population-based study." <u>Journal of Epidemiology and Community Health.</u> July 2007. 61:619-624. Newswise, "Journal of Epidemiology and Community Health," Study, July 2007. www.newswise.com.

(http://www.newswise.com/articles/view/530742/) reported this about the study: "Former military personnel are twice as likely to kill themselves as people who have not seen combat reports a study in the July issue of Journal of Epidemiology and Community Health."

6 Kimberly Hefling, "Iraq, Afghan Vets at Risk of Suicide," Associated Press Writer, 31 October 2007 (Yahoo.com).

7 Edward Tick, <u>War and The Soul</u> (Quest Books, 2005) 3. This excerpt was reproduced by permission of Quest Books, the imprint of the Theosophical Publishing House (www. questbooks.net).

8 Mason, Melvin, Retired Officer, Metropolitan Police Department Washington, DC, February 1987.

9 The Department of Defense Health Board Task Force on Mental Health. "An Achievable Vision: Report of the Department of Defense Task on Mental Health." June 15, 2007.

The group highlighted the urgent need for action to address two "signature injuries" from the current conflicts - Post Traumatic Stress Disorder (PTSD) and Traumatic Brain Injury (TBI).

10 <u>The American Psychiatric Association's Diagnostic and Statistical Manual, Edition III,</u> 1980. <u>www.psych.org</u>.

11 Jim Goodwin, PhD, "The Etiology of Combat-Related Post-Traumatic Stress-Disorders", Chapter 1, Edited by Tom Williams, Psy.D. <u>Post-Traumatic Stress Disorders of the Vietnam Veteran</u>. 1980, Disabled American Veterans, Cincinnati, OH.

12 Ibid. paraphrase.

13 Ibid.

14 "Band of Brothers" is a 10-part television miniseries set during World War II. It first aired in 2001 on HBO. The

miniseries centers on the experiences of Company E of the 506th Parachute Infantry Regiment, U.S. 101st Airborne Division. It begins with Company E's initial training and goes through the American airborne landings in Normandy, Operation Market Garden, the Battle of Bastogne and on to the end of the war. It is based on the book of the same name written by historian and biographer Stephen Ambrose.

Another story about a band of brothers is told in William Shakespeare's, King Henry V, Act IV, Scene III. "This story shall the good man teach his son; and Crispin Crispian shall ne'er go by, from this day to the ending of the world, but we in it shall be remember'd; We few, we happy few, We Band of Brothers, For he to-day that sheds his blood with me shall be my brother; be he ne'er so vile, this day shall gentle his condition; And gentlemen in England now a-bed shall think themselves accursed they were not here, and hold their manhood's cheap whiles any speaks that fought with us upon Saint Crispin's day."

15 Lee Alley, <u>Back From War- Finding Hope & Understanding In Life After Combat</u>, (Exceptional Publishing, 2007) 108. This excerpt was reproduced by permission of The King Consortium (www.thekingconsortium.com).

16 Jim Goodwin, PhD, "The Etiology of Combat-Related Post-Traumatic Stress-Disorders", Chapter 1, Edited by Tom Williams, Psy.D. <u>Post-Traumatic Stress Disorders of the Vietnam Veteran,</u> 1980, (Disabled American Veterans, National Headquarters P O Box 14301 Cincinnati, OH 45214) paraphrase.

17 Edward Tick, <u>War and The Soul</u> (Quest Books, 2005) 74. This excerpt was reproduced by permission of Quest Books, the imprint of the Theosophical Publishing House (www. questbooks.net).

18 The Department of Defense Health Board Task Force on Mental Health. "An   Achievable Vision: Report of the Department of Defense Task on Mental Health." June 15, 2007.

19 Hoge, Charles, M.D. and Castro, Carlo, Ph.D., et.al. "Combat Duty in Iraq and Afghanistan, Mental Health Problems, and Barriers to Care," <u>The New England Journal of Medicine,</u> Vol. 351: 13-22, No. 1, (July 1, 2004).

20 Sue Conant, "God & War – How Chaplains Struggle to Keep Faith Under Fire," <u>Newsweek</u>, 07 May 2007, 26 - 34. Richard Oppel, Jr., "A Salute For His Wounded, A Last Touch For His Dead," <u>New York Times,</u> 02 April 2007, 1.

Both articles describe chaplains questioning their faith after being changed by the trauma of war.

21 From HEALING THE SOUL IN THE AGE OF THE BRAIN by Elio Frattaroli, copyright (c) 2001 by Elio Frattaroli. Used by permission of Viking Penguin, a division of Penguin Group (USA) Inc. p 6.

22 Edward Tick, <u>War and The Soul</u> (Quest Books, 2005) 110.   This excerpt was reproduced by permission of Quest Books, the imprint of the Theosophical Publishing House (www. questbooks.net).

23 From HEALING THE SOUL IN THE AGE OF THE BRAIN by Elio Frattaroli, copyright (c) 2001 by Elio Frattaroli. Used by permission of Viking Penguin, a division of Penguin Group (USA) Inc. p 6.

24 From HEALING THE SOUL IN THE AGE OF THE BRAIN by Elio Frattaroli, copyright (c) 2001 by Elio Frattaroli. Used by permission of Viking Penguin, a division of Penguin Group (USA) Inc. p 432.

25 Anonymous, Iraq War Veteran Amputee, Interview of Army Staff Sergeant at Walter Reed Army Medical Center as he endured hundreds of painful hours of physical therapy by his unit chaplain.

26 Ibid.

27 Confucius.

28 Helen Keller, (June 27, 1880 – June 1, 1968), was an American author, activist and lecturer. She was the first deafblind person to graduate from college. She wrote 12 books and numerous articles. For more information about MS. Keller we recommend reading: The Frost King(1891), her autobiography, The Story of My Life (1903), and her spiritual autobiography, My Religion (1927).

29 Virgil, (70-19 B.C.) is one of the most influential Roman authors in history. He continues to have profound effect on modern writers. He died prior to completing his most famous work, The Aeneid. Caesar Augustus insured the incomplete manuscript was published.

30 The Department of Defense Health Board Task Force on Mental Health. "An Achievable Vision: Report of the Department of Defense Task on Mental Health." June 15, 2007.

The 14-member task force spent a year compiling and evaluating research data and testimony from experts and advocates, and conducted site visits to 38 military installations worldwide. It found that mental health problems carry a stigma that remains pervasive in the military and deters those who need care from seeking it. The group highlighted the urgent need for action to address two "signature injuries" from the current conflicts - Post Traumatic Stress Disorder (PTSD) and Traumatic Brain Injury (TBI).

253

31 Ibid. paraphrase of the study.

32 Amy Jo Kim, "The Network is the Game," Social Trends in Mobile Entertainment Game Developers Mobile Conference, 2005. Power Point Presentation.

33 James Thurber, Grover (December 8, 1894–November 2, 1961) was a humorist and cartoonist. He contributed many cartoons and short stories to The New Yorker magazine.

34 Cardinal Newman, The Venerable John Henry, (February 21, 1801 – August 11, 1890) was an English convert to Roman Catholicism. He wrote a number of influential books, including Via Media, Essay on the Development of Christian Doctrine, Apologia Pro Vita Sua, and the Grammar of Assent.

35 Amy Jo Kim, "The Network is the Game," Social Trends in Mobile Entertainment Game Developers Mobile Conference, 2005. Power Point Presentation.

36 Ibid.

In 2005 Nintendo presented Amy Jo Kim's findings about the emerging trends that are relevant to understanding the critical placement and integration of a technology platform that today's youth trust, engage, have immediate and sustained access to, and shows only increasingly larger and larger global participation. Connected communities are changing: We are no longer 'place-centric' but rather 'people-centric'- social networks; buddy lists on mobiles are collections of people- but not 'in person' rather virtually. Emerging connection in communities is now rapidly moving from PC-centric to Cell-phone centric. The home base PC is the first communications device to research, seek, and establish the virtual community. Now, the cell phone is the emerging primary technology that platforms communities.

37 Douglas Lowenstein, President, Interactive Digital Software Association, addressed the 2003 Serious Games Conference, February 5, 2003, Woodrow Wilson Center, Washington, DC.

38 B.C. Forbes, (May 14, 1880 – May 6, 1954) founded Forbes Magazine.

39 Hoge, Charles, M.D. and Castro, Carlo, Ph.D., et.al. "Combat Duty in Iraq and Afghanistan, Mental Health Problems, and Barriers to Care," The New England Journal of Medicine, Vol. 351: 13-22, No. 1, (July 1, 2004).

40 Hoge, Charles, M.D. and Castro, Carlo, Ph.D., et.al. "Combat Duty in Iraq and Afghanistan, Mental Health Problems, and Barriers to Care," The New England Journal of Medicine, Vol. 351: 13-22, No. 1, (July 1, 2004). Reports that too often military personnel and families do not use the traditional settings to seek after help for their hurt and pain. They attribute this to embarrassment over problems, fearfulness of being judged, and generally feeling like people really don't listen deeply anyhow.

41 Mark Griffiths, "Looking Into Online Therapy," Health Matters. Winter 2000/2001, 18-19 (Health Matters Publications, Ltd.), (www.healthmatters.org.uk.).

42 Ibid. paraphrase.

43 Ibid.

44 The Massachusetts Institute of Technology is currently working to place support materials for its entire curriculum online, free for anyone in the world to use. Yet, these lecture outlines and related readings are not intended as a substitute for an MIT education on campus where students and teachers cooperate in the creation of knowledge and in learning how to

develop and apply creative thinking. No system of technology can fully replace the human teacher/counselor/tutor/coach/guide. But for those times and places where no adequate human mentor is available, automated and computer-linked learning assistance can be of enormous value.

45 Mark Griffiths, "Looking Into Online Therapy," <u>Health Matters</u>. Winter 2000/2001, 18-19 (Health Matters Publications, Ltd.), (www.healthmatters.org.uk.).

46 Ibid.

47 The integration of virtual interactive simulations to provide training, education, and counseling sustainment and reinforcement simply represents the templating of an emerging technology platform to principles, which have been clinically written about and identified in research as early as 1961. Those who have reservations about the efficacy of such an approach have only to begin to study the findings of Jerome Frank in his, <u>Persuasion and Healing,</u> (Frank JD, Frank JB, Cousins N (1993), Persuasion and Healing: A Comparative Study of Psychotherapy. Baltimore: The Johns Hopkins University Press).

48 Maxine Hone Kingston, ed., <u>Veterans of War, Veterans of Peace</u> (Koa Books, 2006) 26.

49 Emily Kuhlbars Howden, family member, age 7.

50 Lee Alley, <u>Back From War- Finding Hope & Understanding In Life After Combat,</u> (Exceptional Publishing, 2007) 164. This excerpt was reproduced by permission of The King Consortium (www.thekingconsortium.com).

51 Edward Tick, <u>War and The Soul</u> (Quest Books, 2005)1. This excerpt was reproduced by permission of Quest Books, the imprint of the Theosophical Publishing House (www.questbooks.

net).

52 German proverb.

53 Buddha, (563 BCE to 483 BCE) was the founder of Buddhism. He is universally recognized by Buddhists as the Supreme Buddha of our age. His teachings were passed down by oral tradition for about 400 years after his death until they were finally committed to writing.

54 Emily Kuhlbars Howden, family member, age 4.

John McChesney, "Support Groups for Soldier's Families Struggle" (NPR), 20 June 2007, "Family readiness groups, or FRGs, as they're known in the military, were created to support the loved ones of soldiers at war. But across the country, those groups are getting mixed reviews at best. Many FRGs have been fractured or destroyed by bickering — and critics say military leaders haven't done enough to cool the tensions and provide adequate financial and moral support. It's a problem that easily spills over onto the battlefield as families at home share their problems with soldiers in Iraq."

55 From HEALING THE SOUL IN THE AGE OF THE BRAIN by Elio Frattaroli, copyright (c) 2001 by Elio Frattaroli. Used by permission of Viking Penguin, a division of Penguin Group (USA) Inc. p 6.

56 Francesco Scavullo, (1912 – 2004), was acknowledged as the dominant photographic influence on American fashion and beauty. He photographed almost every celebrated man, woman, and child in the world today. His photographs have graced the covers of magazines such as Rolling Stone, Life, Time, Town & Country, Harper's Bazaar, Vogue, Mademoiselle, Glamour, Cosmopolitan, and Max.

57 Edward Tick, War and The Soul (Quest Books, 2005) "The simplest act may be followed by death, as in this incident recounted by a veteran of the Vietnam War: 'I ask him does he want a cup of coffee. He nods and smiles. . . I bounce over to the entrance to our bunker and duck inside. I grab our canteens, pull off the two cups, and fill them with coffee. . . I carry the two steaming cups outside, cross over to Clyde, and hand him one . . . he smiles and thanks me. We click cups. . .He hands me back his empty cup. I say I'll be right back. He nods and smiles again. I turn and take a step. I hear a bang. My body clenches and stiffens. I spin. A bullet is crashing into Clyde's face. It is blowing apart. . I hit the ground as he does. I grab my rifle . . . I want to kill. I have to. I crawl to Clyde. I put my hands on him. I try . . . to stop the blood and save his face. But there is no face. It is gone. There is nothing I can do. Nothing'. Because the simplest matters, stepping away to refill a canteen can be linked to such dire and unalterable consequences, they take on a transcendent quality." 27. This excerpt was reproduced by permission of Quest Books, the imprint of the Theosophical Publishing House (www.questbooks.net).

58 Richard Pryor, III, (December 1, 1940 – December 10, 2005) was an American comedian, actor, and writer. His body of work includes such concert movies and recordings as Richard Pryor: Live and Smokin' (1971), ...Is It Something I Said? (1975), Richard Pryor: Live in Concert (1979), Richard Pryor: Live on the Sunset Strip (1982) and Richard Pryor: Here and Now. He collaborated on many film projects with actor Gene Wilder. He won an Emmy Award in 1973, and five Grammy Awards.

59 Plato, (427?–347 B.C.), His teachings have been among the most influential in the history of Western civilization. He was the second of the great trio of ancient Greeks; he succeeded Socrates and preceded Aristotle. The three of them laid the philosophical foundations of Western culture.

60 Gregg Zoroya, "Scientists: Brain Injuries From War Worse Than Thought", <u>USA Today</u>, 03 September 2007, (www. usatoday.com)

61 Viktor Frankl, (I. Lasch, Trans.), Autobiography, <u>Man's Search for Meaning. An Introduction to Logotherapy</u>, Beacon Press. (1963).

Viktor Emil Frankl, M.D., Ph.D., (March 26, 1905 - September 2, 1997) was a psychiatrist and a Holocaust survivor. He founded logotherapy and Existential Analysis. They are called the "Third Viennese School" of psychotherapy. His book, <u>Man's Search for Meaning,</u> describes his experiences as a concentration camp inmate and describes his psychotherapeutic method of finding meaning in all forms of existence, even the most traumatic and horrible, and thus a reason to continue living.

For more information we suggest reading: <u>Man's Search for Meaning , The Will to Meaning- Foundations and Applications of Logotherapy,</u> and <u>Man's Search for Ultimate Meaning.</u>

62 Martin Luther King, Jr., (January 15, 1929 – April 4, 1968) was a Baptist minister who played a key role in the civil rights movement. His most influential and well-known public address is the "I Have A Dream" speech. In 1964, King became the youngest man to be awarded the Nobel Peace Prize.

63 Harold Kushner, (born 1935), is a prominent American rabbi and author. For more information we recommend reading his best selling book on the problem of evil, <u>When Bad Things Happen to Good People. He also wrote How Good Do We Have to Be?,</u> and <u>To Life!</u>

64 From HEALING THE SOUL IN THE AGE OF THE BRAIN by Elio Frattaroli, copyright (c) 2001 by Elio Frattaroli. Used by permission of Viking Penguin, a division of Penguin

Group (USA) Inc. p 11.

65 Sammy Davis, Jr., (December 8, 1925 – May 16, 1990) was a famous entertainer and is best known for being a member of the 1960s Rat Pack led by Frank Sinatra.

66 Tim O'Brien, "The Things They Carried," (Houghton Mifflin, 1990).

67 Lao-Tse, (604 BC) is considered the first philosopher of the Taoist school. His writings teach the philosophy of the Tao, or the Way. According to Lao-Tse the Tao can be found by experiencing the oneness in all things, fulfilling life as one with nature and as one with the inner self.

68 Pamela Paul, "Getting Inside Gen Y," American Demographics, Sept. 2001, 42-49. Paul suggests that today's generation of Warfighters fall into what is being described as "Generation Y." Paul goes on to make these observations about the orientations, values, and principles of how today's youth conduct their lives: they do not remember the Cold War and have never feared nuclear war; the expression "You sound like a broken record" means nothing to them; and there's no such thing as a busy signal or no answer at all.

Gen Y, also known as Echo Boomers, has been heralded as the next big generation, an enormously powerful group that has the sheer numbers to transform every life stage it enters - just as its parents generation did.

69 Sigmund Freud, (1856–1939), was the founder of psychoanalysis. He was a contemporary of Adler and Jung. His theories have also influenced the following fields: anthropology, education, art, and literary criticism.

70 Plato, (427?–347 B.C.), His teachings have been among

the most influential in the history of Western civilization. He was the second of the great trio of ancient Greeks; he succeeded Socrates and preceded Aristotle. The three of them laid the philosophical foundations of Western culture.

71 Paul Watzlawick, Richard Fisch, and John Weakland, "Change: Principles of Problem Formation and Resolution," (W. Norton and Co/NY: 1974) of the Mental Research Institute in Palo Alto, CA have studied how people change.

72 Edward Tick, War and The Soul (Quest Books, 2005) 23. This excerpt was reproduced by permission of Quest Books, the imprint of the Theosophical Publishing House (www. questbooks.net).

73 John Adams, Jr., (October 30, 1735 – July 4, 1826) was the first Vice President (1789–1797) of the United States and its second President (1797–1801).

74 The differences between Complicated and Uncomplicated Grief are defined below.

Normal, or uncomplicated, grief reactions are those that, though painful, move the survivor toward an acceptance of the loss and an ability to carry on with his or her life. Survivors with uncomplicated grief may feel very saddened by the death of an intimate, but they, nevertheless, are able feel that life still holds meaning and the potential for fulfillment. In contrast with the uncomplicated grief reactions described above, survivors experiencing complicated grief reactions question who they are, how they will survive, and their prospects of future fulfillment in the absence of the deceased person.

75 Elisabeth Kübler-Ross, M.D., (July 8, 1926 – August 24, 2004) was the author of On Death and Dying. She developed the Five Stages of Grief concept. Many believe her work was

instrumental in forming the hospice care movement.

76 Elisabeth Kübler-Ross, M.D., <u>On Death and Dying - What the Dying Have to Teach Doctors, Nurses, Clergy, and Their Own Families,</u> (Macmillan Publishing Company Inc, NY, NY. 1969).

77 Gandhi, Mahatma, (October 2, 1869 – January 30, 1948) was an influential spiritual leader. He was born a Hindu and practiced Hinduism all his life. Most of his beliefs are from the teachings of Hinduism. He believed all religions to be equal, and rejected all efforts to convert him to a different faith. He read extensively about all major religions. He pioneered the resistance of tyranny through mass non violent civil disobedience. His form of "protest" inspired movements for civil rights and freedom across the world. To learn more about his philosophy and way of life we suggest reading his autobiography, <u>The Story of My Experiments with Truth.</u>

78 Edward Tick, <u>War and The Soul</u> (Quest Books, 2005) 72-73. This excerpt was reproduced by permission of Quest Books, the imprint of the Theosophical Publishing House (www.questbooks.net).

79 Ibid. 74. This excerpt was reproduced by permission of Quest Books, the imprint of the Theosophical Publishing House (www.questbooks.net).

80 From HEALING THE SOUL IN THE AGE OF THE BRAIN by Elio Frattaroli, copyright (c) 2001 by Elio Frattaroli. Used by permission of Viking Penguin, a division of Penguin Group (USA) Inc. p 283.

81 Leonardo Buscaglia, Ph.D., (31 March 1924 – 11 June 1998) wrote a number of best-selling inspirational books on love. His most famous books are: <u>The Fall of Freddie the Leaf, Living</u>

Loving and Learning, and Love.

82 Edward Tick, War and The Soul (Quest Books, 2005) 217. This excerpt was reproduced by permission of Quest Books, the imprint of the Theosophical Publishing House (www. questbooks.net).

83 Miguel de Cervantes.

84 Peter Madison, Personality Development in College, (Addison Wesley Longman Publishing Company, 1969) offered for several years a college course in personality development based on an autobiography, a daily journal, and readings about case studies.

85 Logan Smith, (October 18, 1865 – March 2, 1946) was an essayist and critic. For more information on his life we suggest reading his autobiography, Unforgotten Years (1938).

86 Gillian Koenig.

87 Pimentel and Teixeira , Virtual Reality: Through the New Looking Glass, (McGraw-Hill, 1994), explain the phenomenon of how computers are fundamentally changing our experiences in life.

Guy Saddy, in his article, "Do Computers Change How We Think?" suggests that computers and our interactions with them in day-to-day lifestyles and decision-making processes are essentially altering us in several ways.

88 As of August 2004, 80% of the American population have daily access to the Internet. According to AOL's CEO, Malcolm Bird suggests that today's teens will be among the first to embrace new, Web-based video technology…the community, scheduling, friends, holidays - all will be in a (virtual) online

environment.

89 Lee Alley, <u>Back From War- Finding Hope &</u>
<u>Understanding In Life After Combat,</u> (Exceptional Publishing,
2007) 132. This excerpt was reproduced by permission of The
King Consortium (www.thekingconsortium.com).

90 Ibid. 117.

91 Maxine Hone Kingston, ed., <u>Veterans of War, Veterans</u>
<u>of Peace</u> (Koa Books, 2006) 1.

For more information on the book and the work of Ms. Kingston
visit: www.vowvop.org. You can find the biographies of the
@80 writers who contributed to this book. A few have website
information listed in their biography. A number of the writers
who contributed essays and poetry to the book are doing
significant work for others.

92 Lee Alley, <u>Back From War- Finding Hope &</u>
<u>Understanding In Life After Combat,</u> (Exceptional Publishing,
2007) 119. This excerpt was reproduced by permission of The
King Consortium (www.thekingconsortium.com).

93 Margaret Kornfeld, <u>Cultivating Wholeness - A Guide</u>
<u>to Care and Counseling in Faith Communities,</u> (Continuum
Publishing Group, May 1998).

94 William McFee, (June 15, 1881 - July 2, 1966) was a
prolific writer.

95 Leo Tolstoy, (1828 –1910), was a Russian writer –
novelist, essayist, dramatist and philosopher. His writings
influenced Ghandi and Martin Luther King, Jr. For additional
information on Tolstoy we suggest reading: <u>War and Peace,</u>
<u>Anna Karenina,</u> and <u>The Kingdom of God is Within You.</u>

96 Viktor Frankl, (I. Lasch, Trans.), Autobiography, <u>Man's Search for Meaning. An Introduction to Logotherapy</u>, Beacon Press. (1963). 88.

97 Ibid. 99.

98 Jesus Christ, (8 BC to 29 AD), is the central figure of Christianity. He was a teacher and a healer. For information on the teachings' and life of Jesus we suggest reading the four New Testament Gospels of Matthew, Mark, Luke, and John.

99 Hoge, Charles, M.D. and Castro, Carlo, Ph.D., et.al. "Combat Duty in Iraq and Afghanistan, Mental Health Problems, and Barriers to Care," <u>The New England Journal of Medicine,</u> Vol. 351: 13-22, No. 1, (July 1, 2004).

100 Billy Graham, (born November 7, 1918) is a well-known and beloved evangelist.

101 Viktor Frankl, (I. Lasch, Trans.), Autobiography, <u>Man's Search for Meaning. An Introduction to Logotherapy</u>, Beacon Press. (1963).

102 Albert Schweitzer, M.D., OM, (January 14, 1875 – September 4, 1965), was a theologian, musician, philosopher, and physician. He received the 1952 Nobel Peace Prize for his philosophy of "reverence for life."

103 Viktor Frankl, (I. Lasch, Trans.), Autobiography, <u>Man's Search for Meaning. An Introduction to Logotherapy</u>, Beacon Press. (1963). 88.

104 Ibid.

105 Gandhi, Mahatma. (October 2, 1869 – January 30, 1948) was an influential spiritual leader. He was born a Hindu

and practiced Hinduism all his life. Most of his beliefs are from the teachings of Hinduism. He believed all religions to be equal, and rejected all efforts to convert him to a different faith. He read extensively about all major religions. He pioneered the resistance of tyranny through mass non violent civil disobedience. His form of "protest" inspired movements for civil rights and freedom across the world. To learn more about his philosophy and way of life we suggest reading his autobiography <u>The Story of My Experiments with Truth.</u>

106 John McQuiston II, "Finding Time for the Timeless: Spirituality in the Workweek," (Skylight Paths Publishing, 2004) 142 – 157.

107 Harold Kushner, (born 1935), is a prominent American rabbi and author. For more information we recommend reading his best selling book on the problem of evil, <u>When Bad Things Happen to Good People. He also wrote How Good Do We Have to Be?,</u> and <u>To Life!</u>

108 Eleanor Roosevelt, (October 11, 1884 – November 7, 1962), was First Lady from 1933 to 1945. She was married to President Franklin D. Roosevelt. She was actively involved in human rights issues throughout her public life.

109 Allen B. Clark, <u>Wounded Soldier, Healing Warrior</u>, (Zenith Press, MBI Publishing Company, St. Paul, MN, 2007)

110 Viktor Frankl, (I. Lasch, Trans.), Autobiography, <u>Man's Search for Meaning. An Introduction to Logotherapy</u>, Beacon Press. (1963).

111 Dana Priest and Anne Hull, "The War Inside - Troops Are Returning From the Battlefield With Psychological Wounds, But the Mental-Health System That Serves Them Makes Healing Difficult," <u>Washington Post,</u> 17 June 2007; A01 (Washingtonpost.

com).

112 Albert Schweitzer, M.D., OM, (January 14, 1875 – September 4, 1965), was a theologian, musician, philosopher, and physician. He received the 1952 Nobel Peace Prize for his philosophy of "reverence for life."

113 Albert Einstein.

114 Shakespeare, Henry V, Act 4, Scene 3.
William Shakespeare (baptized 26 April 1564 – 23 April 1616) was an English poet and playwright. His surviving works consist of 38 plays, 154 sonnets, two long narrative poems, and several other poems. His works include: <u>Hamlet, King Lear,</u> and <u>Macbeth.</u>

SELECTED BIBLIOGRAPHY

Alley, Lee, <u>Back From War- Finding Hope & Understanding In Life After Combat.</u> Exceptional Publishing. 2007.

Baldwin, The Honorable Valerie L. "Virtual Leadership in a Virtual Private Network Environment." (Resource Management, 2005: Comptroller Proponency Office, Office of the Assistant Secretary of the Army).

Barlow, John Perry, and Rheingold, Howard. "Cyberhood Vs. Neighborhood." <u>UTNE READER,</u> March/April 1995, 50-56.

Becker, Craig, et.al. "The Usability And Effectiveness Of A Self-Management Intervention, " <u>American Journal of Health Studies, Spring, 2004.</u>

Bergin, A.E. "Values and Religious Issues in Psychotherapy and Mental Health." <u>American Psychologist,</u> 1991. *46,* 394-413.

Bien, T. H., Miller, W. R., & Tonigan, J. S., "Brief Interventions For Alcohol Problems: A Review." <u>Addiction.</u> 1993. *88,* 315-335.

Blanchard EB, Jones-Alexander J, Buckley TC, Forneris CA. "Psychometric Properties Of The PTSD Checklist (PCL)." <u>Behavior Response Therapy.</u> 1996. 34:669-673.

Briggs, John C. "The Promise of Virtual Reality." <u>Futurist.</u> Sept. /Oct. 1996. 13-18. World Future Society, 7910 Woodmont Avenue, Suite 450, Bethesda, MD. 20814.

Briley, R. Fowler, P. & Teel J. "How Are We Doing?" <u>Journal of Environmental Health.</u> 1999. 62(5) 35-46.

Britt, TW. "The Stigma Of Psychological Problems In A Work Environment: Evidence From The Screening Of Warfighters Returning From Bosnia." Journal Applied Social Psychology. 2000. 30:1599-1618.

Bryant, R. A. & Harvey, A. G. Acute Stress Disorder: A Handbook Of Theory, Assessment, And Treatment. Washington, DC: American Psychological Association. 2000.

Bryant, R. A., Harvey, A. G., Basten, C., Dang, S. T., & Sackville, T. "Treatment Of Acute Stress Disorder: A Comparison Of Cognitive-Behavioral Therapy And Supportive Counseling." Journal of Consulting and Clinical Psychology. 1998. 66, 862-866.

Bryant, R. A., Sackville, T., Dang, S. T., Moulds, M., & Guthrie, R. "Treating Acute Stress Disorder: An Evaluation Of Cognitive Behavior Therapy And Supportive Counseling Techniques." American Journal of Psychiatry. 1999. 156, 1780-1786.

Callander, Bruce D. "Training in Networks." Air Force Magazine. Aug. 1999. 84-88.

Castro CA, Bienvenu RV, Hufmann AH, Adler AB. "Soldier Dimensions And Operational Readiness In U.S. Army Forces Deployed To Kosovo." Int Rev Armed Forces Med Serv. 2000. 73:191-200.

Catherall, D. R. Back From The Brink: A Family Guide To Overcoming Traumatic Stress. New York: Bantam Books. 1992.

Chalder, T., Hotopf, M., Unwin, C., Hull, L., Ismail, K., David, A; Wessely, S. "Prevalence Of Gulf War Veterans Who Believe They Have Gulf War Syndrome: Questionnaire Study." British

Medical Journal. 2001. 323, 7311, 473-476.

Clark, Allen B., Wounded Soldier, Healing Warrior. Zenith Press, MBI Publishing Company, St. Paul, MN. 2007.

Clasper, Paul, Eastern Paths And The Christian Way. New York: Orbis Book, 1982.

Colglazier, Scott, R., A Larger Hope-Opening the Heart to God. Chalice Press, 2002.

Comeaux, P. "The Impact Of An Interactive Distance Learning Network On Classroom Communication." Communication Education. 1995. 44, 353-361.

Conant, Sue, "God & War – How Chaplains Struggle to Keep Faith Under Fire." Newsweek. May 07, 2007. pp. 26 -34.

Curran, E. "Fathers With War-Related PTSD." National Center for PTSD Clinical Quarterly. 1997. *7(2),* 30-33

Damasio AR. Descartes' Error: Emotion, Reason, and the Human Brain. New York, NY: GP Putnam's Sons; 1994.

DiPietro, Monty. "Coming of Age, Virtually." The East: May/June 2000, pp. 34-39.

Donta, S. T., Clauw, D. J., Engel, C. C., Guarino, P., Peduzzi, P., Williams, D. A., et al. "Cognitive Behavioral Therapy And Aerobic Exercise For Gulf War Veterans' Illnesses: A Randomized Controlled Trial." Journal of the American Medical Association, 2003. 289, 1396-1404.

Engel, C. "Outbreaks Of Medically Unexplained Physical Symptoms After Military Action, Terrorist Threat, Or

Technological Disaster." Military Medicine. 2001. 166(12) Supplement 2, 47-48.

Figley, C. Helping Traumatized Families. San Francisco: Jossey-Bass. 1989.

Finholt, T., & Sproull, L. "Electronic Groups at Work." Organization Science 1990. 1, 41-64.

Foa, E. B., Keane, T. M., & Friedman, M. J. Effective treatments for PTSD: Practice guidelines from the International Society for Traumatic Stress Studies. New York: Guilford. 2000.

Foa, E. B., & Rothbaum, B. O. Treating The Trauma Of Rape: Cognitive-Behavioral Therapy For PTSD. New York: Guilford. 1998.

Frankl, Viktor. (I. Lasch, Trans.), Autobiography, Man's Search for Meaning. An Introduction to Logotherapy, Beacon Press. (1963).

Frattaroli, Elio M.D. Healing the Soul in the Age of the Brain. Penguin Books, N.Y. N.Y., 2001.

Friedman MJ, Schnurr PP, McDonagh-Coyle A. "Post-Traumatic Stress Disorder In The Military Veteran." The Psychiatric Clinics of North America 1994.17:265-277.

Gimbel, C., & Booth, A. "Why Does Military Combat Experience Adversely Affect Marital Relations?" Journal of Marriage and the Family. 1994. 56, 691-703.

Goldenberg, H., & Goldenberg, I. Counseling Today's Families. (2nd ed.). Pacific Grove, CA: Brooks/Cole. 1994.

Goodwin, James, PhD, "The Etiology of Combat-Related Post-Traumatic Stress-Disorders", Chapter 1, Edited by Tom Williams, Psy.D. "Post-Traumatic Stress Disorders of the Vietnam Veteran." 1980. (Disabled American Veterans, National Headquarters P O Box 14301 Cincinnati, OH 45214).

Gorham, J. "The Relationship Between Verbal Teacher Immediacy And Student Learning." Communication Education. 1988. 37, 40-53.

Griffiths, Mark. "Looking Into Online Therapy." Health Matters. Winter 2000/2001. 18-19 Health Matters Publications, Ltd. www.healthmatters.org.uk.

Hackman, M. Z., & Walker, K. B. "Instructional Communication In The Televised Classroom: The Effects Of System Design And Teacher Immediacy On Student Learning And Satisfaction." Communication Education. 1990. 39, 196-206.

Harkness, L., & Zador, N. Treatment of PTSD in Families and Couples. In J. Wilson, M. J. Friedman, & J. Lindy (Eds.), Treating Psychological Trauma And PTSD . New York: Guilford. 2001.

Hefling, Kimberly. "Iraq, Afghan Vets at Risk of Suicide." Associated Press. 31 October 2007 (Yahoo.com).

Helzer JE, Robins LN, McEvoy L. "Post-Traumatic Stress Disorder In The General Population: Findings Of The Epidemiologic Catchment Area Survey." New England Journal of Medicine. 1987. 317:1630-1634.

Hoge, Charles, M.D. and Castro, Carlo, Ph.D., et.al. "Combat Duty in Iraq and Afghanistan, Mental Health Problems, and Barriers to Care," The New England Journal of Medicine, Vol. 351: 13-22, No. 1. July 1, 2004.

Hoge CW, Lesikar SE, Guevara R, et al. "Mental Disorders Among U.S. Military Personnel In The 1990s: Association With High Levels Of Health Care Utilization And Early Military Attrition." American Journal Psychiatry. 2002.159:1576-1583.

Hyams, C., Wignall, S., & Roswell, R. "War Syndromes And Their Evaluation: From The U.S. Civil War To The Persian Gulf War." Annals of Internal Medicine. 1996.125, 398-405.

James, William. The Varieties of Religious Experience. New York: Collier Books. 1961.

Jardin, Xeni. "Virtual Reality Therapy for Combat Stress." NPR. March 2, 2006. www.npr.org.

Jensen, P. S., & Shaw, J. A. "The Effects Of War And Parental Deployment Upon Children And Adolescents." R. J. Ursano & A. E. Norwood (Eds.), Emotional Aftermath Of The Persian Gulf War: Veterans, Families, Communities, And Nations. 1996. 83-109. Washington, DC: American Psychiatric Press.

Kabat-Zinn J. Wherever You Go, There You Are: Mindfulness Meditation in Everyday Life. New York, NY: Hyperion; 1994.

Kang HK, Natelson BH, Mahan CM, Lee KY, Murphy FM. "Post-Traumatic Stress Disorder And Chronic Fatigue Syndrome-Like Illness Among Gulf War Veterans: A Population-Based Survey Of 30,000 Veterans." American Journal of Epidemiology. 2003. 157:141-148.

Kaplan, Karen. "A Virtual world is Taking Shape in Research Labs." Los Angeles Times: Feb. 5, 2001, pp. C1+.

Kaplan Mark S., Huguet Nathalie, McFarland Bentson H., and Newsom Jason T., "Suicide among male veterans: a prospective population-based study." Journal of Epidemiology and Community Health. July 2007. 61:619-624. Newswise, "Journal of Epidemiology and Community Health," Study, July 2007. www.newswise.com.

Maxine Hone Kingston, ed., Veterans of War, Veterans of Peace. Koa Books. 2006.

Kirkland, F. R. "Postcombat Reentry." F. D. Jones, L. Sparacino, V. L. Wilcox, J. M. Rothberg, & J. W. Stokes (Eds.), War Psychiatry. 1995. 291-317. Washington, DC: Office of the Surgeon General.

Kornfeld, Margaret, Cultivating Wholeness - A Guide To Care And Counseling In Faith Communities." Continuum Publishing Group. May 1998.

Koshes, R. J. "The Care of Those Returned: Psychiatric Illnesses Of War." R. J. Ursano & A. E. Norwood (Eds.), Emotional Aftermath Of The Persian Gulf War: Veterans, Families, Communities, And Nations. 1996. 393-414. Washington, DC: American Psychiatric Press.

Kim, Amy Jo 'AJ'. "The Network is the Game." Social Trends in Mobile Entertainment Game Developers Mobile Conference. 2005.

Kubany, E. S. "Cognitive Therapy for Trauma-Related Guilt." V. M. Follette, J. I. Ruzek, & F. R. Abueg (Eds.), Cognitive-Behavioral Therapies For Trauma. 1998. 124-161. New York: Guilford.

Kübler-Ross, Elisabeth. "On Death and Dying - What the Dying Have to Teach Doctors, Nurses, Clergy, and Their Own Families," Macmillan Publishing Company Inc, NY, NY., 1969.

Kurzweil, Raymond. "Soul on Silicon." The Executive Educator, February 1994. 24-29.

Langer EJ. Mindfulness. Reading, Mass: Addison-Wesley Publishing Co Inc; 1989.

Madison, Peter. Personality Development in College Addison Wesley Longman Publishing Company. 1969.

Machlis, Sharon. "Visions of the Future: Man-Machine Barriers Begin to Crumble." Design News. Nov. 4, 1996. 182f.

McGuire, Meredith B. "Health And Spirituality As Contemporary Concerns." Annals of the American Academy of Political & Social Sciences May 1993. 527, 144-155.

McQuiston II, John. Finding Time for the Timeless: Spirituality in the Workweek. Skylight Paths Publishing. 2004. 142 – 157.

Montgomery, Kathryn C. "Children in the Digital Age." American Prospect. July/Aug. 1996. 69-74. New Prospect, Inc.

Najavits, L. M. Seeking Safety: A Treatment Manual For PTSD And Substance Abuse. New York: Guilford. 2002.

Newswise. "Journal of Epidemiology and Community Health." Study. July 2007. www.newswise.com.

Nhat Hahn T. Peace Is Every Step: The Path of Mindfulness in Everyday Life. New York, NY: Bantam Books; 1992.

Nin A. The Diary of Anais Nin, 1939-1944. New York, NY: Harcourt Brace & World; 1969.

Norwood, A. E., Fullerton, C. S., & Hagen, K. P. "Those Left Behind: Military Families." R. J. Ursano & A. E. Norwood (Eds.), Emotional Aftermath Of The Persian Gulf War: Veterans, Families, Communities, And Nations. 1996.163 -196. Washington, DC: American Psychiatric Press.

O'Brien, Tim. The Things They Carried. Houghton Mifflin. 1990.

Oppel, Richard A., Jr., "A Salute for His Wounded, A Last Touch For His Dead." New York Times. April 02, 2007. p.1

Ouimette, P., & Brown, P. J. Trauma And Substance Abuse: Causes, Consequences, And Treatment Of Comorbid Disorders. Washington, DC: American Psychological Association. 2002.

Paul, Pamela. "Getting Inside Gen Y." American Demographics. Sept. 2001. 42-49.

Pimentel and Teixeira. Virtual Reality: Through the New Looking Glass. McGraw-Hill, 1994.

Postman, Neil. "Virtual Students, Digital Classroom." Nation. Oct. 9, 1995. 377f. The Nation Company, L.P.

Prigerson HG, Maciejewski PK, Rosenheck RA. "Population Attributable Fractions Of Psychiatric Disorders And Behavioral Outcomes Associated With Combat Exposures Among US Men." American Journal Public Health. 2002. 92:59-63.

Prigerson HG, Maciejewski PK, Rosenheck RA. "Combat Trauma: Trauma With Highest Risk Of Delayed Onset And Unresolved Posttraumatic Stress Disorder Symptoms, Unemployment, And Abuse Among Men." Journal Nervous Mental Disorder. 2001.189:99-108.

Mental Disorder. 2001.189:99-108.

Proctor, S. P., Heeren, T., White, R. F., Wolfe, J., Borgos, M. S., Davis, J. D., et al. "Health Status of Persian Gulf War Veterans: Self-Reported Symptoms, Environmental Exposures and The Effect Of Stress." International Journal of Epidemiology. 1998. 27, 1000-1010.

Rheingold, Howard. "Virtual Reality's Promise—and Threat." Christian Science Monitor. Jan. 2, 1992, p. 15.

Risen, James. "Back From Iraq, Contractors Face Combat-Related Stress." New York Times. July 5, 2007. 1.

Ryan, R. M. & Deci, E. L. "Self-Determination Theory And The Facilitation Of Intrinsic Motivation, Social Development, And Well-Being." American Psychologist. 2000. 55(1), 68-78.

Ryle G. The Concept of Mind. New York, NY: Barnes & Noble; 1949.

Ruzek, J. I. "Concurrent Posttraumatic Stress Disorder and Substance Use Disorder Among Veterans: Evidence And Treatment Issues." P. Ouimette & P. J. Brown (Eds.), Trauma And Substance Abuse: Causes, Consequences, And Treatment Of Comorbid Disorders. 2003. 191-207. Washington, DC: American Psychological Association.

Schon DA. The Reflective Practitioner. New York, NY: Basic Books; 1983.

Scurfield, R. M., & Tice, S. "Acute psycho-social intervention strategies with medical and psychiatric evacuees of "Operation Desert Storm" and their families. Operation Desert Storm Clinician Packet." White River Junction, VT: National Center for PTSD. 1991.

Shay, J., M.D., Ph.D., L. Goerner (Ed.), <u>Achilles In Vietnam: Combat Trauma and the Undoing of Character.</u> New York, NY: Macmillan Publishing Company. 1994.

Steil, R., & Ehlers, A. "Dysfunctional Meaning of Posttraumatic Intrusions In Chronic PTSD." <u>Behavior Research and Therapy,</u> 2000. 38, 537-558.

Streng FJ. <u>Emptiness: A Study in Religious Meaning.</u> Nashville, Tenn: Abingdon Press; 1967.

Sternberg, R., Forsythe, G., Hedlund, J., Horvath, J., Wagner, R., Williams, W., Snook, S., and Grigorenko, E., <u>Practical Intelligence in Everyday Life.</u> New York: Cambridge University Press. 2000.

Sonnenberg, S. M. "The Problems Of Listening." R. J. Ursano & A. E. Norwood (Eds.), <u>Emotional aftermath of the Persian Gulf War: Veterans, families, communities, and nations.</u> 1996. 353-367. Washington, DC: American Psychiatric Press.

Suzuki S. <u>Zen Mind, Beginner's Mind.</u> New York, NY: Weatherhill; 1980.

Swigger, K., & Brazile, R. "Evaluating Group Effectiveness Through A Computer-Supported Cooperative Problem-Solving Environment." <u>International Journal of Human-Computer Studies.</u> 1995. 43, 523-528.

Swigger, K., Brazile, R., Lopez, V., & Livingston, A. "The Virtual Collaborative University." <u>Computers in Education,</u> 1997. 29, 55-61.

Teasdale, Wayne. The Mystic Heart. Novato, CA: New World Library. 1999.

The Centers for Disease Control Vietnam Experience Study Group. "Health Status of Vietnam Veterans." I. Psychosocial characteristics. JAMA. 1988. 259:2701-2707.

The Department of Defense Health Board Task Force on Mental Health. "An Achievable Vision: Report of the Department of Defense Task on Mental Health." June 15, 2007.

The Iowa Persian Gulf Study Group. "Self-Reported Illness And Health Status Among Gulf War Veterans: A Population-Based Study." JAMA. 1997. 277:238-245.

Thomas, Keith. "God in the Computer." The New York Review of Books. Dec. 17, 1998. 78-80.

Tick, Edward, Ph.D. "War and The Soul." Quest Books. 2005.

Torrance, Robert. The Spiritual Quest: Transcendence In Myth, Religion, And Science. Berkley, CA: Univ. of California Press. 1994.

Usoh, Martin and Slater, Mel. "An Exploration of Immersive Virtual Environments." Endeavour. March 1995, pp. 34-38.

Varela FJ, Thompson E, Rosch E. The Embodied Mind: Cognitive Science and Human Experience. Cambridge, Mass: Massachusetts Institute of Technology Press; 1991.

Vargas, Jose Antonio. "Video Gaming Not Just a Boys' Club Anymore." Toronto Star. July 31, 2004, p. J12.
Walther, J. B. "Relational Aspects Of Computer-Mediated Communication: Experimental Observations Over Time."

Organizational Science. 1995. 6, 186-203.

Walther, J. B., & Burgoon, J. K. "Relational Communication in Computer-Mediated Interaction." Human Communication Research. 1992.19, 50-88.

Watzlawick Paul, Fisch Richard, and Weakland John. "Change: Principles of Problem Formation and Resolution." W. Norton and Co/NY: 1974. The Mental Research Institute in Palo Alto, CA.

Weathers FW, Litz BT, Herman DS, Huska JA, Keane TM. "The PTSD checklist (PCL): reliability, validity, and diagnostic utility." San Antonio, Tex.: International Society of Traumatic Stress Studies. October 1993.

Wessely S, Unwin C, Hotopf M, et al. "Stability of Recall of Military Hazards Over Time: Evidence From The Persian Gulf War Of 1991." Br Journal Psychiatry. 2003.183:314-322.

Westberg J. Teaching Creatively With Video: Fostering Reflection, Communication, and Other Clinical Skills. New York, NY: Springer Publishing Co. 1994.

Westberg J, Jason H. "Fostering Reflection and Self-Assessment." Family Medicine. 1994. 26; 278-282.

Williams III, Gurney. "Virtual Reality: Enter the World of Simulated Reality." The American Legion Magazine. Feb. 1993. 24f.

Wolfe, J. W., Keane, T. M., & Young, B. L. "From Soldier To Civilian: Acute Adjustment Patterns Of Returned Persian Gulf Veterans." R. J. Ursano & A. E. Norwood (Eds.), Emotional Aftermath Of The Persian Gulf War: Veterans, Families,

Veterans." R. J. Ursano & A. E. Norwood (Eds.), <u>Emotional Aftermath Of The Persian Gulf War: Veterans, Families, Communities, And Nations</u> 1996. 477-499. Washington, DC: American Psychiatric Press.

Yerkes, S. A., & Holloway, H. C. "War And Homecomings: The Stressors Of War And Of Returning From War." R. J. Ursano & A. E. Norwood (Eds.), <u>Emotional Aftermath Of The Persian Gulf War: Veterans, Families, Communities, And Nations</u>. 1996. 25-42. Washington, DC: American Psychiatric Press.

Zoroya, Gregg. "Scientists: Brain Injuries From War Worse Than Thought." <u>USA Today</u>. September 03, 2007. <u>www. usatoday.com</u>

Visit www.SilentWounds.com
to purchase our book and assessment software or for more information about our products and services

"Silent Wounds: The Hidden Cost of War" ($20.00)
Authors - James W. Daniels, Jr., Emily Kuhlbars Howden, Richard Arden Kuhlbars

Learning for all begins with understanding the core issue...the silent wounds. Everyone associated with combat trauma should familiarize himself or herself with what it means to be silently wounded in the Soul. Our concern is about the combat trauma symptoms that we call the silent wounding. We suggest that this deep silent wounding affects the whole person and if left untreated may lead to pre-mature death by suicide.

"Healing the Soul: A Self Guide to Our Own Healing" ($199.99)
Developed and Produced by Richard Arden Kuhlbars, II

This is an interactive software package that helps Veterans, Soldiers, and family members perform a personal, private, and non-judgmental self-examination to determine the effects of their silent wounding. This is also an effective self-guided suicide prevention tool. Self-directed and repeatable, this interactive program offers a safe, private experience, encouraging reflective assessment in relationships, financial issues, career development, personal habits, leisure activities, spiritual values, and decision-making.

"Silent Wounds" Lecture/Presentation

This is a format where we provide a lecture or presentation

normally less than two hours in length for classes, meetings, worship, lunch or dinner presentations, or other organizational settings. The lecture would cover the highlights of the issues and concepts of "Silent Wounds: The Hidden Costs of War."

"Silent Wounds" Workshop

This is a 20-hour workshop format. Each of the five modules of the book "Silent Wounds: The Hidden Cost of War" are dealt with in an appropriate format with exercises and presentations. This format is ideal for a weekend session that would begin Friday at noon and conclude Sunday afternoon.

"Silent Wounds" Training

This is a full-length five-day training event that covers each of the five modules of the book "Silent Wounds: The Hidden Cost of War." The configuration is five one-day sessions scheduled at the convenience of the sponsoring organization. Each day is dedicated to one training module topic.

Personal Notes

Personal Notes

Personal Notes

Personal Notes

Personal Notes

Personal Notes

Personal Notes

Personal Notes

Personal Notes